RSPB
HANDBOOK OF
GARDEN
WILDLIFE

second edition

PETER HOLDEN AND GEOFFREY ABBOTT

B L O O M S B U R Y   W I L D L I F E
LONDON · OXFORD · NEW YORK · NEW DELHI · SYDNEY

giving
nature
a home

BLOOMSBURY WILDLIFE
Bloomsbury Publishing Plc
50 Bedford Square, London, WC1B 3DP, UK

BLOOMSBURY, BLOOMSBURY WILDLIFE and the Diana logo are trademarks of
Bloomsbury Publishing Plc

First published in the United Kingdom 2008
This edition published 2017

A catalogue record for this book is available from the British Library

Library of Congress Cataloguing-in-Publication data has been applied for

ISBN: PB: 978-1-4729-6461-8; ePub: 978-1-4729-3085-9

2 4 6 8 10 9 7 5 3 1

Typeset and designed by Susan McIntyre
Printed in China by C&C Offset Printing Co. Ltd.

MIX
Paper from
responsible sources
FSC® C008047

To find out more about our authors and books visit www.bloomsbury.com
and sign up for our newsletters

For all items sold Bloomsbury Publishing will donate a minimum of 2% of the publisher's
receipts from sales of licensed titles to RSPB Sales Ltd., the trading subsidiary of the RSPB.
Subsequent sellers are not commercial participators for the purposes of
Part II of the Charities Act 1992.

Contents

ACKNOWLEDGEMENTS

Producing a book like this requires the time and commitment of a large number of people to bring an initial idea to its natural conclusion. We are grateful to both Bloomsbury and the RSPB for listening to our ideas and sharing our vision and thanks also to all those who advised on the selection of species.

This edition has benefited from the people who contributed to the first edition and in addition our editor, Katie Read, and the designer, Susan McIntyre. Throughout the production of both editions Julie Bailey has been our guide and mentor and brought her extensive knowledge of natural history publishing to this volume.

Once again we thank our respective families for their forbearance in allowing us to negotiate our way around family commitments as we gathered the material and kept to our deadlines.

We have drawn on numerous sources of information. Lifelong personal wildlife observations have been augmented by reference to many existing books, journals and scientific papers to ensure the material we have presented here is both accurate and up to date. We are thankful to field naturalists both past and present who have published their material and made it available to the world at large.

For readers who would like more information, there are a great number of books specialising in individual topics that are very accessible; particularly those published by T & AD Poyser, Christopher Helm, Bloomsbury and the Collins *New Naturalist* series. In addition, the websites plantpress.com and rspb.org.uk are particularly recommended.

Peter Holden and Geoffrey Abbott

Swallow chicks in an outbuilding.

FOREWORD
BY MIRANDA KRESTOVNIKOFF

DOES YOUR GARDEN GIVE NATURE A HOME?

With so much of the countryside taken up for human needs, many of our birds and other species are being squeezed out. This is why the RSPB urges us all to give nature a home – and where better to start than in your garden, balcony or even window box? The UK's gardens together cover a huge area and can make a real difference to wildlife.

It's not only the wildlife that will benefit. Giving nature a home brings a garden to life in a way no costly water feature or lighting ever could. Even routine weeding becomes a pleasure when a Robin appears – watching keenly for worms or spiders to be unearthed. Sitting quietly in a dusk-shrouded garden watching a Hedgehog lead her family out under cover of darkness is both a pleasure and a privilege. And what can compare with the song of a Blackbird breaking the still of an early summer evening?

All of these are species that will happily live in gardens. Sadly Hedgehogs, one of our once familiar garden animals, are vanishing at an alarming rate and struggle to get past hard fences and walls to make their necessary nightly journeys from garden to garden. Even 'common' garden birds, such as House Sparrows, Starlings and Song Thrushes, have disappeared from many gardens. Meanwhile bees sometimes struggle to find the nectar and pollen they need in modern strains of garden flowers.

As well as our most noticeable garden visitors, butterflies, bees, frogs, bats, ladybirds and beautiful shiny beetles are just a few of the many species the whole family can enjoy in a more wildlife-friendly garden.

The good news is we don't need to choose between having a beautiful garden and a nature-friendly wilderness – even subtle changes to our gardens can make a real difference to wildlife. So, read on to discover ways you can welcome nature in your garden and learn how to recognise all the exciting species when they appear...

Miranda Krestovnikoff, RSPB President

The RSPB

The RSPB is the country's largest nature conservation charity, inspiring everyone to give nature a home.

Together with partners, it protects threatened birds and wildlife so our towns, coast and countryside will teem with life once again. It also plays a leading role in a worldwide partnership of nature conservation organisations.

The threats that nature faces are vast, which is why the RSPB asks everyone – individuals, businesses, schools, farmers and the Government – to do their bit to give nature a home. By buying this book, you are helping, so thank you.

Thanks to the support of over a million members, the RSPB manages over 200 nature reserves, which are home to 80 per cent of the UK's rarest or most threatened bird species.

Sound science is at the heart of the RSPB, with conservationists monitoring how well (or not) different species are doing, identifying any problems, researching the reasons, then coming up with solutions to ensure the wildlife that we all love will be around for future generations to enjoy.

One such success is the Bittern – a heron-like wading bird that lives in reedbeds. In the 1990s, there were only 11 male Bitterns left in the UK. Now, thanks to new, clean wetlands being created and carefully managed, there are more than 100 males in the UK. Bitterns are, literally, booming again.

The RSPB campaigns for better laws and policies for nature and makes sure that environmental issues are on our politicians' agenda. It works with farmers and landowners to ensure there is space for nature across the UK countryside.

Educating and inspiring the next generation is also important, as our children will be the custodians of our environment in the future.

You can find out more about the work of the RSPB at rspb.org.uk

giving
nature
a home

RSPB Arne in Dorset, one of more than 200 wild places managed by the RSPB, and free to enjoy for members.

INTRODUCTION
TO THE SECOND EDITION

Garden Spider.

It is eight years since we wrote the first edition of this handbook and we are delighted that so many people have found its contents useful.

Gardens are special places. We create them for our own pleasure and no two are alike. Some are neat and tidy while others are – how shall we put it – more natural! Some have vegetable plots, but most have only lawns and flower borders. Some have mature trees while others are recent creations, with no trees or shrubs at all. With so much variety, it is not surprising that there is no definitive list of garden wildlife.

No wild plants or animals are found exclusively in gardens – they have not had time to evolve to match the requirements of this rather new and varied habitat completely. However, many species, from woodpeckers to woodlice, do visit us regularly and some stay to rear their offspring. Wild plants also occur in gardens: we often think of these as 'weeds', although the authors prefer to regard them as wild flowers that are simply in the wrong place!

Since the first edition, wildlife has continued to come under pressure. New houses tend to have smaller gardens. Hedgehogs, Starlings and House Sparrows have further declined, and non-native species such as Ring-necked Parakeets are more dominant in some areas. Gardens are increasingly regarded as important for nature conservation and we have expanded the contents to reflect reflect the latest thinking in garden conservation.

Our gardens can be intricate webs of life, and understanding the web – and improving it from year to year – is the real aim of this book.

A Nature Reserve on Your Doorstep

Water is important to birds for bathing as well as drinking.

As our countryside comes under pressure from agriculture and leisure activities, much of its wildlife is struggling to cope. As a result, gardens have become more important for the survival of all sorts of species, from the familiar Robin, to the elusive Blackcap, and from the urban Fox to the agile Common Frog. Just as nature reserves are specially managed for wildlife, so you can plan and maintain your garden to create the best possible conditions for the widest selection of species. Like a reserve warden, the wildlife gardener should know what is on his or her 'patch', makes plans to develop a space that appeals to as many species as possible, and manages the site to maintain a balance that suits both its human owners and its wildlife occupants.

Species that live in gardens can't survive in isolation. A garden is a miniature ecosystem, and understanding its whole food web is important. For example, the Song Thrush is a popular garden visitor and Garden Snails constitute some of its food. In autumn, the thrush is likely to be eating berries, but when that crop is exhausted, earthworms and other invertebrates become essential to its diet. Retaining some snails in the garden, planting berry-bearing shrubs and having plants that are home to invertebrates are all key to a successful wildlife garden and will ensure this species survives throughout the year.

The wildlife potential of a garden can be enhanced by carrying out structural improvements, such as erecting nest boxes and bird tables, constructing a pond or even making small modifications to a building. You might also enjoy keeping a record of the species you identify in your garden but, most importantly, you need to have a master plan. If you do all this, we are certain you will be surprised and enthralled at the results.

MAKING A WILDLIFE GARDEN

GET TO KNOW YOUR GARDEN

It may sound obvious, but the first step towards creating a successful wildlife garden is getting to know what is already there. Find out which plants are established, which grow well, and which animals visit and at what time of year. Make lists of the plants, insects, birds and animals you see, including the months in which they flower or visit. If you are unsure where to start, you could use the index of this book as the basis of your personal checklist.

Look out for any birds that might be nesting in or near your garden, as well as other animals like Hedgehogs or bats that could also breed there. If possible, wait a whole year before making any significant changes to your garden, otherwise you may inadvertently lose some key features that are already attracting wildlife.

PLANNING

Next, draw up a garden plan. This may be a simple map indicating the key features of the garden. Be sure to include any features outside the garden boundary that might influence your plans, such as a mature tree with overhanging branches. Mark areas that are shady, and also note those that get direct sunlight. Indicate the main compass points too, as orientation is important in the siting of structures such as nest boxes.

Mark on the plan ideal sites for nest boxes, bat boxes and a pond. Even if you have a small garden, consider leaving part of it untouched with more native plants, which can become your own wildlife haven. If possible, decide which area of the lawn is least used and cut the grass here less frequently.

Even small gardens can include birdfeeders and a variety of plants that feed and support insects.

BOUNDARIES, BORDERS AND LAWNS

BOUNDARIES

Around the edge of your garden there will be some kind of boundary, usually a fence, wall or hedge. Animals do not recognise our self-imposed partitions so, for obvious reasons, hedges are the most wildlife-friendly option, especially if they comprise native shrubs such as Holly, Wild Privet, Hazel or Hawthorn. The inclusion of additional shrubs such as Dogwood, Blackthorn, Spindle and Beech can provide even more interest and be better still for wildlife – like the old mixed hedges of farmland. Planting new conifer hedges, such as Leyland Cypress, should be avoided as they have limited wildlife benefit and drain the soil of nutrients and moisture. However, think carefully before removing any pre-existing conifers, as they might be home to nesting or roosting animals. Even if a garden in surrounded by walls or fences, small hedges can be introduced as dividers or as a backdrop to a garden pond.

Fences and walls have limited wildlife value except as supports for climbing shrubs and plants and for nest boxes. Fixing trellis to a fence or wall will help plants climb up it, and these in turn will help to support open nests, such as those of the Blackbird or Song Thrush. The vertical face of a wall can be used for growing Ivy and Honeysuckle, both of which are popular with insects, excellent for House Sparrows, and make for a great foraging and nesting habitat for birds. A dense cover of more exotic varieties of jasmine, wisteria and Barberry have their own value for roosting and nesting birds.

Well-chosen species planted along a boundary can also give added security: plants with thorns, like Holly, Hawthorn, Blackthorn and Barberry, are likely to deter trespassers, and a thick growth of Bramble is as effective a deterrent as barbed wire. No wonder so many small birds nest in such places!

FLOWER BORDERS

Just because the emphasis here is on wildlife, there is no reason to banish many of the usual garden flowers. Indeed, a traditional herbaceous border is not only colourful but is also very good for producing nectar for insects, especially bees and butterflies.

To create a wildlife-friendly border or flower-bed, choose a sunny aspect and select plants that attract insects. Lavender, marigolds, valerians, Foxglove, Sunflower, Red Hot Poker, catmint, flowering tobaccos and spiraeas all flower in summer, while stonecrops and

Thick climbing shrubs provide shelter for nesting birds and roosting places in winter.

Elephant Hawkmoth.

Michaelmas Daisy are ideal for autumn. A good ground-cover species that is also popular with bees in spring is Lungwort. Of course, the actual plants that grow well will depend on your soil and their position in the garden. In small gardens, similar effects can often be created with cleverly planted tubs and hanging baskets.

LAWNS

The dominant feature in most gardens is the lawn. It is used by birds such as thrushes and Starlings, which probe into the surface for worms and other invertebrates. It may also be home to some common wildflowers such as Daisy and clovers.

Perfect-looking lawns that are raked, fertilised and weed-free are not good for wildlife. Weedkillers and artificial fertilisers should not be used, as some weeds like clovers feed the lawn with nitrogen and their flowers provide nectar for insects. Wildlife-friendly

(top) A well-stocked herbaceous border attracts insects like butterflies, moths, bees and hoverflies.

(inset) Robins are often a gardener's companion.

lawns should be cut less frequently and left to grow a little longer, and one area should be left to grow even longer and seed naturally, before cutting in autumn or, even better, the following March. In larger gardens a wildflower meadow can be planted and then cut after the main flowering season. Finally, never water a lawn as it is too wasteful of this precious resource. Managing your lawn in the manner described can save you time, money and energy, as well as benefiting wildlife!

THE IDEAL LAWN

The ideal lawn arrangement in terms of benefits to wildlife includes areas of short grass where birds can feed, and longer grass that provides seeds and also a habitat for insects and their larvae. Mow the lawn with the blades set at a height of 3.5–5 cm, and stop mowing the area that is to be kept long in May and leave it alone until September. At this time, rake off the 'hay' but leave some tall grass until the following March, when it can be cut and raked. If you have more than one area of long grass, cut them in rotation at different times of the year. Cutting long grass can be difficult without a strimmer or powerful mower, although smaller areas may be cut by hand.

TREES

Some new trees will appear naturally in the garden as small seedlings, while others need to be planted. Those that appear naturally are generally species whose seeds are dispersed by the wind, such as the maples, including Sycamore, or those with berries that are dispersed by birds, such as Rowan. To germinate, some seeds need to pass through an animal's digestive system. Acorns and chestnuts may also be buried by squirrels or Jays, and inevitably some are never retrieved and go on to germinate.

Introducing trees to a garden can be challenging, but don't be quick to remove existing trees. Studies have shown that trees over 2 m high are one of the priorities for wildlife gardens. And, if your available space will permit them, trees add height and interest to any garden, and are hugely beneficial, providing food, shelter, nest sites and shade to a host of different species. They are, of course, generally slow-growing, and care needs to be taken during planting to ensure they are not placed close to a building or somewhere their roots could damage drains or underground cables. Whenever possible, it is advisable to consult a site plan that shows the locations of services before planting trees.

(right) Silver Birch trees produce catkins in spring, and an abundance of seeds (food for tits and finches) in autumn.

(below) Mistle Thrushes may visit to feed on windfalls.

Trees need to suit the size of the garden. Generally speaking, the larger the garden, the larger the trees that can be introduced. To help wildlife, try to select mostly native species, especially those that grow wild locally. Oak and Beech are valuable, but they need plenty of space and take several generations to mature. Rowan and Silver Birch, on the other hand, grow more quickly. Most conifers are not suitable, for the reasons already outlined (*see* p10), but the native Scots Pine may have a place in some gardens, as does the evergreen Holly.

Fruit trees may also be planted in larger gardens. A traditional cultivated Apple, pear or plum tree adds diversity, is good for early bees, provides a fruit crop in autumn, and the windfalls are food for a variety of birds, mammals and insects.

SHRUBS

Shrubs provide food and shelter for insects, which in turn attract a wide variety birds, such as Blue Tits hunting for caterpillars in summer.

As with trees, the number and species of shrubs that can be accommodated in a garden will be dictated by the size of the plot. And, like trees, some shrubs may arrive naturally – birds may bring Holly or Hawthorn, for example, depositing seeds from berries eaten elsewhere amongst their droppings. A mixture of native species and non-native berry-bearing shrubs will help attract insects, give cover for nesting and roosting birds, and provide autumn and winter food for birds and small mammals. Aside from the many native berry-bearing species such as Dog Rose, Elder, Hawthorn, Spindle and Dogwood, attractive shrubs like Barberry and Firethorn are especially good for a variety of birds as they provide them with both food and shelter.

The ground below the shrubs is also important to wildlife. The old leaves that collect here can be home to many tiny invertebrates that are a vital component of the garden food web. A positive sign is when you observe a Blackbird flicking over the dead leaves in search of its prey.

Some shrubs grow quickly and so require regular pruning, but be careful not to prune during the nesting season (March–August), when trimming can expose nests to unnecessary dangers. Also avoid reducing the size of the bush too much in the face of winter, as dense shrubs are often secret night-time roosts for many of our small birds.

Peanuts, Scraps and Slug Pellets

Peanuts

Peanuts are a highly nutritious bird food; however putting them in gardens can sometimes be a risk to the health of wild birds:

- Poorly kept nuts sometimes contain aflatoxin. To avoid this risk only purchase from a reputable dealer (such as the RSPB).
- Whole nuts in the breeding season can potentially choke young birds so should be avoided at this time, or used in mesh feeders where adults can only take very small portions.

Also, there are usually many more 'airmiles' linked to peanuts compared with locally grown Sunflower seeds, which are also popular with many small birds.

Kitchen scraps

Before commercial bird food was available people generally fed garden birds with 'kitchen scraps' and, with care, this is still beneficial – and also contributes to our domestic recycling.

You should avoid desiccated coconut, and long bacon rinds should be chopped short. Cake and breadcrumbs have only limited benefits, but pastry is excellent. Meat and fat chopped and put out in containers will be popular with birds such as Starlings, while thrushes will generally eat soft fruit and food with currants and raisins (although these should be out of reach of cats and dogs).

Be aware that garden birds cannot metabolise salt and that it can be toxic to them in high quantities. For this reason, salted food should never be offered to birds, and nor should salt be used to de-ice birdbaths.

Generally it's good to remove any uneaten meat before nightfall to prevent rats and Foxes taking it (unless you are feeding Hedgehogs – see p26).

Mesh feeders ensure that birds can only take small pieces at a time reducing the risk of choking when adults feed their chicks.

Slug pellets

The RSPB encourages gardeners to use non-chemical forms of slug control as much as possible. However, in the event of non-chemical solutions being unsuitable or impractical, the RSPB welcomes and endorses 'The Slug Pellet Code'. The code is as follows:

- Use slug pellets wisely and, before use, always read the instructions on the pack.
- It is essential that slug pellets are sprinkled thinly on the soil and around the plants being protected – not all plants are favoured by slugs and snails.
- Individual pellets should be placed 10–15 cm apart around the plant. Never pile them up.
- Always secure the container and store safely out of reach of children and pets.

LOG PILES AND COMPOST HEAPS

Composting plant material is an excellent way to avoid waste and feed garden plants.

LOG PILES

Dead wood is a miniature habitat. It supports fungi as it slowly decays, while the spaces inside and under a wood pile will be colonised by invertebrates such as woodlice, ants and snails. Insects hibernate inside log piles or under the peeling bark, and small mammals such as voles may also be attracted to them. Larger piles may provide nest sites for Wrens and a few other species.

To create a log pile, use local wood from garden tree branches and avoid bringing logs in from woods and other natural sites. If a tree or woody shrub dies in your garden, leave it in situ and let nature take it over, or plant Honeysuckle around it to create a feature.

COMPOST HEAPS

A feature of a good garden is its compost system, which recycles garden and household waste in an effective and eco-friendly way. Modern composters are plastic containers that have limited wildlife value until their contents are eventually fed back into the garden. More traditional compost piles or heaps, on the other hand, have a greater wildlife value, attracting insects, birds that probe them for food, and even reptiles, which may be drawn to the heat generated from the rotting vegetation within.

To prevent rats or Rabbits from digging into a compost heap, it is best to construct a retaining wall of robust wire, burying the lower edge 10 cm or so into the soil. The dimensions of the heap can be 1 sq m or more, and the waste that can be added to it includes grass cuttings, soft garden prunings, leaves, uncooked kitchen vegetable waste, and some newspaper and household shreddings. In general it takes a year for most materials to decompose, although some – such as large amounts of grass cuttings and leaves – will take longer. For this reason some gardeners use a system of several different piles that mature at different times.

WILDFLOWER MEADOWS

In larger gardens it may be possible to create a wildflower meadow, either by managing part of the lawn in a different way or by creating a new 'meadow'. The area does not have to be large, but it does require a sunny position. Access to larger garden meadows can be made more practical and interesting by mowing a narrow winding path through the area.

Creating a meadow can be as simple as letting the grass grow and encouraging wild flowers like clovers and Daisies to spread. However, by introducing wildflower seeds, which can be bought from many suppliers, you will achieve a larger mix of species. Flowers like Cowslip (spring), and Field Scabious and Knapweed (summer) all look attractive and are popular with insects, especially butterflies.

Wildflower seeds may be sown such as these colourful annuals.

The secret to a wildflower area is knowing how and when it should be cut. This depends on the plants you want to encourage, but the general advice is to cut early in the year (March or at the start of April) and again after the flowers have dropped their seeds (June or July). After cutting, leave the 'hay' on the meadow for a few days, to allow the last seeds to fall, before raking it off and adding it to your compost. This will ensure that you have spread seeds for the next year. Also, give the area a last cut before the winter (early October) or leave it until early spring. If you have a large garden meadow you may choose to leave one part mainly for butterflies, cutting it only once a year in March.

Buildings

Given the chance, some wildlife will share our homes. With careful planning this can give us pleasure while at the same time helping a species to survive. Once, when buildings were less well maintained, they contained plenty of gaps where birds and other animals could creep in. Starlings and House Sparrows nested in the eaves, bats roosted in the attic and, of course, spiders appeared in the bath! Some of these species now need our help, and it is possible to erect nest boxes under the eaves – special boxes for Swifts and artificial nests to attract House Martins. If there is a hole under the roof that is regularly used by House Sparrows, Swifts or Starlings, leave it as it is, and regard it as a rare privilege to have these species under your roof.

Garden sheds have always been popular with Robins as nesting sites and, in country gardens, Swallows may take over anything that passes for a barn. There is little we can do to help these species in their nesting, but inadvertently closing a door or window after the birds have started nesting can be disastrous unless you leave a permanent entrance they're happy to use, like a missing window pane.

It is not only birds that want to share our roof. Insects will also enter a house or out-building to hibernate, including ladybirds and Peacock butterflies. House walls may support climbing plants such as Honeysuckle or Ivy, and these also provide shelter for insects and potential nest sites for birds. Barberry planted around a window, for example, can provide security (it is very thorny), produces nectar to feed early bees, may support the nest of a Song Thrush or Blackbird, and also supplies winter berries for Blackcaps.

(inset) Long-eared Bats will often roost in roofs of houses and other buildings.

(below) Robins frequently enter sheds and garages to build their nests.

WATER FEATURES

Creating a water feature in a garden will provide great satisfaction and an endless source of entertainment. It will attract many forms of wildlife, as even non-aquatic species need to drink and birds, of course, will also regularly bathe. A natural-looking pond will be most successful in terms of attracting wildlife, but even a modern water feature bought at a garden centre provides some benefits so long as it allows birds to drink and bathe safely.

There is no perfect size for a pond, and even the smallest container kept full throughout the year will attract some wildlife. However, larger water bodies can support a greater variety of plants and, therefore, provide a much richer wildlife habitat. Water boatmen and diving beetles will soon colonise such a pond, and House Martins, Swallows and thrushes will use mud from the water's edge to construct their nests. Larger ponds are also less likely to dry out in summer – although the rate of water loss will depend on the density of plants emerging from the water. If necessary, additional water can be provided by capturing

(inset) Frogs arrive in garden ponds very early on in spring.

(below) Regular bathing is a vital aspect of plumage care.

water running off a nearby roof and diverting it into the pond. While the dimensions of a garden pond may vary, its depth is critical. Ponds that are more than 50 cm deep in the centre are less likely to freeze solid in winter, so the creatures hibernating at the bottom are more likely to survive.

The more a pond resembles a natural habitat, the more successful it will be. Planting emergent species will both look good and attract more wildlife, and sloping the edges to the pond will allow species that enter it to get out again. A pond with fish and frogs may also attract Grey Herons. However, introducing Goldfish is not recommended as they reduce the value of the pond to wildlife.

Finally, avoid planting trees or shrubs too close to a pond, but do add edging rocks and boulders, or even some paving, to provide shade and cover for amphibians. (*See also* pp246–7 for more details on garden ponds.)

A well-established garden wildlife pond.

Bog GARDEN

Safety is an important consideration when it comes to garden water features. Although ponds can be fenced off or have netting placed over them, they can still pose a danger to young children. A safer alternative that may appeal is a bog garden.

The principle behind the construction of a bog garden is similar to that of a pond, except there is no open water and the depression is filled with a mixture of soil and sand, into which a variety of native plants are introduced. Plants such as Yellow Iris, Common and White comfrey, Ragged Robin, Purple Loosestrife and Marsh Marigold are all well suited to the wet conditions. The area will need to be kept moist during early summer, but most of these plants can withstand a short period of drought.

A wide variety of attractive, native and nectar-rich species flourish in boggy conditions.

SEASONAL MANAGEMENT

Like any garden, a wildlife garden requires care and maintenance, but some of the actions are different from those in conventional gardening.

On lawns, grass may be left to grow longer and can be cut less frequently, the big cuts taking place after the main flowering season. Short grass clippings can be left to add humus to the lawn, but longer cut grass should be raked off and composted. While fallen leaves can look untidy on a lawn, some should be left as they will become food for earthworms.

Shrubs, including hedges, should not be cut during the nesting season (March–July) and pruning should encourage dense growth wherever possible. Also avoid drastic cutting and pruning in autumn – remember that some dense cover in a garden provides safe places for wildlife to shelter and roost. Don't always cut right back to the old wood, and consider cutting some shrubs in rotation – one part in one year and the other part the following year.

Flowering plants should be left to go to seed. When they are eventually cut, after the winter, they can be left in piles with other vegetation for a day or two so that insects can emerge and return to their habitats before the cuttings are composted.

The management of ponds is more difficult as there is never a 'right' time to tidy them up. Probably the best tactic is to remove any excessive plant growth in late summer or autumn, before any small creatures start to hibernate. Leave piles of cut vegetation on the edge of the pond for a few days to allow any

In winter, Long-tailed Tits will return to the same roost in dense cover each evening.

animals caught up in it to crawl back to the water, then add the piles to your compost.

Finally, stand back at the end of the year and ask yourself if the results of your planning and planting are what you expected. Has the wildlife improved in your garden? Have some plants dominated others or grown too quickly? Always be prepared to change your plan or take drastic action to remove certain plants to achieve the desired balance.

Before lighting a bonfire, check that no Hedgehog has crept underneath for cover.

MONTHLY GUIDE

Month	Wildlife highlight	Tasks
January	Robins start 'spring' song Blackcaps visit garden bird tables	Start a new wildlife log for the year Join in the RSPB's Big Garden Birdwatch
February	Early Brimstone and Comma butterflies come out of hibernation Tawny Owls are heard calling First frogspawn in ponds	Put up nest boxes for small birds (this is your last opportunity for the year) Prune shrubs and hedges late in the month
March	Early broods of birds Winter thrushes leave and early summer migrant birds start arriving Robins display	Sort compost ready for the new season Carry out your annual cut of wildflower areas Construct a pond – this is the best month
April	Hedgehogs emerge from hibernation The majority of summer migrant birds return to the UK Swarms of St Mark's Flies gather in sheltered places	Plant up a children's corner in the garden Set up nest boxes ready for Swifts
May	The dawn chorus is at its best Peak nesting season for small birds Wildflower meadows are at their best Nettle beds have many small caterpillars	Do not cut hedges and shrubs until the end of summer as birds may be nesting in them Make a home for bees and leave it near your flowering plants
June	Pipistrelle bats breed – often in large colonies Herbaceous borders attract butterflies and bees Damselflies and dragonflies may visit gardens Painted Ladies appear in large numbers in some years	Make and erect a bat box Introduce nectar-rich flowering plants to window boxes, tubs and borders
July	Starling flocks start to form once breeding is over Wolf Spiders are seen carrying eggs on bare soil Gardens visited by butterflies in search of nectar and to lay eggs	Keep bird feeders topped up during the summer Use 'grey' water from the house to water garden plants
August	Swifts leave Zebra Spiders rest on warm brickwork Ants swarm on calm, warm days	Leave garden plants to go to seed
September	Blackberries ripen in the hedges Many moths are attracted to lighted windows House Martins have their second or third broods	Cut areas of long grass for the last time Clear excess vegetation out of ponds Make a Hedgehog hibernation box
October	Hedgehogs start their hibernation Most summer migrant birds leave Winter migrant birds start to arrive Berries in hedges attract thrushes Tawny Owls are heard calling	Prepare winter bird feeders Plant trees and shrubs for wildlife
November	Small Tortoiseshell and Peacock butterflies hibernate in sheds Windfall apples attract migrants Small birds travel the countryside in flocks in search of food	Compost fallen leaves, but leave some under trees and shrubs Lightly trim shrubs, leaving sufficient cover for birds to roost Start a log pile with tree prunings
December	Pied Wagtails roost in some urban areas Gulls may visit inland gardens in cold weather Siskins may visit bird feeders Winter Moths are seen flying	Keep bird tables and feeders stocked with bird food and kitchen scraps

PREDATION IN THE GARDEN

Predators aren't always warmly received by gardeners wanting to encourage wildlife, but others consider it a testament to the health of the ecosystem they've nurtured. If your garden is attracting and supporting native predators then it's probably also home to a rich variety of wildlife at every level of the food web.

Domestic cats are instinctive bird catchers. If they belong to you then a collar with a bell will help by warning birds of their presence, but it's important for the cat's own safety that any collar has a quick release buckle. If the cat belongs to a neighbour, you'll need to find another way to protect the birds. CATWatch is an ultrasonic cat deterrent that has been shown to be very effective at keeping cats away from a particular area. If cats continue to be a problem then some modifications to your garden plan may be necessary. All bird food should be put on a high-level table or suspended from the thinnest branches of trees, but certainly kept at least 2 m clear of the shrubbery where wily cats can lurk. By covering a nest box with chicken wire you'll ensure that only the small birds can gain entry to the nest, but sometimes just the presence of a cat nearby will dissuade parent birds from using that box.

Squirrels are even more agile than cats. To prevent them from stealing food meant for

Domestic cats are responsible for killing large numbers of garden birds and small mammals.

birds, suspend the feeder from the finest of wires and fit a squirrel-proof collar around the bird table. Several designs of squirrel-resistant feeders are now sold by the RSPB and other outlets. In gardens with Grey Squirrels, nest boxes can be fitted with metal plates around the holes to prevent them from being enlarged and these rodents reaching the eggs or young.

Sparrowhawks and Magpies have become more common in urban gardens in recent years. They are a more natural threat, of course, being indigenous species, but are unwelcome to some people nonetheless. Again, there are some simple modifications that may scupper their ambushes. Feeders hung among tree branches will slow down a Sparrowhawk attack, or they can be placed near bushes where birds can take shelter. Plenty of dense cover will help to deter Magpies from raiding nests.

Invertebrate 'pests' may be welcomed in a wildlife garden as a sign of success and are also important prey for a wide variety of animals. However, if a particular species becomes a nuisance (such as slugs, ants or wasps), try wildlife-friendly solutions to deter them, and then only in moderation. The same is true of unwelcome rodents: mice and rats in a house need to be dealt with in a humane way. Live traps can be used to catch mice, although professional advice should be sought if rats are seen regularly.

Keeping Grey Squirrels away from bird food is one of the most difficult problems for the wildlife gardener.

THE GREEN GARDENER

More of us are now seeking ways to lead a greener lifestyle, and wildlife gardening can play a part in this.

COMPOSTING AND KITCHEN SCRAPS

Most organic material can be returned to the environment through composting. A good system absorbs not only garden waste but also uncooked kitchen scraps, newspaper and shredded paper (in reasonable quantities), fluff from wool carpets, human and animal hair, and litter from pets such as hamsters. The compost heap is home to many invertebrates and is a feeding place for birds and small mammals (*see* p15).

Cooked kitchen scraps may not compost, but they might be useful on the bird table. *See* p14 for more information on this.

ENERGY USE

Unless you use a hand-mower you will require petrol or electricity to cut your lawn. Such energy use can be reduced by cutting lawns less frequently and leaving some areas to go wild, or use a push mower – good exercise too! Any area of lawn that is turned into a shrubbery or a pond will also, obviously, reduce mower use.

WATER USE

Introducing a water butt is one way of making the most of rainwater. Position the butt to catch water running off the house or garage roof, where it will soon fill up during a shower of rain; the water collected can then be used as required. Ponds and bog gardens can also be positioned so that they receive water from a nearby roof (perhaps using a length of piping), thereby easing the problem of them potentially drying out in summer.

Watering garden plants is a waste of water, so instead introduce species that thrive in a dry climate. The plants mentioned in this book will not require too much attention and there are many other herbs that will also provide diversity in a dry summer. If you do water plants, use 'grey' water that has already been used in the house, such as the washing-up water or even bath water.

CHEMICAL-FREE GARDENING

We are now used to buying food that has been grown organically, so why not extend this by adopting an organic approach to wildlife gardening? Reducing or eliminating the use of chemicals in the garden and adding natural nutrients through compost is both responsible and cheap. There are also natural methods of pest control that do away with the need for commercial sprays and powders – the tactical use of coffee grounds and crushed egg shells to keep slugs and snails away from favourite plants is one example.

PEAT-FREE GARDENING

It is a tradition that gardeners add peat to flower-beds and containers, and use it to bring on small plants. While peat is undoubtedly good as a soil enricher, it is an unsustainable material that is taken from a unique and endangered habitat – peat bogs, which take centuries to form and just days to destroy. Using home-made compost is a far better option, or there are commercial peat-free alternatives available for purchase. Always check that plants you select have not been grown in peat.

LEISURE AT HOME

One of the biggest contributions to our carbon footprint is travel, so time spent in the garden at home has the benefit of being carbon-neutral. In addition, the fresh-air exercise of gardening is good for our health – a double benefit over driving to the gym!

Sunflowers are fun to grow and their seed heads provide food for birds in the autumn.

Secret Garden

In our modern world, nature often seems a long way away and irrelevant to everyday life. While older generations may look back with affection to the school nature tables of their childhood and the freedom they had to roam the countryside, today's children are more likely to experience nature secondhand via the TV, computer or device screens. The wildlife garden can change all this, allowing young people to experience nature at first hand in safety – to use their senses of sight, hearing, touch and smell by watching ants, avoiding wasps, planting seeds or picking up ladybirds.

Involvement

If you have children at home or who come to visit, involve them in garden activities as much as possible, helping to plan, to plant and to manage. These activities will teach them about the animals and plants that inhabit the garden and, most importantly, how they relate to and depend on one another – exactly the sort of information that you will find on the following pages.

Study

Children usually have keener eyesight than adults and enjoy looking closely at small animals. Such simple pleasures can be expanded into a study of insects with a hand lens or 'bug box'.

A desire in younger children to collect things can be harnessed to teach them about the garden through investigating fallen leaves and discarded feathers. Older children might enjoy keeping written records, for instance a checklist of the birds or butterflies they see in the garden illustrated with drawings or collages. The RSPB's annual Big Garden Birdwatch is also very popular with children. It can be done from home as a family activity and at school. For more information, visit rspb.org.uk/birdwatch.

Care

A passion for nature often leads to a desire to look after it. Encouraging children to feed birds and to provide homes for species that breed and feed in the garden will engender an attitude of caring, which is the first step towards conservation. Being given custodianship of a small plot of flowers or vegetables can introduce children to the concepts of basic gardening – planting, tending and harvesting – sparking an interest that may grow into a hobby or even a passion in years to come.

Games

Play is vital in the development of the child, and games in the garden are both healthy and great fun. They can vary from I spy (which teaches plant and animal names) to Kim's game (which helps in remembering objects). A version of sleeping giants can explain why owls have to use their ears to hunt, and searching for different coloured wools distributed around the garden can illustrate the advantage of camouflage in a most enjoyable way!

Birth and death

All life is represented in the garden – animals live, breed, produce young and die. These are concepts that children need to learn and become familiar with on their journey through their own life, and ladybirds on roses or caterpillars on cabbages may provide practical lessons that will stay with them for years to come.

A simple way for children to take part in eco-friendly gardening is by using 'grey' water recycled from the household to water plants.

MAMMALS

HEDGEHOG *Erinaceus europaeus*

Length 26 cm
Common throughout Britain
and Ireland.

IDENTIFICATION

Stout animal that is both familiar and unmistakable. Back, sides and top of head are completely covered with dense, stiff, sharp spines. Each spine is about 20 mm long and pale brown with a dark band below the tip, giving an overall flecked effect. Face is hairy rather than spiny. Muzzle is pointed, with a shiny black nose. Ears are visible in front of the spines. Legs appear short and tail is inconspicuous.

Hedgehogs usually emerge to feed at dusk.

HABITS

The largest of our insectivores. Nocturnal, but often active at dusk in woods, hedgerows and gardens. Moves slowly when hunting, but can raise itself higher on its legs and run more quickly when necessary. Can also climb and swim. When alarmed, will first stop and crouch with raised spines, then roll up completely, pulling the head and legs within the ball of spines. Very noisy when hunting, with much snuffling and grunting.

Hedgehogs leave long (up to 50 mm) cylindrical droppings on lawns and paths. These are black, with the fragments of insects usually clearly visible. They hibernate in a nest of dead leaves, under dense bushes such as Bramble or piles of cut brushwood. They can become very fat and slow before hibernation, and must attain a good body weight of 400 g or more to survive the whole winter. Hibernation usually lasts from late October to early April, but this varies with temperature.

Breeds May–October, in a large nest. Produces an average of 5 young, which are born blind and with very soft white spines. Hard, dark spines appear as the young develop. They are weaned by 6 weeks, after which they disperse.

FOOD

Feeds on ground-living invertebrates, including slugs, earthworms, caterpillars and beetles. Also eats small frogs, Slow-worms, mice, voles, occasionally eggs or young birds, and sometimes dead animals.

IN THE GARDEN

Hedgehogs hunt their invertebrate prey over a wide range and a hole in your garden fence will make this necessary travel possible. You can introduce a feeding station and provide mealworms, Sunflower hearts, minced meat, wet cat food, cooked potato or crushed nuts, but never bread or milk.

Nest-building can be encouraged by leaving patches of dense Bramble at ground level, or piles of shrub trimmings, along with a plentiful supply of dead leaves. Alternatively, a purpose-built hibernation box for Hedgehogs can be bought or built (*see* p245). Unfortunately, Hedgehogs will nest or hibernate in bonfires, so these should always be dismantled and relocated before burning. Some Hedgehogs also drown in garden ponds, and these should therefore include areas of shelving bank to allow the animals to escape.

Hedgehogs have between 2 and 7 young.

MOLE *Talpa europaea*

Length 11–16 cm
Widespread in Britain, but absent
from Ireland.

IDENTIFICATION

Familiar mammal, although seldom seen. Its presence is usually indicated by mounds of earth, or 'molehills'. It is the size of a small rat with a short, stubby tail (30 mm), usually held upright. Fur is black, short, dense and velvety. Legs are extremely short, the front pair with broad, flat 'hands' that have large straight claws. Has a pointed snout and very small eyes, almost hidden by the fur of the face. No ears are visible.

HABITS

The Mole is a specialised burrowing animal found in many habitats, especially grassland and deciduous woodland. It is active both day and night, alternating about 4 hours of activity with 4 hours of sleep. It excavates and inhabits a network of tunnels, from just below the surface down to 70 cm or more. In tunnelling, the soil is loosened and pushed back by sideways movements of the hands and claws. The loosened soil is then pushed up through a hole to form a molehill. Molehills are, therefore, spoil heaps, not the homes of Moles. Once a system of tunnels has been established, it is not necessary for many new molehills to be produced. In damp soil or leaf mould, a Mole may simply push along just below the surface, forming a shallow ridge. A nest of dried grass or leaves is made in a round chamber within the tunnel. Where the ground is damp or shallow, the nest may be at ground level, in a large molehill or 'fortress'.

Moles hunt by travelling through their existing tunnel system, finding animal prey that has entered it. Occasionally prey is caught by digging, or on the surface. They have long, narrow jaws, with sharply pointed teeth. Their hearing and sense of smell are good, but their sight is very poor. The main sense they rely on is touch, and sensing vibrations in the soil, especially by the snout and tip of the tail.

Breeds March–May. A single litter is produced, of 3 or 4 young. These are born blind and naked, but grow fur and are weaned by 5 weeks. They leave the female's territory and may travel overground, when they are vulnerable to predation.

FOOD

Moles are carnivorous, their main food being earthworms, and the larvae of insects such as craneflies, millipedes and slugs.

IN THE GARDEN

Moles are unpopular visitors to conventional gardens and have traditionally been trapped or poisoned. Non-lethal deterrents are also available, although these are less effective. Removing the molehills and allowing the animals to continue their activities underground is one practical solution.

BATS

Bats are the only true flying mammals. Their wings are derived from highly adapted hands, with a membrane of skin stretched between the fingers, back to the hind leg, and joining the tail.

Famously, bats navigate and find their prey in the dark by means of ultrasounds – high-pitched sounds, inaudible to the human ear, that they project and register as they bounce back. Each species uses its own wavelength and pattern of sound.

Bats are hard to identify in flight unless you have a bat detector. Having a pond in your garden, having night-scented flowers and putting up bat boxes will turn your garden into a bat haven.

BROWN LONG-EARED BAT *Plecotus auritus*

(COMMON LONG-EARED BAT)
Body length 5 cm
Found throughout Britain and Ireland,
except in the north of Scotland.

Long ears give a distinctive profile.

IDENTIFICATION
Small bat, although slightly larger than the Pipistrelle. Distinguished by enormously long ears (over 28 mm, or almost ¾ the length of the head and body), which can often be seen in flight. Fur is light brown, paler on the underside.

Brown Long-eared Bats are most common in wooded areas.

HABITS
Nocturnal, usually emerging after dark mainly in wooded areas, so not easily seen. By day, roosts in roof spaces and tree hollows, within small crevices. Has a weak, fluttering flight, usually around trees, and often hovers among leaves. Insects are sometimes taken in flight, but more often directly from leaves. It hibernates in buildings and hollow trees, from November until late March. Females begin breeding at 2 or 3 years old, and produce only a single offspring each year.

FOOD
Mainly moths.

IN THE GARDEN
In the past, bats suffered from the use of persistent insecticides. Such chemicals should be avoided. If bats are suspected of using a roof space, care must be taken not to disturb them as it is illegal to do so (*see box opposite*). Any timber treatment or building work that needs to be carried out requires consultation with a bat expert. Brown Long-eared Bats may make use of bat boxes as temporary daytime roosts (*see p249 for construction details*).

Body length 4–5 cm
Widespread throughout most
of Britain and Ireland.

Pipistrelles emerge soon
after sunset.

IDENTIFICATION

Very small, with an erratic, flittering flight. Fur is dark brown, sometimes darker and greyer in juveniles, and lighter on underside. Tail only just projects from beyond wing membrane. Two other pipistrelle species, the **Soprano Pipistrelle** (*P. pygmaeus*) and the **Nathusius Pipistrelle** (*P. nathusi*) are now known to occur in Britain, and are best distinguished by their different echolocation calls and genetic differences. The Soprano and Nathusius tend to prefer waterside habitats.

HABITS

The Common Pipistrelle is our smallest and commonest bat, and the most likely to be seen around houses and gardens. Nocturnal, emerging at dusk about 20 minutes after sunset, when it is still just light enough to watch the bats flying out of their roost. Sometimes seen flying in daylight when emerging during a warm spell in winter. They spend the daytime roosting, usually in a building. Common roosting sites are roof spaces and wall cavities – the bats can enter and leave through a surprisingly small opening. The sites may change from time to time. At rest, they cling to a surface rather than hanging free by the back legs.

Pipistrelles feed in flight, locating insect prey by echolocation. They also make a high-pitched squeak, which can just be heard, in addition to the inaudible ultrasounds.

Winter months (usually late October–March) are spent hibernating in a building or hollow tree, which is often a different location from the summer roost. Occasionally they emerge during warm weather.

Young are born during June or July. Females gather in large nursery colonies, each individual producing only a single offspring in a year. Pipistrelles have been recorded living up to 11 years.

FOOD

Small night-flying insects, midges, moths, etc. These are caught in flight and, except for larger items, are also eaten in flight. Will often visit outside lights to take the insects these attract.

IN THE GARDEN

Roosting and wintering sites in houses are extremely important for pipistrelles. Nothing should be done to prevent them from using these and they do no harm. Special precautions are needed when deciding on timber treatment, for which expert advice should be sought. Persistent insecticides have affected them in the past and should be avoided. Pipistrelles may make temporary use of bat boxes as daytime roosts (*see* p249 for construction details).

Roof spaces and wall cavities are common roosting sites.

BAT CONSERVATION

All bats are legally protected and must not be disturbed at the roost or handled without a licence. Any cases of injured bats, or questions of roosts being disturbed by building or timber preservation, must be referred to a licence-holder. Check the Bat Conservation Trust's website for details at bats.org.uk – they also have a bat helpline. Because of the risk of lyssavirus, you should never handle a bat yourself – leave it to the experts.

IDENTIFICATION OF MOUSE-SIZED MAMMALS

COMMON SHREW (page 32)

Very small. Long, thin, pointed nose. Small eyes. Ears short, almost hidden by fur. Sometimes has white ear patches. Brown upperparts, contrasting greyer underneath. Almost hairless tail just over half body length.

PYGMY SHREW (page 32)

Extremely small. Long, thin, pointed nose. Small eyes. Short ears, almost hidden in fur. Grey-brown, above and below. Tail two-thirds length of body, rather hairy.

BANK VOLE (page 33)

Short, blunt nose. Very short ears covered with fur. Small beady eyes. Rich reddish-brown fur, greyer underneath. Tail short, about half the length of the body

FIELD VOLE (page 33)

Short, blunt nose. Very short ears covered with fur. Small, beady eyes. Fur greyish or yellowish-brown. Tail very short, about one third the length of the body.

WOOD MOUSE (page 34)

Long nose, large bulging eyes and
very large, almost naked ears.
Long tail, longer than the body.
Body rich brown above, white
underneath, often with a
small yellow breast spot.

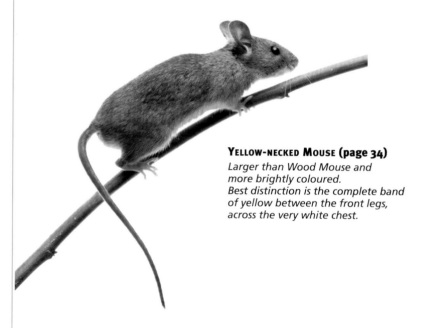

YELLOW-NECKED MOUSE (page 34)

Larger than Wood Mouse and
more brightly coloured.
Best distinction is the complete band
of yellow between the front legs,
across the very white chest.

HOUSE MOUSE (page 34)

Body light grey.
Pointed nose, large ears and
small beady eyes.
Tail long, almost as long as body.

COMMON SHREW   *Sorex araneus*

Body length 6–8 cm
Common and widespread in most habitats in Britain, but not in Ireland.

IDENTIFICATION

Small and mouse-sized. Fur is short and velvety, dark chocolate-brown above and grey below. Head has a long, sharp snout, eyes are very small, and ears are very short and embedded in fur. Tail is about half the body length and smoothly hairy.

HABITS

Shrews are not rodents, but are related to the Mole and Hedgehog in the order of mammals called Eulipotypha. The Common Shrew weighs only 6–13g. It is active year-round, and although on the go both day and night is secretive and seldom seen. It moves rapidly, in a network of tunnels and runways beneath vegetation.

Its nest is made from dry grasses, pulled into a ball, and sited underground or under the cover of logs and the like. It produces 2 or more litters of 5–8 young. These are born blind and naked, but grow quickly and are weaned after about 22 days, becoming mature the next season. Lifespan is only 18 months.

FOOD

Invertebrates, especially spiders, beetles, wood-lice, earthworms, small slugs and snails, and insects.

IN THE GARDEN

Shrews need adequate cover – leaves, long grass or other vegetation. They depend on good invertebrate populations for food.

PYGMY SHREW   *Sorex minutus*

Body length 5 cm
Less common than the Common Shrew, but its range is more extensive, including Ireland.

IDENTIFICATION

Distinguished from the Common Shrew by smaller size and longer, hairy tail, which is ⅔ its body length. The smallest mammal in the British Isles, weighing 3–4 g.

HABITS

Very similar to Common Shrew. Active by day as well as night, but rarely seen. Moves and hunts in underground tunnels, and along surface runways under cover of leaves and thick vegetation.

NOTE

Shrews are protected by law, and should not be caught or handled without a licence.

FOOD

Depends entirely on invertebrates, including spiders, beetles and woodlice.

IN THE GARDEN

Requires thick cover in the form of dead leaves or rough vegetation, and benefits from a rich invertebrate community for feeding.

Bank Vole   *Myodes glareolus*

Body length 9–11 cm
Found throughout Britain and parts
of south-west Ireland. Absent from the
Northern Isles, Western Isles and
Isle of Man.

Identification

Mouse-sized but with shorter legs, a blunter nose, smaller, fur-covered ears and smaller, beady eyes. The tail is also much shorter. Distinguished from the Field Vole by its reddish-brown colour and creamy-white underside (greyer in juveniles), and a tail that is about half the body length.

Habits

This is the most likely vole to occur in gardens. Elsewhere it lives in woodland, scrub and hedges, where there is good ground cover. It is active by day and night, although is seldom seen. It digs a system of burrows, and although it forages above ground it generally remains under cover. Voles are mostly ground-living animals, running quickly, but also climb up into shrubs. Their gnawing front teeth allow them to chisel open hard items such as nut shells.

They make a nest of grass and moss below ground or under cover, such as beneath dead wood. There may be 4 litters per year, with an average of 4 young in each. These are born blind and naked, but are weaned in less than 3 weeks. Voles can live for over 2 years.

Food

Almost all plant food: seeds and nuts, such as Hazel; fruits and berries, especially blackberries; and softer shoots and leaves.

In the Garden

They benefit from a good deal of cover and undergrowth, plus a wide variety of seed- and berry-bearing shrubs.

Field Vole   *Microtus agrestis*

Body length 9–11 cm
Found all over Britain except the
Northern Isles and Isle of Man.
Absent from Ireland.

Identification

Similar in appearance to the Bank Vole, but with brown fur and a grey underside. Tail is shorter, up to a third of its body length.

Habits

Widespread in grassland, but less common in gardens than the Bank Vole. It makes burrows and shallow runways among grass roots, leaving characteristic piles of cut grass stems in the runways along with piles of small droppings.

Food

Eats the leaves and stems of grasses almost exclusively. Field Vole teeth are specially adapted to its diet, the cheek teeth growing continuously to cope with the heavy wear.

In the Garden

As grassland specialists, Field Voles will normally come into gardens only if an area of rough or unmown grass is present.

WOOD MOUSE · *Apodemus sylvaticus*

(LONG-TAILED FIELD MOUSE)
Body length 8–9.5 cm
Common and widespread in the British Isles.

IDENTIFICATION

Large mouse with a pointed snout, large bulging eyes and large, thinly haired ears. Has a long tail that is at least as long as the body, and large, powerful hind legs and feet. It is rich brown in colour with a white underside, and usually has a small yellow spot between the front legs. Juveniles are greyer.

HABITS

Found in a wide range of habitats, especially woodland. Almost entirely nocturnal. Moves by running and jumping, but is also an agile climber and will visit bird tables. Has a network of runways and underground burrows. Nest is constructed of shredded grass and is usually below ground. Often stores nuts or seeds in hollow logs, etc.

If a Wood Mouse is caught by the tail, the skin pulls off from that point, and the mouse can escape.

FOOD

Plant food: mainly fruits and berries, seeds and nuts, buds and seedlings. Also eats some invertebrates: mainly snails and insects.

IN THE GARDEN

Sometimes enters houses. Benefits from a variety of seed- and berry-bearing plants.

> **NOTE**
> The rarer Yellow-necked Mouse, *A. flavicollis*, also visits gardens and houses in Wales and southern England. It is distinguished by its larger size (length 10–13 cm) and brighter colour, but mainly by a yellow band across the white chest.

HOUSE MOUSE · *Mus musculus*

Body length 7–9 cm
Found throughout Britain and Ireland, including towns.

IDENTIFICATION

Smaller than the Wood Mouse, with a tail that is almost as long as the body. Has shorter hind feet, smaller ears and less prominent eyes, and is grey above and below. Presence may be indicated by its distinctive musty smell.

HABITS

A familiar mouse, and the ancestor of the pet and laboratory breeds. Usually occurs in houses and other buildings, although small numbers live outdoors (these may also come inside in colder weather). Mostly nocturnal. Can gnaw through wood, and gain access to cavities in walls, lofts and below floors. Nest is often made of artificial materials such as shredded paper. Runs quickly and is an agile climber.

FOOD

Outdoors, it eats grain, grass and weed seeds, other plant foods, and occasional insect larvae, worms and other invertebrates. Indoors, it eats almost any human foods, but preferably cereals, fats and meat products.

IN THE GARDEN

They will visit sheds and take bird food, They may become prey for Foxes or owls.

BROWN RAT *Rattus norvegicus*

(COMMON RAT)
Body length 24–28 cm
Widespread and common throughout
Britain and Ireland.

IDENTIFICATION
Much larger than a mouse. Tail is slightly shorter than body and scaly in appearance. Has a pointed face with large, slightly furry ears. Fur is rough-looking, brownish-grey above and paler grey beneath.

HABITS
A relative newcomer to our fauna, arriving in the 18th century by ship. Associated with human habitation, but also found in cultivated land and on riverbanks. In many places it is considered a pest, owing to the damage it causes by gnawing and its contamination of foods and the health hazards associated with this. The species is the original ancestor of pet and laboratory rats.

Mainly nocturnal, but may be seen in daytime where not disturbed. Moves by running along the ground, but can climb and swim. Does not hibernate, but tends to seek more sheltered situations, such as outbuildings, in winter. Often associated with humans, so will occur in gardens, but does not normally go inside houses.

Very cautious and suspicious of any new object or food. This makes rats notoriously difficult for pest-control officers to trap or poison. Their senses are good, especially smell and hearing. Digs a system of burrows underground, often under sheds and chicken houses. Also makes tracks and runways above ground, which are quite easy to see if regularly used. The nest (usually underground) is a bulky mass of material such as dry grass, or artificial materials such as paper.

Usually breeds in summer and autumn, although in warm environments it will do so at any time. Females can have 3–5 litters per year, with the litter size averaging 7 or 8. Young are born blind and naked, but they grow quickly and can leave the nest after only about 3 weeks.

FOOD
Almost anything organic. Usually carries food items to a safe place before eating them. Has a preference for cereals and large seeds, and also eats fruit and invertebrates. Human food remains, both vegetable and meat, will be scavenged from compost heaps or bird-feeding areas.

IN THE GARDEN
Brown Rats transmit some human diseases, especially in wet areas, and so should not be encouraged. Compost heaps should be made rat-proof with chicken wire, and bird food should not be left on the ground overnight.

GREY SQUIRREL   *Sciurus carolinensis*

Body length 26 cm, tail length 22 cm
Common in England, Wales, southern
Scotland and central Ireland.

IDENTIFICATION

Silvery-grey fur and a long, bushy tail. In summer it is brownish, with reddish-brown along the flanks. Underside is white.

HABITS

Found in deciduous and mixed woodland, parks and gardens. A North American species that was introduced into Britain from the USA and Canada a number of times between 1876 and 1929. Has since spread from about 30 sites and is still spreading.

Active during the daytime. A skilled climber of trunks and branches. Also leaps from branch to branch. On the ground, it moves in short bounds.

Constructs a large spherical nest (called a drey) in a tree from twigs and leaves, lining it with moss or grass. Breeding and winter dreys are often close to the trunk; temporary summer dreys are less substantial and may be located among the branches.

Courtship involves chasing along the ground and up and around tree trunks. Squirrels produce 2 litters a year, in January–March and May–July. Young are born blind and naked. They are weaned by 10 weeks.

Food is picked up and held between the front paws. Surplus food is buried in the ground, or in tree holes and later found by smell.

FOOD

Large seeds and nuts, especially acorns, Hazel nuts (it splits the shells open), Sweet Chestnuts, Beech mast and pine cones (the woody scales are stripped off, leaving the core). Also berries, bulbs, tree buds, bark stripped from branches, fungi, insects and, occasionally, birds' eggs and nestlings. Well known for visiting bird feeders.

IN THE GARDEN

Where present, Grey Squirrels will visit bird feeders and nest boxes, where they can be serious predators of small birds and eggs. This invasive species also damages trees and has significantly impacted native Red Squirrel populations.

RED SQUIRREL   *Sciurus vulgaris*

Body length 22 cm, tail length 20 cm
Absent from most of England and Wales
except for a few small areas, e.g. the Isle
of Wight, Lake District and Anglesey.
Still present in Scotland and Ireland.

HABITS

It is native to Europe, but has declined in modern times. Most often found in large conifer forests.

IDENTIFICATION

Summer coat is chestnut-red, with the tail the same colour or paler. Winter coat is greyer, with a dark brown tail. Underside is white year-round. Long, thick ear tufts develop in winter. Slightly smaller than the Grey Squirrel.

FOOD

Mainly the seeds of conifers. Otherwise eats similar foods to the Grey Squirrel.

IN THE GARDEN

There are a few areas where Red Squirrels visit gardens, but where they do they can be encouraged by supplying nuts such as Hazel nuts at feeding stations off the ground.

RABBIT *Oryctolagus cuniculus*

Body length up to 40 cm
Common and widespread
throughout Britain and Ireland,
including most islands.

IDENTIFICATION

A familiar animal in appearance. The fur is greyish-brown, more reddish-brown on the nape, white or light grey on the underside. The ears are long, 6–7 cm, with round tips. Quite large, prominent dark eyes. Long hind legs with large back feet. Short upturned tail, showing white on the underside.

HABITS

Well established here as a wild animal, but actually introduced (from southern Europe) by the Normans (11th century), kept by them, and through the Middle Ages, in managed colonies called warrens.

A social animal, living in colonies in underground burrows, often on banks or slopes. The entrances are between 10 and 50 cm across, and often show signs of fresh digging. The droppings are the typical small, round, rather dry dark pellets, usually many deposited in the same spot.

Feeding is mainly crepuscular or nocturnal, although may also be active during daylight if undisturbed. Breeding mainly between January and August. Young are produced in a short burrow, called a 'stop'. This is lined with soft vegetation and fur from the female's belly, while the entrance is blocked up with soil. 3–7 young per litter, several litters per year. Female visits to suckle once per day. Young are born blind and almost naked. Their eyes open at 10 days, they begin to emerge from burrow after 18 days, and are weaned after three weeks.

Main predators are Foxes and Stoats, and birds of prey such as Buzzards. Dead Rabbits taken as carrion by Buzzards, Red Kites and members of the crow family. Smaller Rabbits also taken by Weasels and domestic cats.

Rabbit fleas are unusual in living around the edge of the ear of their host.

FOOD

Vegetation, selecting those plants that are the most nutritious: commonly grasses and clover. Especially grazes short turf where fresh growth has a higher food value.

Rabbits have a special feeding habit called refection: in addition to the normal pellets, they produce special soft droppings which are immediately re-eaten. Grass is difficult to digest, and this two-stage system allows for more efficient digestion of some of their plant food.

IN THE GARDEN

In rural areas, Rabbits may come into gardens from adjacent fields. If not excluded, as well as grazing on lawns and digging scrapes, they will eat a great variety of tender garden plants.

Fox *Vulpes vulpes*

(Red Fox)

Body length 65 cm, tail length 40 cm
Widespread in most of mainland Britain and Ireland.

Nowadays Foxes are a common sight in towns and cities.

Identification

Large dog-like mammal with a narrow muzzle and sharply pointed ears. Coat is reddish-brown, with white on the underside, throat and muzzle. Tail tip is also usually white. Lower legs, feet and backs of ears are black. Its normal movement is walking or trotting. Makes a variety of calls, mainly soon after dark. The commonest of these is a short, sharp, high-pitched bark, usually repeated three times. Also a high wailing scream is made by the female in the breeding season.

Tracks left in snow or soft mud show 4 toes and the pad arranged in a diamond pattern, with the two outer toes further back than those of a dog. Fine lines show that the pad is covered by fur. Its droppings are long, twisted and pointed, showing indigestible fur or feathers and the hard remains of prey, and are left in prominent positions on paths etc.

Habits

Our only wild member of the dog family (male is called a dog fox, female is a vixen). Found in countryside, suburban and urban areas, where it is a visitor to many gardens. Nocturnal, emerging at dusk, but sometimes seen in daylight. Can roam across a large area each night. Territory in suburbs may cover about 50 ha. It is marked with musty-scented urine, which can easily be detected by humans.

By day, Foxes lie up in many types of cover, such as Brambles or dense shrubs. The den, or earth, is often dug underneath some structure such as a garden shed. There is a single litter, usually of 4 or 5 young, produced in spring. They are born blind but have fur, and emerge from their earth at 4 weeks, playing around it while gradually weaning. The male brings much of the food at first. Young leave the earth completely at about 8 weeks, and are fully grown at 25 weeks.

Food

Mainly a predator on small mammals, especially voles and Rabbits, but also takes birds, insects, and earthworms on lawns on damp nights. Scavenges on dead animals. Often disliked for killing domestic poultry. A great opportunist, scavenging on almost anything and known for raiding rubbish bins in towns.

In the garden

A country animal that has moved into towns. If left alone it will breed in dense cover or under buildings. If you often see Foxes in your garden then they have probably found a good food supply, so don't leave any out for them. Don't try to make them tame and never hand feed them.

Young foxes emerge from their earth at 4–5 weeks old.

BADGER *Meles meles*

Length 92 cm
Widespread in mainland Britain
and Ireland.

IDENTIFICATION

Unmistakable. Large mammal with a long head and short tail. Body is grey, and head is black and white. The black extends in 2 stripes from in front of the eyes, past the ears to the neck. Ears have white tips. Legs and underside are blackish. Has large feet with 5 powerful claws. Although the overall colour is grey, individual hairs (which may be found in places where Badgers squeeze under fences) are pale with a dark band below the tip.

HABITS

Favours woodland, hedgerows and pasture, in areas of well-drained soil. Visits gardens in some areas. Nocturnal, coming out from dusk onwards. Normally shy, although in some gardens has become bolder. Does not hibernate but is less active in the winter. Movement involves ambling or trotting on its short legs, although it can run faster if alarmed and can also climb tree trunks to some extent.

Carries out a great deal of digging, with the flexible snout used for probing. It digs when foraging for food, and also for excavating the burrow, or sett. This can be a large and complex system of burrows and underground chambers with several entrances, these at least 20 cm wide, surrounded by worn tracks. Old bedding (dry grass etc.) is thrown out from time to time. Droppings are deposited in specially dug dung pits. The male is known as a boar, and the female a sow.

The female has a single litter of 1–4 cubs a year, born between January and March.

The young first appear above ground after 8 weeks, initially staying in the vicinity of the sett. Weaning may take 4 months, and the cubs stay with their mother until at least the autumn. They take about 2 years to reach maturity.

FOOD

Omnivorous, eating animal and plant foods. Earthworms are often an important dietary item, but many other invertebrates are also taken, including beetles, wasp larvae from nests, slugs and snails. Vertebrate prey includes frogs, young Rabbits and small mammals, such as Moles and Hedgehogs. They also eat carrion. Plant food consists of berries, fallen fruit, bulbs, some grasses and clover.

IN THE GARDEN

If Badgers visit the garden, it is simple to set up a viewing window as they will learn to find food like sun-flower hearts and may even get used to lights. While they are accused of creating mess or damage in gardens, such as digging holes in lawns, most people feel privileged to have them close by, but your neighbours may not, so be wary of encouraging them to become reliant on supplementary food.

Muntjac and Roe Deer

Muntjac *Muntiacus reevesi*

(Reeves' Muntjac, Barking Deer)
Body length up to 80–85 cm.
Shoulder height 45–48 cm.
Originally introduced from S.E. China over a period from 1894. Now well established in southern England, with some found in northern England, Wales and Scotland.

Identification
Our smallest deer. Reddish-brown with a smooth, glossy coat. Head often held low, giving a rather dog-like appearance with a rounded back. Head rather pointed, with two dark stripes running down the face. Antlers, on male (buck) only, short and straight, occasionally with one very short branch, pointing backwards along the head. Antlers are shed in late spring, and re-grown in late autumn. The upper canine teeth form short tusks, longer and more visible in the buck than in the doe.

Habits
Solitary. Prefers areas with woodland and scrub, where it does considerable damage to native plants. Active during both day and night, but most likely to be seen a little before dusk.

Voice is a short, sharp bark, uttered at regular intervals. Scent glands on the head, especially visible in front of the eyes, are used to mark the territory.

Females (does) give birth to a single fawn, which can become adult by 7 months. No defined breeding season. Does can produce a fawn about every 8 months.

Natural predators include Foxes which take young. Also killed by traffic and domestic dogs.

Food
Browses on a variety of vegetation, particularly Bramble and Ivy. Also eats leaves and flowers of many ground plants, with grass particularly in the spring. Takes nuts and fallen fruit from the ground.

In the garden
Will very often enter larger gardens. A selective feeder, eating flowers and shoots of a number of garden plants such as cyclamens, bluebells and tulips.

Roe Deer *Capreolus capreolus*

Body length about 110 cm.
Shoulder height about 65 cm.
Our smallest native deer. Found throughout most of England, parts of Wales and all of Scotland. Absent from Ireland.

Identification
Reddish-brown in summer, darker greyish-brown in winter. White or buff rump patch. Head with a black muzzle and white chin. Antlers, on buck only, small (about 30 cm when mature), typically with three small branches (tines).

Habits
Solitary or in small groups. Rather secretive, staying in cover during the day. Mainly active at dawn and dusk. Has a single kid, usually in May or June. Bucks defend territories throughout the summer.

Food
Mainly browse from low branches of broad-leaved trees. Also eat grasses and other ground plants.

In the garden
Although our commonest deer, apart from large gardens in rural areas, the Roe Deer is not often seen in gardens.

BIRDS

GREY HERON *Ardea cinerea*

Length 90–98 cm
Widespread in Britain and Ireland.

IDENTIFICATION

Long-legged, long-necked grey bird with a dagger-like bill and black marks on wings, neck and above eyes. Has a long, black wispy crest and long, fine plumes on its lower breast in the breeding season. Young are greyer and plainer than adults, and lack crest and plumes. Flight is slow, on long, broad, rounded wings, with neck curled back into the breast and long legs projecting at the rear.

HABITS

Resident. Nests in colonies called heronries, which are usually in tall trees. The population varies from year to year, and cold winters in the past have caused big losses to this species, as snow, ice and freezing conditions have reduced feeding opportunities. However, a series of mild winters in recent years has seen heronries growing, new ones starting and the population increasing.

FOOD

Individuals spread out from the heronries to find food, usually visiting the banks of lakes and rivers, and sometimes the coast. When hunting, they stand motionless or move stealthily. They hunt fish but will also take mammals, birds and amphibians. They also spend some time standing doing nothing, either alone or in groups.

IN THE GARDEN

This is a difficult species to attract to the garden deliberately. However, the hunt for fish will sometimes bring Grey Herons into gardens, and some individuals appear to specialise in visiting garden ponds, where they take Goldfish and other prey. It is possible to net a pond against herons, but this usually reduces the wildlife value: some people prefer to give up with fish and create a wildlife pond instead, where herons are welcome.

Juvenile Grey Herons (above) are less well-marked than the adults (right).

SPARROWHAWK *Accipiter nisus*

Length male 30 cm, female 38 cm
Widespread in Britain and Ireland.

The male Sparrowhawk
(below) is smaller than the
female (left).

IDENTIFICATION

Small bird of prey, the female noticeably larger than the male. Tail is long, and broad wings are rounded. Adult male has a blue-grey back with orange cheeks and often breast. Female and especially juvenile are browner, with a white stripe over the eye that gives them a fierce expression, and have barred underparts.

HABITS

Breeds in woodland, but relatively common in farmland and open country and increasingly seen in towns. Its flight consists of several flaps and a glide, but is fast and dashing when chasing prey. It sometimes circles high up on broad rounded wings, especially when displaying in late winter. At most other times it is secretive, watching the activities of small birds. After a rapid dash it strikes at its prey with needle-sharp talons. Often when hunting, it will fly along one side of a hedge and then slip over the top, trying to surprise birds on the other side.

FOOD

Feeds almost exclusively on birds, from small species such as tits and sparrows up to anything the size of a Collared Dove. Females generally prefer larger prey.

IN THE GARDEN

Sparrowhawks are recovering from a population crash 50 years ago, caused by the use of toxic chemicals in agriculture. They are now returning to their old haunts and are increasingly seen in gardens. A good wildlife garden that is home to lots of birds will help this species in its recovery, but emotions can run high when its food is the local Robin or Blue Tit!

NOTE

Female Sparrowhawks are sometimes confused with the Kestrel, *Falco tinnunculus* (female shown here), but the latter species is a bright chestnut brown and has narrower, more pointed wings. Although it often nests in towns, the Kestrel has never favoured gardens, preferring roadside verges and wasteground instead. When hunting, it hangs motionless, hovering with its head into the wind and using its sharp eyes to scour the ground for its prey of insects, small mammals and, only rarely, birds.

PHEASANT *Phasianus colchicus*

Length 53–89 cm
*Resident throughout most of Britain
and Ireland.*

IDENTIFICATION

Male is large, colourful and unmistakable, with a red face, dark green neck and iridescent copper-coloured body. He has dark scallops on the breast and flanks, and a very long, pointed tail. Female is brownish-yellow with darker marks on the back and flanks, and also has a long, pointed tail, although this is not as long as the male's. Juveniles resemble females but have shorter tails. Commercial breeding may result in variable plumage in the male, and some varieties have a bold white neck-ring.

HABITS

A cock Pheasant may guard a harem of 2, or sometimes many more, females. He will take no part in looking after the young, but his far-carrying 'kor-ork-ok-ok' call is a familiar sound of the countryside as he declares his territory.

The Pheasant is at home in a variety of habitats, usually close to woods, fields and hedges, and is also common in fenland. The species is native to central Asia and south-east Russia, and appears on Roman mosaics around the Mediterranean. It was probably introduced to Britain by the Normans in the 11th century.

FOOD

Eats a wide range of vegetable food, especially grain and other seeds, berries, leaves and, in summer, insects – especially ants and beetles.

IN THE GARDEN

Although not a typical garden species, Pheasants will visit gardens in areas where they are common from time to time, especially the males. They will sometimes feed under bird feeders or on food that has been dropped by other birds. In areas where Pheasants do visit gardens, they may deplete food intended for smaller species.

*Female Pheasants (left) lay up to 14 eggs.
Male Pheasants (below) often have a harem
of several females.*

GULLS

Several members of this opportunistic family have developed an affinity with humans that is not always welcomed.

IDENTIFICATION

Gulls are large and long-winged. Generally grey and white. Black wing-tips often incorporate white spots. Bills are long, strong, and formidable on large species. Young are grey or brown and may take up to 5 years to reach adult plumage.

HABITS

Aggressive yet wary, they will sometimes rob other species. The Herring and Lesser Black-backed Gulls now nest inland on buildings.

FOOD

Omnivorous and scavenging, often visiting rubbish tips and loitering where human food may be discarded.

IN THE GARDEN

Usually wary in enclosed areas. Will visit gardens to take kitchen scraps from the ground.

BLACK-HEADED GULL

Chroicocephalus ridibundus

Length 32–37 cm
Found throughout British Isles
Chocolate brown head in breeding season
Red bill and legs
Pearl-grey wings, white leading edge
in flight

HERRING GULL

Larus argentatus

Length 55–67 cm
Found in many towns and
cities and near the coast
Large and fierce-looking
Yellow bill with red spot
Flesh-coloured legs
Grey back, black wing-tips
with white spots

LESSER BLACK-BACKED GULL

Larus fuscus

Length 52–67 cm
Slowly colonising some towns,
both inland and coastal
Much darker grey back than Herring Gull
Yellow legs
White spots on black wing-tips

COMMON GULL

Larus canus

Length 40–42 cm
Occasional visitor
Smaller than Herring Gull
Grey back with white spots on black
wing-tips
Gentle appearance with dark eyes
Greenish-yellow legs and bill

TAWNY OWL *Strix aluco*

Length 37–39 cm
Widespread and resident in Britain;
absent from Ireland.

Female Tawny Owls can be aggressive when defending their nests.

IDENTIFICATION

Thickset bird with a large round head, very large dark eyes set in a facial disc of stiff feathers, and a small hooked bill. The brown plumage is streaked and speckled, giving excellent camouflage in woodland. It flies on broad rounded wings, often quite high and straight.

HABITS

This is the owl that gives the familiar 'too-wit-tuwoooo' call, but it also utters some harsh 'kewick's. These sounds are usually the first indication of a bird's presence as the species is remarkably secretive and strictly nocturnal. It may occasionally be seen leaving a daytime roost at dusk, and can sometimes be found during the day by following the alarm calls and mobbing behaviour of small birds. It can be aggressive in defence of its nest making swooping attacks on intruders, so care is needed if you suspect this species is breeding nearby.

FOOD

Eats small mammals, especially mice, voles and shrews, but also larger ones like Moles and rats. It also catches insects, birds, frogs, earthworms and, surprisingly, sometimes fish.

IN THE GARDEN

This is the owl that is most likely to visit towns and gardens – it even lives in some of the wooded squares in central London. It is unwise to encourage Tawnies as they can be very aggressive in the breeding season. However, make sure water butts are covered as this owl is often found drowned.

NOTE

Two-thirds the size of a Tawny, the Little Owl, *Athene noctua,* is more likely to be seen in daylight. It is active at dawn and dusk, and will often bob when it knows it is being watched. Its flight is deeply undulating on rounded wings. It likes parkland or water meadows with old willows, copses and agricultural land, and may occasionally visit rural gardens.

WOODPIGEON *Columba palumbus*

Length 40–42 cm
Common resident across Britain and Ireland.

IDENTIFICATION

Our largest pigeon. It has a blue-grey back and head with darker wings and tail. The upper breast is flushed pink and adults have a green/purple sheen and an obvious white mark on sides of neck. Head is small and body is plump. In flight, white crescents show on open wings. Call is a soothing 'orr-oo-cooo, oo-cooo'.

The display flight is a wing clap followed by a graceful downward glide.

HABITS

Found in farmland, woods and copses, as well as in town parks. Large flocks gather in winter and spring, most of them made up from local birds as British and Irish Woodpigeons are largely sedentary – unlike those in northern and eastern Europe, which are highly migratory.

FOOD

Eats a wide range of plant material, especially buds, leaves, shoots, seeds and acorns and its liking for farm crops has brought it into conflict with farmers. It will also eat some insects, such as beetles.

IN THE GARDEN

Woodpigeons have increased by over 30 per cent in 20 years, and many now breed in towns, frequently visiting parks and gardens, although seldom in the density of numbers of the Feral Pigeon. It is most likely to occur in gardens with mature trees or dense shrubs.

Woodpigeons can be encouraged in gardens by scattering bird food that contains seeds and grain on the ground. They are also more than happy to devour vegetable crops such as peas or lettuce, so gardeners with vegetable plots may need to use nets or other protection for their plants.

Woodpigeons will nest at any time of year

FERAL PIGEON   *Columba livia*

Length 31–34 cm
Familiar resident of towns and cities in
most parts of Britain and Ireland.

IDENTIFICATION

Smaller than the Woodpigeon, and varying in colour from all white to almost black. The most common form resembles the wild Rock Dove (from which these birds are descended), with a grey body, darker head and breast, and a greenish-purple sheen on the neck. Some birds show the white rump of their wild ancestors. The call is a soft 'orr-roo-coo'.

HABITS

Breeds at any time of year, but especially in spring and autumn. The nest is usually situated in a semi-dark cavity in a building or rock face.

This species has a long history of domestication dating back to around 4500 BC in ancient Iraq, and it was probably the Romans who introduced domesticated birds to Britain. In Norman and medieval England, dovecotes were common and the young birds produced in them provided fresh food for the rich, especially in winter. More recently, the species has been used for carrying messages in times of war, for racing (homing) and in the breeding of fancy varieties. The white fantail variety has even become a fashion accessory in some gardens. Over the years, many domesticated birds have escaped to build feral populations in cities all over the world.

FOOD

Many Feral Pigeons scavenge on streets and other places where there are easy pickings. They are mainly vegetarian and in gardens are likely to feed on grain and seed, but will also eat the seeds of wild flowers such as Shepherd's Purse.

IN THE GARDEN

These are highly opportunistic birds, and if they find a regular supply of food they will return to the spot again and again. As a result, they are not very popular with wildlife gardeners, especially those who do not really consider them to be wild birds. They certainly can become a pest if too many appear too often and take food intended for smaller species. To avoid such a build-up it is best to limit the amount of food (especially grain and scraps) put on the ground.

COLLARED DOVE *Streptopelia decaocto*

Length 31–33 cm
Widespread resident; more likely to inhabit gardens in rural areas than in towns.

The Collared Dove spread across Europe in the 20th century.

IDENTIFICATION

Smaller than a Woodpigeon. Has a pinkish-buff head and underparts, and a darker pinkish-brown back. Adults have a small black half-collar on the sides of their necks. The longish tail has white outer margins when seen from above, but has a broad white terminal band when seen from below. The call is a harsh 'krurrr', and the song is a loud, repetitive 'coo-oo-cuk, coo-oo-cuk', sometimes mistaken for the call of a Cuckoo.

In flight, wings show a band of pale grey.

HABITS

A very visible species, feeding on lawns or other open areas, and singing from rooftops and overhead wires. Its display involves flying up steeply and then parachuting down on fanned wings and tail.

The Collared Dove is a relatively new arrival in Britain and Ireland, first nesting in the 1950s following a spectacular population expansion from south-eastern Europe to the north and west. Its long breeding season can last from February to October, and it is possible for a pair to raise 5 broods in a year.

FOOD

Its main food is grain, seeds from grasses and other wild plants, and berries. Some green plant material is also eaten, and insects are taken in summer.

IN THE GARDEN

Bird food scattered on the ground will attract these birds if they are already in the neighbourhood. They will frequently feed under hanging bird feeders and bird tables, and benefit from food dropped by other species. Collared Dove nests are often in conifer trees, so having a mix of trees, including 1 or 2 dense conifers, will be appreciated.

SWIFT   *Apus apus*

Length 16–17 cm
Widespread in Britain and Ireland
in summer.

Swifts will travel many kilometres to avoid storms.

IDENTIFICATION

Sooty-brown bird that often looks black, with a slightly forked tail (compared to the Swallow) and very long, narrow, pointed wings that curve back into a crescent in flight. The most aerial of species, spending months at a time in flight when not nesting.

HABITS

The Swift arrives in western Europe in late April or early May from Africa and leaves to return to Africa in August. Although not really a garden bird, it can often be seen feeding high over towns and villages, sometimes singly but usually in groups. Some groups form 'screaming parties' and perform breathtaking aerial chases over and between buildings. This is thought to be a social activity that helps keep a colony unified.

FOOD

Eats flying insects, including flies, beetles, aphids, hoverflies, craneflies, moths, butterflies, thrips, leafhoppers, ants and lacewings, and also small spiders drifting on gossamer. Prey is caught in flight in the bird's large gape, and 10,000 insects may be caught in a day when feeding young.

IN THE GARDEN

Swifts originally nested in holes in trees and rocks but now prefer buildings, usually under the eaves of a house where there is a suitable access hole, and also in old buildings such as churches. In eastern Europe Swifts frequently use Starling-sized nest boxes, a habit that has also recently been observed in Scotland.

The species has come under threat as nesting holes have been blocked up and buildings netted to deter pigeons. To attract nesting Swifts, leave holes or gaps under eaves or tiles to allow them access to the roof space, and try putting 1 or 2 Starling-sized nest boxes under the eaves. In addition, encourage insects in the garden, as these are the main food of Swifts. Playing tapes of Swift calls in spring may also help to attract birds to potential nest sites.

Young swifts have more scaly-looking plumage than adults.

Ring-necked Parakeet *Psittacula krameri*

(Rose-ringed Parakeet)
Length 38–42 cm
Introduced species, found mainly in
south-east England.

Identification

A Starling-sized bird with a long, tapered tail and green body. Close up, the typical red bill is obvious, as is the black and pink neck-ring of the adult male. The rapid, flickering flight is distinctive, as are the pointed blackish wings, which appear to be positioned towards the front of the body.

Habits

A noisy bird, making frequent high-pitched screeches – often in flight. It tends to be gregarious, with groups gathering in the tops of tall trees and roosting communally.

The species originates in Asia and Africa, and its arrival in Britain is rather mysterious; some may have escaped from captivity while others may have been deliberately released. It was first known to breed in the wild in Britain in 1969, and numbers have increased rapidly since then in urban areas in south-east England. Garden bird tables may have helped its winter survival, and its liking for soft fruit and apples means it can be a pest in areas where these crops are grown commercially.

Ring-necked Parakeets are now common in parts of south-east England.

Food

Fruit and berries, and also Sunflower seeds from bird tables and feeders.

In the garden

These parakeets were first noticed in the Greater London area, where they took to using gardens and parks for feeding and breeding. They take food intended for native species and may displace other cavity-nesting birds.

Waxwing *Bombycilla garrulus*

Length 18 cm
Winter visitor, especially in
eastern Britain

These attractive winter migrants come to us from northern Scandinavia and Siberia. They feed on insects in summer, but rely on berries in winter. They are nomadic in their hunt for these fruits and numbers visiting Britain vary considerably from year to year.

GREEN WOODPECKER *Picus viridis*

Length 31–33 cm
Resident in the countryside in England,
Wales and southern Scotland; absent
from Ireland.

IDENTIFICATION

Our largest woodpecker, with a grey-green
back and a lighter green breast and belly.
The rump in flight is vivid yellow-green and
the top of the head is red. The bill is typical
of the woodpeckers, being long and strong.
The distinctive flight is bounding, with the bird
apparently closing its wings periodically. At
close quarters males can be recognised by their
red rather than black cheek stripe. Young birds
are duller and are heavily spotted and barred.

HABITS

Like other members of the family, the Green
Woodpecker spends a lot of time in trees and
nests in holes in trunks or large branches,
which it excavates for itself. Unlike other
woodpeckers, however, this species is also
frequently encountered on the ground as it
searches for insects in short turf – especially
ants and their larvae.

(right) The call is a laughing 'peeu peeu peeu',
but drumming is rather feeble.

(below) Young can fly at about 21 days old.

FOOD

Its long tongue has a sticky tip and can reach
into the tunnels of wood-boring insects to
extract adults and larvae, and to take ants from
their nests. It will also eat beetles, flies and
caterpillars.

IN THE GARDEN

This woodpecker will visit gardens with large
lawns or other grassy areas, particularly if there
are old trees nearby. It is more likely to be seen
in rural locations or on the edges of towns.
It is not usually interested in supplementary
bird food, preferring instead to search for
ants and other invertebrates in grassy areas.
A wildflower meadow or a lawn with a few
ants' nests may therefore provide the right
habitat, and if there are old trees nearby these
may be potential nest sites.

GREAT SPOTTED WOODPECKER *Dendrocopos major*

Length 22–23 cm
Resident throughout Britain where there are mature trees; absent from most of Ireland.

FOOD

It eats insects in summer, and seeds and other fruits in autumn and winter. It opens hard nuts and pine cones by wedging them in crevices and hacking at them. It also takes nestlings of other species, sometimes making a hole in the side of a nest box in order to reach the young of birds such as Blue Tits.

IN THE GARDEN

Great Spotted Woodpeckers frequently visit gardens, usually in search of food. They can be tempted with fatty bird food and live food such as mealworms. Some will also visit plants for nectar, including the Red-hot Poker. Other visits are less welcome, when they raid garden nest boxes in an attempt to remove young birds.

(left) Young birds can be recognised by their red crowns.

(below) The rapid 'drumming' of the woodpecker is a form of communication and is not 'drilling' a nest hole.

IDENTIFICATION

The largest of our 2 black and white woodpeckers, being the size of a Blackbird (the Lesser Spotted is much rarer and is only the size of a sparrow). It has large white oval patches on its wings and dirty white underparts. It has crimson under its tail and the males also have crimson on the back of their heads. The frequent call is a distinctive sharp 'keck, keck', and the spring communication is a short burst of mechanical drumming on a branch that echoes through the woods.

HABITS

Seldom seen on the ground. It spirals up tree trunks and extracts invertebrates from under the bark or from inside dead wood with its long tongue. This has a hard, sharp tip and is equipped with small harpoon-like spines. Often it will chip away at dead wood to reach new prey. In recent years the species has become more common, while its smaller relative, the Lesser Spotted, has become much rarer.

SWALLOW *Hirundo rustica*

Length 17–19 cm
Summer visitor to rural areas
throughout Britain and Ireland.

IDENTIFICATION

Small, agile bird with a deeply forked tail and very long tail-streamers. The back is an iridescent blue-black, the underparts are whitish and the face is a dull red. Male has slightly longer streamers than female, and in juveniles they are almost entirely lacking. The bill is short and the mouth wide for catching prey. The call is a sharp 'twisit' and the song is a twittering trill.

HABITS

Most Swallows arrive in April and the bulk of the population has left by October. They are usually seen in flight, swooping near the ground or low over water as they catch insects in the air. They sometimes fly higher, but seldom as high as Swifts. They frequently perch on overhead wires, and they also visit puddles and other wet areas to gather mud for building their cup-shaped nest.

Swallows take about six weeks to reach their winter quarters in southern Africa.

Swallows like a roof over their nest, so construct it on a beam or support in buildings such as barns or sheds, not under eaves like a House Martin. They produce 2 or 3 broods before returning to South Africa for the winter.

FOOD

Feeds on a variety of flying insects, including flies, aphids and flying ants, all of which are caught in the air. Its agility to catch its prey is amazing, and it may need 6,000 insects a day to rear its brood of 3–6 young.

IN THE GARDEN

Swallows pass through or over towns on migration, but gardens in rural locations are most likely to attract them. It is not possible to feed these birds, but an insect-rich garden may help a little. Providing a muddy puddle or pond will assist birds with nest-building, and if they use an outbuilding for their nest site, do take care not to shut them inside accidentally.

Swallows will return to the same nest year after year.

HOUSE MARTIN *Delichon urbicum*

*Length 12.5 cm
Common visitor April–October to
towns and villages throughout
Britain and Ireland.*

IDENTIFICATION

Small and plump with delta-shaped wings and a short forked tail, but no tail-streamers. The back is blue-black, with a very obvious bold white rump. The underparts are white. The flight is more direct than that of the Swallow. Its song is a soft twittering often given in flight, and the call is a hard 'prrit'.

HABITS

Insect food is caught on the wing – House Martins may be seen catching prey at low or medium heights, often over water. They sometimes perch on overhead wires and occasionally in trees, but at night many sleep on the wing at high altitudes.

House Martins are sometimes seen on the ground, especially when gathering small pellets of mud to build their cup-shaped nests, usually constructed under the eaves of houses. The nest sites tend to be in loose colonies, and old nests of previous years are often reused. They produce 2 or 3 broods a year.

FOOD

Almost all the House Martin's food comprises small flying insects, such as aphids, caught on the wing.

House Martins rearing their second or third brood may be assisted by their first-brood youngsters.

IN THE GARDEN

The wildlife gardener can really help this species as it needs people who are prepared to allow it to nest on their property. Artificial nests placed under the eaves, or at least a rough surface here to assist nest attachment, will sometimes attract House Martins. If birds build their own nests, these should be left in place as they are often reused another year (it contravenes wildlife protection laws to knock down these nests when in use). Nesting birds can leave a bit of a mess, but this problem can be solved by erecting a small shelf under the nest.

Buildings with white walls and overhangs are favourite nest sites.

PIED WAGTAIL   *Motacilla alba*

Length 18 cm
Common resident over much of Britain and Ireland; northern populations move south in winter.

IDENTIFICATION

A neat black and white bird with a long black and white tail that is eye-catching as it is constantly 'wagged' up and down. Males have a black back, while in females it is grey. Juveniles are more drab, with brownish upperparts and yellowish face and underside. The call, often uttered in flight, is a sharp 'twissi-vit', while the song is a pleasant twittering, sometimes given during a fluttering song-flight. The flight is typically bounding.

HABITS

A very active species that is at home on the ground in open locations, where it runs quickly after insects. Often seen near water, but is also found a long way from lakes and rivers – it has a liking for car parks, playgrounds and even motorway service stations! Large communal roosts of hundreds of birds may gather

Both parents help to rear a brood of young Pied Wagtails (right), while in winter, a male (below), may defend its own small territory.

before dusk from late summer, through winter and into early spring. Some roosts are in reed beds and other wild areas, while still others are in town centres.

FOOD

Feeds mainly on insects such as flies and midges, and also on caterpillars. Will sometimes fly up and snatch a flying insect from the air.

IN THE GARDEN

Pied Wagtails often feed on short grassy areas and sometimes visit larger garden lawns. If they visit regularly they may be tempted to stay and nest in an open-fronted nest box, although they are not a common garden breeding species. A lawn that is not treated with herbicides or pesticides and is cut regularly may attract them, as will a wildflower meadow after cutting, when small insects are emerging.

DUNNOCK *Prunella modularis*

Length 14.5 cm
Common resident throughout Britain
and Ireland.

IDENTIFICATION

The size of a Robin, its back is brown with darker streaks, the head and breast are blue-grey, and it has dark streaks on its flanks. The bill is small and pointed. The male and female look alike, but the juvenile is browner and a little more stripy. Has a piping 'tseep' call and a short, fast, warbling song.

HABITS

The Dunnock tends to be rather unobtrusive, staying close to cover or moving in a mouse-like fashion with its body close to the ground. As it walks it appears to shuffle along and often flicks its wings. In courtship displays, the wing flicking is more pronounced as it waves one wing above its back.

The breeding behaviour is rather unusual: while some males and females form pairs, other females may attract and mate with 2 or more males, and a few males may have 2 or more females. This social life leads to some interesting courtship rituals as individuals try to establish dominance – a drama that is played out in many gardens every year.

FOOD

Mostly takes invertebrates, but will also eat berries and small seeds.

GARDEN CONSERVATION

This is a common garden bird but is often overlooked. A feeding station is likely to attract Dunnocks, although it is rare for them to feed on a bird table – they are more likely to be on the ground picking up tiny food items dropped by other species. They commonly nest in gardens, and require densely growing shrubs or a traditional hedge containing Bramble, roses, Hawthorn or similar species to provide cover and protection to the cup-shaped nest.

Dunnocks regularly flick each wing separately in display, but will sometimes wave both wings.

WREN *Troglodytes troglodytes*

Length 9–10 cm
One of our most numerous species,
resident in most parts of Britain
and Ireland.

IDENTIFICATION

Tiny hyperactive bird with a reddish-brown back and buff underparts, fine barring all over (most obvious on wing and tail), and a white stripe over the eye. The wings are short and rounded, and the tail is often cocked over the back, especially during singing. The song is amazingly powerful for such a small creature and usually ends in a rapid trill. The call is a loud 'tic-tic-tic'.

HABITS

A secretive but energetic species that often remains in dense cover or flies low and fast between bushes. When singing, however, it will sometimes use an exposed branch. The male builds several 'cock' nests, from which the female selects her choice. She then lines this and uses it for 1 or 2 broods during the summer.

Wrens are strongly territo-rial for most of the year, but will roost together communally in an old nest or nest box for extra warmth in cold weather. Some of these cold weather roosts have been known to number almost 100 birds.

FOOD

Feeds mostly on invertebrates such as flies, aphids, beetles and spiders. Surprisingly, Wrens have also been seen to catch small fish and even tadpoles.

IN THE GARDEN

Dense vegetation with plenty of insect food will attract Wrens. They seldom take traditional bird food, although can sometimes be tempted by mealworms and, reputedly, grated cheese scattered under bushes. They may use open-fronted nest boxes as a site for their domed nests, and in winter they sometimes roost House Martins' nests.

Wren populations may 'crash' during
prolonged cold winter weather.

ROBIN _Erithacus rubecula_

Length 14 cm
Familiar resident throughout Britain
and Ireland, especially in rural areas.

IDENTIFICATION

The male and female look alike. The orange-brown breast, brown back and white underside make the Robin unmistakable when seen properly. Depending on whether its feathers are fluffed up, its shape can change from plump in cold weather to sleek at other times. Juveniles lack the red breast and are quite spotted. The song is also variable: slow and wistful from autumn until midwinter, then suddenly changing to a brighter, faster song as spring approaches. The call is a sharp 'tic-tic'.

Young Robins out of the nest are spotted, giving camouflaged protection.

HABITS

Unlike most other birds, Robins continue to sing for much of the year as they are resident and continue to defend territories, even in winter. Pairs usually split up outside the breeding season and hold separate territories. Courtship is quite elaborate as the birds display and posture, using their red breasts as visual signals to help sort out rivals from potential mates. Prior to and during egg-laying, males can be seen 'courtship feeding' females who beg with squeaky calls and fluttering wings.

FOOD

Eats invertebrates such as flies, spiders, beetles and worms. Will take berries and other fruits in autumn and winter.

IN THE GARDEN

Robins once followed large animals foraging in woodland in order to feed on newly disturbed invertebrates. Today, they are more likely to follow a gardener for the same reason – to pick up food from recently disturbed soil. Thus garden Robins often become very tolerant of people and learn to take food such as mealworms from the hand. Some Robins are now adapting to feed from bird feeders. They can sometimes be encouraged to nest in an open-fronted nest box, although they are just as likely to enter a garden shed and nest among the paint tins.

Male and female Robins defend separate winter territories.

SPOTTED FLYCATCHER *Muscicapa striata*

Length 14.5 cm
Summer visitor to open woods and large gardens; has declined across Britain and Ireland in recent years.

IDENTIFICATION

Small grey-brown bird with an off-white breast. Looks very 'upright' when perched. The crown and upper breast have dark streaks. Male and female are similar, while young are more spotted. Wing feathers have pale edges. The bill is quite long and the gape wide to catch prey. Call is thin 'teeze' and the song an indistinct warble.

HABITS

Catches insects in the air by flying from a perch with a swooping, erratic action. It is one of the last summer visitors to return, having wintered in Africa, south of the equator. It is not clear if the issues causing its recent decline are in Europe, Africa, or along its migration route.

FOOD

Flying insects, including flies and butterflies, form the main part of its diet, but it will also take aphids and other smaller prey from plants, and sometimes feeds on small snails and other invertebrates on the ground.

GARDEN CONSERVATION

This species has only ever been common in larger rural gardens with mature trees and suitable cover for nesting. Its rapid decline now makes it a very special visitor. Its needs are quite easily arranged, as it will nest in an open-fronted nest box, on a sheltered ledge on a wall, or among climbing plants such as Ivy or Honeysuckle.

PIED FLYCATCHER *Ficedula hypoleuca*

Length 13cm
Summer visitor to western Britain.

Slightly smaller than House Sparrow. Plump. Males are black and white in spring, females are white in wings and tail. An unusual garden bird but may use nest boxes close to woodland in the west or north of Britain. Recent decline as a breeding species.

Male Pied Flycatchers (left) are polygamous, mating with two or more females, although he will usually only help to feed one family.

BLACKBIRD *Turdus merula*

Length 24–25 cm
Common resident throughout Britain
and Ireland; additional migrants
arrive for winter.

IDENTIFICATION

Adult male is sooty black with a yellow bill and eye-ring. Female is dark brown and some have speckles on the breast, although these are never as obvious as in Song Thrushes. Juveniles are similar to the female, but are more spotted and sometimes have a ginger head. Young males are black, but lack the yellow bill and eye-ring. Calls are an urgent 'chink, chink-chink' or a high-pitched 'seep', and the song, given from an open position, is a rich, rather slow flute-like warble that tails off at the end.

HABITS

The nervous 'chinking' calls of Blackbirds at dusk are a typical sound heard in many gardens. Some of the bird's actions are also distinctive: as it lands, its tail is cocked and lowered slowly; and at other times it will energetically turn over leaves under bushes in its search for food.

Nesting may start very early, during mild spells in late winter, but most young are reared in spring and summer, with some pairs producing two or even three broods in a season. Cup-shaped nests of grass, straw and fine twigs are built in bushes and incorporate some mud in their structure.

FOOD

Invertebrates and fruit are the species' main foods. Insects are taken in summer, berries and other fruits are important in autumn and winter, and earthworms are pulled from moist soil at any time.

IN THE GARDEN

This is a woodland species that has adapted well to gardens. It likes dense shrubs for nesting, but will feed both under cover, turning over dead leaves, or in the open on lawns, where it searches for worms. To help Blackbirds, plant berry-bearing shrubs for autumn and winter food, and leave thick shrubs alone from February onwards to encourage nesting.

(above) Both parents help rear the young, but only the female incubates the eggs.

Local Blackbirds may be joined by migrants from the north and east in autumn and winter. This is a male.

These images are not to scale.

MALE BLACKBIRD (page 61)
Sooty black. Breeding adult has yellow bill and yellow eye-ring.

FEMALE BLACKBIRD (page 61)
Dark brown with darker wings and tail. Some birds have markings on the brown breast.

SONG THRUSH (page 64)
Medium-brown upperparts. Small dark spots on buff breast and flanks. Small buff wing marks. Orange underwing in flight.

MISTLE THRUSH (page 65)
Large thrush. Greyish-brown upperparts. Larger dark spots on whitish breast. Pale edges to wing-feathers. White underwing and white outer tail feathers visible in flight.

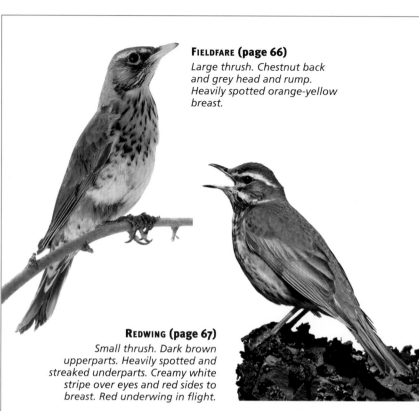

FIELDFARE (page 66)
Large thrush. Chestnut back and grey head and rump. Heavily spotted orange-yellow breast.

REDWING (page 67)
Small thrush. Dark brown upperparts. Heavily spotted and streaked underparts. Creamy white stripe over eyes and red sides to breast. Red underwing in flight.

All five thrush species (clockwise from top): Fieldfare, Song Thrush, Blackbird, Redwing, Mistle Thrush.

Song Thrush *Turdus philomelos*

Length 23 cm
Common resident in lowland Britain and Ireland; additional migrants arrive from Europe in winter.

IDENTIFICATION

Only slightly smaller than a Blackbird, with a medium-brown back, small dark spots covering the off-white and buff underparts, and pale orange under its wings. The sexes are alike, while the young have a lightly spotted back. Its song, given from an open position, is variable but always loud. It comprises a series of notes or short phrases repeated 3–5 times before changing to another series of notes that are also repeated, and so on until the original series returns. The call, usually given in flight, is a thin 'tsic'.

HABITS

The Song Thrush's best-known habit is its unique way of dealing with snails, which are smashed open on a stone or other hard object (usually referred to as an anvil). Like the Blackbird, it nests in deep cover and may rear more than one brood in a summer. Its cup-shaped nest of straw and feathers has an inner lining of hard mud.

Song Thrushes have declined rapidly in recent years. One reason for this appears to be shortage of food in the wider countryside for young birds in autumn and winter.

Song Thrushes will often use a favourite 'anvil' several times to crack snail shells.

FOOD

While the Song Thrush is an expert at opening snails, it also feeds on a variety of other foods, including insects in summer, berries in autumn and winter, and earthworms and other invertebrates all year round.

IN THE GARDEN

The use of snail and slug pellets (*see* p14) will kill off some of the Song Thrush's essential food and may well harm the bird itself. An organic approach to wildlife gardening will therefore help this and other species. A pond or wet area for mud, thick bushes for nesting, and plants that produce berries in autumn are all garden features that will help support a local Song Thrush population.

MISTLE THRUSH *Turdus viscivorus*

Length 27 cm
Resident in much of Britain and Ireland, especially where there are mature trees.

IDENTIFICATION

Our largest thrush. Rather upright, with grey-brown upperparts and large dark spots on its pale breast and belly. The wing feathers have pale margins, giving the appearance of a pale panel on the closed wing. The wing underside is white and the bird also has distinctive white tips to the outer-tail feathers, which are obvious in flight. The call is a loud rattling, and its song is powerful and melodious, rather like that of a Blackbird, but louder, slower and more repetitive.

HABITS

Starting early in the year, it sings from high and often bare branches. It is territorial when nesting, but may be seen in small, loose flocks in other seasons as it travels widely in search of food. Some residents in winter will aggressively defend a food supply, such as a berry-laden Holly tree. Its old country name of 'Storm-cock' is well deserved, as its far-carrying song is often the only one to be heard during windy and stormy conditions.

FOOD

Like other thrushes, the Mistle Thrush feeds on invertebrates such as insects, worms, slugs and snails, and also fruits such as berries and windfall apples in orchards and gardens.

IN THE GARDEN

Not a common garden bird, although it will nest in some larger gardens with mature trees or visit larger lawns to feed on worms and other invertebrates. In autumn and winter, small groups may visit gardens that contain good crops of berries or windfalls that have been left to rot under fruit trees.

(top) Mistle Thrushes defend a food supply in winter.

(right) Mistle Thrushes are aggressive towards other species that approach their nests in spring.

FIELDFARE *Turdus pilaris*

Length 25.5 cm
Winter migrant to Britain and Ireland from northern Europe; widespread November–March.

IDENTIFICATION

A large and quite colourful upright thrush with a heavily spotted buff breast, chestnut back, grey head, grey rump and black tail. The male and female look alike. Its call is a loud 'chacker chack chack'. In flight, the white underwing is very noticeable.

HABITS

Migrant Fieldfares travel around in loose flocks and sometimes mix with Redwings. It is often their chuckling calls that draw attention to their presence. When feeding, they spread out over an area of grass or plunder the berries in hedgerows or other shrubs. They cross the North Sea from the Continent, arriving on the east coast in October, and spread rapidly inland. Occasionally a pair stays and nests in northern Britain.

FOOD

The crops of berries in our hedgerows are a magnet for these birds, but they are just as likely to be seen feeding on windfall apples and other fruit, or as a flock scattered over areas of short grass hunting for worms. At other times of year they will also eat insects.

Migrants are generally first seen in eastern Britain, before spreading across the countryside.

IN THE GARDEN

Although widespread across Britain and Ireland in some winters, the Fieldfare is not a common garden bird. Larger gardens with big lawns may attract a visiting flock, as will fruit trees with fallen fruit. Garden hedges or shrubs with berries may also attract an itinerant group, especially during hard weather. To help these and other thrushes in cold weather, it is good to hold back some windfall apples until December or even January and then put them out with other bird food.

REDWING *Turdus iliacus*

Length 21 cm
Winter migrant to most of Britain and Ireland; widespread October–March.

IDENTIFICATION

Slightly smaller than a Song Thrush, with a brown back, speckled breast, bold white stripe over the eye, smaller white stripe under the eye, and orange-red under the wing that also continues onto the flanks (although this can sometimes be hard to see on birds on the ground). The call is a high-pitched 'seep', which is often given in flight.

HABITS

One of the first signs of migrating Redwings is the sound of their 'seep' calls after dark on clear autumn evenings, as the birds travel in flocks. They feed on areas of short grass, or in bushes and trees that hold ripe berries.

A few Redwings may nest in Scotland, but most of our winter visitors migrate here from Scandinavia and other parts of north-western Europe, and from Iceland. They are generally seen in small flocks and frequently mix with Fieldfares and other thrushes. They roost communally at night, in groups of hundreds or, occasionally, thousands.

Thin 'seep' flight calls can sometimes be heard after dark, as these birds migrate at night.

FOOD

Redwings feed on berries and other fruits in autumn, and they also take earthworms from areas of short grass. At other times of year insects and even small snails are eaten.

IN THE GARDEN

Most likely to be seen in the countryside, or in flight over larger towns. It is not a frequent garden visitor, but in hard weather it may seek refuge and food in gardens (even in the suburbs) if these contain fruit such as apples, or sheltered places where worms can be obtained. Berry-bearing shrubs may also tempt these birds closer to our houses once the natural berry crop in the countryside becomes exhausted.

All our thrushes like a supply of windfall fruits.

BLUE TIT *Cyanistes caeruleus*

Length 11.5 cm
Common resident throughout Britain and Ireland.

IDENTIFICATION

Familiar small bird with a blue cap and wings, white cheeks, a black line through the eye, a blue-green back and yellow underparts. It has a pale patch on the nape and a small white wing-bar. The male and female look alike, but juveniles in summer resemble washed-out versions of their parents and have yellow cheeks. The call is a high-pitched 'see see see' and the song is a thin 'see see see-chu chu chu'.

HABITS

Famous as an acrobat, as it feeds upside-down expertly on hanging bird feeders in gardens – a normal habit for a species that regularly hangs on flimsy twigs in its search for its natural food. It is territorial when nesting, but at other times will travel around woods, hedges and gardens in small flocks, often accompanied by other small birds such as Long-tailed Tits and Goldcrests.

Its natural nest site is a hole in a tree, but it will also use other cavities. It is the most likely species to be attracted to a specially made nest box, providing the hole is the correct size (*see* pp242–3).

FOOD

In summer it feeds on insects, especially caterpillars and aphids, and also on spiders and other invertebrates. In winter it takes seeds, such as birch, small nuts, fruits and berries. In gardens it will feed on peanuts, Sunflower seeds and kitchen scraps (*see* p14). In woodland in summer, a pair of Blue Tits may feed up to 1,000 caterpillars a day to their family of nestlings.

IN THE GARDEN

This is a species that is relatively easy to attract to most gardens, as it will search for food there in winter, and in summer may stay and nest. Commercial bird foods such as peanuts and Sunflower seeds are popular, but the species will also take household scraps, such as fat from bacon rind and meat from bones. Urban Blue Tits may sometimes have difficulty in finding sufficient food to rear their young in gardens in summer; a variety of insect-rich bushes and trees will help, but supplying additional bird food is now recommended.

Blue Tits readily use nest boxes, particularly when natural tree holes are in short supply. These should face north or east, and should be positioned about 2 m above the ground. To prevent a build-up of parasites, nest boxes should be cleaned out annually, soon after any young have left (*see* pp242–3).

GREAT TIT *Parus major*

Length 14 cm
Common resident throughout Britain
and Ireland.

IDENTIFICATION

This is the largest member of the tit family, and
has a black head and white cheeks. The back is
greenish and the tail grey-blue. The underparts
are yellow with a black stripe running down the
centre, which is generally wider and bolder in
males than females. It also has a white stripe
in its blue-grey wings. Juveniles in late summer
are like pale imitations of the adults. Great
Tits utter a wide variety of different calls, the
most familiar being a scolding 'charr, charr'.
The most commonly-heard song is a loud,
repetitive 'teacher, teacher', sounding rather
like a squeaky bicycle pump, but some Great
Tits have a variety of other songs.

HABITS

This is a woodland species that is also at home
in gardens, especially in winter. It is dominant
around bird feeders and will frequently chase
off other species. It is territorial when nesting,
but its territories break down once the young
leave the nest; at this time family parties roam
the countryside, often joining with other tits
and other small birds. It nests in holes in trees
and other cavities, and some birds occasionally
use man-made structures such as road signs and
letter boxes for the purpose. Great Tits make a
wide variety of calls and there is evidence that
these may vary with the habitat in which the
birds live; urban birds, for example, sing at a
higher pitch in noisy areas.

FOOD

Feeds on fruits, seeds and nuts, including Hazel
nuts, which it can chisel open. It will eat peanuts
and Sunflower seeds (see p14) in gardens,
as well as taking kitchen scraps. In summer it
feeds on insects, especially caterpillars.

IN THE GARDEN

A common visitor to garden bird
feeders and bird tables. Natural
food shortages can occur at
any time so garden feeders
can help, but avoid loose
peanuts, dry, hard
foods, large chunks
of bread, or
fats during
the spring
or summer.

Great Tits lay an egg a day, but do not incubate
until the clutch is complete, so all the young hatch
at the same time.

Native trees and shrubs will help provide cover
and food for more insects, which in turn are
eaten by Great Tits.

Great Tits can be encouraged to stay in
gardens to nest if a box with a suitable sized
hole is provided (see pp242–3). Deep boxes
are preferred, with at least
19 cm from the bottom of
the hole to the floor of the
box. A nest box that has
been used should always
be cleaned out after the
nesting season.

*The male (right)
has a wider stripe
on the breast than
the female.*

COAL TIT *Periparus ater*

Length 11.5 cm
Widespread resident in Britain
and Ireland.

IDENTIFICATION
Small member of the tit family, with a blue-grey back, pale buff underparts and two small but obvious wing-bars. Its tail is short. The rather large black head has white cheeks and an obvious white patch on the nape. In birds resident in Ireland, the white on the head and nape tends to be tinged yellow. The 'pee-chew, pee-chew' song is similar to that of a Great Tit but is faster and higher pitched, while the call is a high 'see-see'.

Coal Tits rarely use nest boxes, preferring natural holes.

HABITS
The Coal Tit is usually associated with conifer trees, and so is a relatively unusual visitor to most gardens, unless there happens to be a conifer wood nearby. Outside the nesting season it will range further afield, and often joins roving bands of small birds. It is at this time that it is most likely to visit gardens.

It is very agile and always on the move. It often feeds by hanging upside-down at the ends of thin twigs or hovering to reach under branches and leaves. If it does visit a garden, it may carry off peanuts or Sunflower seeds and hide them away in small crevices, returning time and again to the food source to collect more and more food. This secret cache of food may be revisited later when other food is in short supply, and there is evidence that the bird can often remember where it was hidden.

It nests in holes in trees and in other cavities (even in the ground in mouse-holes), but only rarely uses nest boxes.

FOOD
It mostly feeds among the highest branches of trees, but will sometimes exploit a food supply on the ground, such as fallen Beech mast. Its summer food is larvae, especially caterpillars, and adult insects, as well as spiders. In winter it eats seeds and will visit gardens for commercial bird food, such as Sunflower seeds.

IN THE GARDEN
The best way to attract this relatively unusual garden bird is by providing a regular supply of good commercial bird food in winter. It may follow a flock of other small birds into a garden, especially during hard weather or when there is shortage of food elsewhere.

NOTE
The similar-looking Marsh Tit, *Poecile palustris*, has no white on the nape or wings and is a much rarer garden visitor.

LONG-TAILED TIT *Aegithalos caudatus*

Length 14 cm
Common resident throughout
Britain and Ireland.

IDENTIFICATION

Tiny bird with a small round body, hardly any neck and a very long tail. Its body is black and pinkish-brown above and white below, with a pink tinge on the flanks. The head is black and white. Juveniles have more black on their head than adults and lack any pink. The call is a high-pitched 'see, see, see', interspersed with a short dry 'thrupp'. The flight is weak on short rounded wings.

HABITS

A Long-tailed Tit's nest is usually built in a thick bush or small tree and is a wonderful structure, forming a complete ball of moss, lichen and spiders' webs, and camouflaged with lichen on the outside. It is lined with feathers and has an entrance hole at the side. The nest is soft and flexible with a natural elasticity that allows the 8–12 young to move around inside without the danger of it collapsing. Individuals (especially males) from pairs that fail to produce young will sometimes help rear the offspring of a neighbouring pair.

After fledging, birds from several families form itinerant flocks that travel around woods and hedges, the individuals making their distinctive calls to help keep in touch with one another. At night they roost together in a tight 'huddle'.

FOOD

The Long-tailed Tit's main food is invertebrates, including small insects such as moth caterpillars, and also spiders. In winter, the eggs of insects and spiders are taken from bark and buds. It will also eat seeds.

IN THE GARDEN

Until recently, Long-tailed Tits would not have been considered garden birds except in the most rural of gardens. However, in the 1990s the species was suddenly seen in gardens more often as it adapted to visiting hanging bird feeders. Whether this change in behaviour was a response to increased numbers, to a shortage of natural food or to the improved quality and variety of commercial bird food is uncertain.

A regularly maintained feeding station offering small seeds such as Nyjer and black Sunflower seeds and also 'fat balls' may attract this species. In areas where breeding habitat is scarce, birds may sometimes nest in thick, spiny garden shrubs. Maintaining tall hedges that contain native shrubs would therefore be a good way to help the species, especially if there are fields, parks or wasteland nearby.

Small flocks of Long-tailed Tits may visit gardens outside the breeding season.

BLACKCAP *Sylvia atricapilla*

Length 13 cm
Summer migrant arriving mainly in
April across Britain and Ireland;
others from Europe arrive in autumn
and winter.

*Females and juveniles resemble
males but have reddish caps.*

IDENTIFICATION

Small, slim bird with a grey-brown back and paler underparts. The male has a distinctive sooty-black cap, while the female and juvenile have reddish-brown caps. The call is a sharp and hard 'tac, tac'. The song, made up of distinct phrases, rich clear notes and a varying tempo, is both loud and melodic, and is thought by many to be one of the most attractive songs of any native British bird.

HABITS

A common summer visitor to woods and copses, arriving in March or April and leaving in September or October. However, during the last 30 years increasing numbers of Blackcaps have been seen in Britain, often in gardens, in winter. Ringing these birds has shown that most are not summer visitors that have stayed on, but are in fact migrants from northern or eastern Europe.

Although relatively common, the Blackcap can also be secretive. It is easier to hear than to observe in summer when leaves are on the trees, as it mostly sings from within dense cover. The winter visitors are often attracted to bird tables and feeding stations in gardens, or may be seen eating late-autumn berries.

FOOD

In summer the Blackcap's food consists mainly of invertebrates such as flies, caterpillars and beetles, as well as nectar. In autumn and

The migration direction of Blackcaps has changed so that increasing numbers visit British gardens.

winter, fruits and berries from trees and shrubs such as Elder, Apple, Bramble, Honeysuckle and Holly are eaten, and birds visiting gardens also take commercial bird food and kitchen scraps (*see* p14).

IN THE GARDEN

Gardens resembling a wood or copse may attract Blackcaps. The more trees and shrubs in a garden, the more insects and fruits there will be to eat and the greater the chance there is of the birds finding a suitable nest site. However, most gardens are not like this, and so the species is likely to be only an infrequent visitor, usually occurring at migration time when birds are on the move. The best chance of seeing one (or sometimes a male and female together) is at a well-stocked bird feeding station in cold weather.

NUTHATCH *Sitta europaea*

Length 14 cm
Woodland species, resident in
England, Wales and parts of southern
Scotland.

IDENTIFICATION

Small bird with a large head, longish bill and very short tail. It has blue-grey upperparts, a whitish breast with chestnut flanks, and a black, bandit-like mask through its eye. Its legs are short and it moves with a series of short jerks up and down branches, often upside-down, and occasionally forages on the ground. The call is a loud 'tweet, tweet tweet' and a loud rattling trill, which echoes through woods in spring.

HABITS

The Nuthatch is famous for being able to climb down tree trunks as well as up them. It has some of the characteristics of a small woodpecker, but is unrelated and does not excavate its own nest hole as a woodpecker would do. Instead, it selects an existing hole (often made by a woodpecker in a previous year) and reduces the size of the entrance to keep out larger birds. To do this the Nuthatch uses mud that sets solid. If a nest box is chosen whose entrance hole is the right size, the bird's instinct is so strong that it will still plaster a coating of mud around the front of the box and sometimes on top as well.

Nuthatches narrow a nest box entrance with mud, which sets hard and deters predators.

IN THE GARDEN

Nuthatches seldom travel far, so it can be very difficult to attract them to gardens. They rarely move from mature trees, so gardens with large trees or those situated close to woods or parks are more likely to be successful. However, the birds will visit bird tables and feeding stations, carrying off Sunflower seeds, which they break open in typical Nuthatch manner.

FOOD

It feeds mainly on insects and spiders in summer, but, as its name suggests, seeds and especially nuts are important in its diet. To extract the edible parts of these, the Nuthatch has evolved the habit of wedging the seed, nut or pine cone in a crevice and hammering it open with its strong bill – hence its common name of Nuthatch, which comes from 'nut-hacker'.

Male Nuthatches have richer red flanks than the females.

CROWS

Members of the crow family are known for their intelligence and adaptability. Three 'black' species visit gardens in addition to Jay and Magpie.

IDENTIFICATION

Large birds with mostly black plumage and broad wings. Some are colonial, while others are more likely to be seen in pairs. Bill is strong and in most species is an adaptation to a varied diet. All are found in all seasons in Britain.

HABITS

Raucous and dominant in the garden. Clever at obtaining food. Some are predators on smaller bird species.

FOOD

Omnivorous and opportunistic. Some take eggs and young in the breeding season and most are carrion eaters. Can be encouraged into gardens with kitchen food scraps (see p14) as well as bird food such as fat balls.

IN THE GARDEN

Not always welcomed in a garden. Dominant, and potential predators on smaller species. Jackdaws can be encouraged to use large nest boxes.

ROOK   *Corvus frugilegus*

Length 44–46 cm

Black with purple sheen. Grey bill. Bare face between bill and eyes. Shaggy leg-feathers.
   Colonial and nests in rookeries at tops of trees. Tends to be more rural in its distribution.

CARRION CROW   *Corvus corone*

Length 45–47 cm

All black with black powerful bill and black eye.
   Tends to be more solitary than the Rook, but flocks may form outside the nesting season.
   Found in urban as well as rural habitats; even city centres.

JACKDAW   *Corvus monedula*

Length 33–34 cm

Black with a grey back to its head and a pale 'watery' eye.
   Colonial species that nests in holes and crevices; often in buildings, especially chimneys.
   Clumsy acrobats when trying to use hanging feeders.

JAY *Garrulus glandarius*

Length 34–35 cm
Relatively common resident where
there are woods and trees, although
scarce in the north and west.

IDENTIFICATION

Attractive member of the crow family, with a pinkish-brown body, dark wings with blue and white patches, a black tail and an obvious white rump. Delicate black streaking on the blue feathers of the wings can be seen at close quarters. Also has a streaked crest that is raised during display or when alarmed. Has a rather laboured flight on broad, rounded wings. Its call is a raucous screech, although it has various others, including occasional 'popping' and mewing, and it is capable of mimicking the calls of other species.

HABITS

Like the Magpie, the Jay has spread from the countryside into towns in recent years, and may sometimes arrive in suburban gardens. Its natural habitat is woodland, where it is a shy bird and more likely to be heard than seen. It was once regarded as vermin by gamekeepers, and was shot and trapped in large numbers because of its habit of eating the eggs of gamebirds. Jays still eat eggs, of course, but much of the countryside is less extensively keepered than it was in the past, giving the species a chance to increase and populate new habitats; habitats that contain few predators able to tackle birds of its size. It is usually resident, seldom moving far afield, but in autumn its liking for acorns will take this bird away from dense woodland in search of oak trees and its favourite food.

If food is plentiful, Jays will hoard some by burying it, returning later when supplies are scarce, but, for many reasons, they don't always recover their hidden caches. The spread of oak woods has been attributed to the burying of acorns by Jays, especially woods that have expanded uphill.

FOOD

An omnivorous feeder, taking insects, other invertebrates, young birds and eggs in summer, and fruit and nuts (especially acorns) in autumn and winter. Also sometimes preys on small mammals.

IN THE GARDEN

The Jay is a visitor to rural gardens and, more recently, also to suburban gardens. It will take peanuts (see p14) and other bird food, but can become unpopular with gardeners as it will dig up newly planted seeds (especially peas) and will sometimes raid the nests of songbirds in search of fledglings to feed to its own young.

MAGPIE *Pica pica*

Length 44–46 cm
Common resident across most of
Britain and Ireland, except for
northern Scotland.

IDENTIFICATION

Familiar black and white crow with a long,
wedge-shaped tail. Close up, the dark feathers
of the wings and tail show an oily blue-green
sheen. The flight is strong
but rather leisurely, on
wings that are broad and
rounded. On the ground it
walks or hops, often with its tail
raised. The call is a noisy, scolding 'chacker
chacker'. It also has a quieter bubbling song
that is seldom heard.

HABITS

Magpies are easily spotted and often perch
on the tops of shrubs and small trees. Most
frequently they are seen in pairs, but they may
sometimes gather in flocks of up to 100.

They build a large domed nest of twigs and
sticks in a bush or small tree. These nests are
obvious in winter, but tend to be well hidden
when there are leaves on the shrubs. When
food is plentiful they will store unwanted items
and retrieve them later. They are also rumoured
to hide shiny objects, although there are no
first-hand accounts of wild birds doing this.

Magpies have moved from the countryside
into towns and cities in recent years. Here
they are not persecuted as much as in the
countryside, and so the population has
increased. Since their move into gardens they
have come under more scrutiny, and their
habit of raiding the nests of smaller birds and
feeding on the eggs and young has earned
them an unsavoury reputation, causing them
to be blamed for the decline of some other
garden birds. Research has exonerated the
Magpie from this charge; that it raids nests is
indisputable, but not to the extent of causing
species to decline. Furthermore, this accusation
does not explain why some of its prey species
are becoming rarer while others are becoming
more common.

FOOD

Omnivorous, eating fruit, invertebrates and
carrion, and also taking some live prey such as
small birds and mammals. It can often be seen
feeding on road kill.

IN THE GARDEN

The Magpie will visit
gardens to feed on bird
food, especially kitchen
scraps put out in winter.
In summer it is more likely
to look for nests to raid. A
wildlife garden with thick
bushes (the bigger and
thicker the better) will help
deter this raider.

*The recent move of the
Magpie into urban areas
is still continuing in some
towns and cities.*

STARLING *Sturnus vulgaris*

Length 21.5 cm
Common resident over most of
Britain and Ireland, with more
arriving from the Continent in winter.

IDENTIFICATION

Gregarious bird, except when nesting. Generally has dark plumage with a greenish sheen and brown wings. In winter it is heavily spotted with white or buff, but most of the spots are lost by the breeding season, especially on the male. The bill is dark in winter and becomes yellow in the spring, with a bluish base in the male. Juveniles are smoky brown at first and gradually adopt adult feathers during late summer; for a time they appear a curious mix of half-adult and half-juvenile, with a brown head and back, but blackish, spotted underparts.

In flight, the wings appear triangular and the tail short. It makes a wide variety of squeaks and whistles, and the warbling song is full of harsh notes and wheezy rattles, as well as mimicry of other sounds that range from farmyard chickens to barking dogs and telephones.

HABITS

In recent years the population has fallen by over 50 per cent, although the reasons for this are far from clear. Starlings nest in holes and sometimes in the roofs of houses. Pairs may have one brood a year, but sometimes manage two. The male and female share the incubation, but some males have several females, and some females dump their eggs in other Starlings' nests. Sometimes, the females lay an egg outside the nest, which explains the single sky-blue eggs that are sometimes found on lawns.

Starling roosts build up from late summer and into winter. These can be very dramatic, as thousands of birds move across the sky in unison before dropping into their night-time roost.

FOOD

Mainly invertebrates in summer, especially leatherjackets (cranefly larvae), which it finds by probing into areas of short grass, including lawns. When flying insects are plentiful, such as ant swarms, it will become quite aerobatic and catch prey in flight. In autumn and winter it eats berries and other fruits.

IN THE GARDEN

Although still a common garden bird, the Starling is far less numerous than it once was. It is important not to block any holes that this species uses for nesting, and to help it by providing suitable nest boxes. While young Starlings can be quite noisy before leaving the nest, this phase does not last long and it is well worth putting up with any inconvenience. Putting out winter food is also important; the birds will take commercial bird food, especially fat balls and similar items, as well as kitchen scraps (*see* p14).

BULLFINCH *Pyrrhula pyrrhula*

*Length 14.5 cm
Once a common resident throughout
much of Britain and Ireland,
but now scarcer.*

The strong bills of these Bullfinches enable them to open small, hard seeds.

IDENTIFICATION

Plump finch. Adult male has a black cap, a rose-pink breast and face, and a grey back, with black wings and tail, and a brilliant white rump. The adult female is similar except her breast and face are much greyer. The juvenile is browner than the female and lacks the black cap of the adult. All Bullfinches have dusky-grey wing-bars and a white rump that shows up well in flight. The call is a soft but distinctive 'pew, pew', while the song is a soft, creaking warble that is seldom heard.

HABITS

Bullfinches live in woods and in thick, un-trimmed hedges, and visit farmland and orchards. In autumn, some additional birds arrive here from the Continent.

The species is unobtrusive, usually keeping within bushes and shrubs. Where common, it forms flocks of less than a dozen birds, unlike most other finches whose flocks are usually considerably larger. Family parties may be seen in late summer as they move around the countryside in search of food. The Bullfinch's habit of picking off fruit buds has made it unpopular with farmers and gardeners, and for years it was treated as a pest in fruit-growing areas. However, the recent rapid decline in the population means it is now fully protected.

FOOD

Adults eat buds, soft fruits, berries, and the seeds of plants, such as Bramble, Dandelion, nettles and docks, as well as the seeds of trees, especially Ash. The young are fed both plant material and invertebrates.

Bullfinches build a flimsy nest in dense cover.

IN THE GARDEN

There was a time when the Bullfinch was regarded as a garden pest, but this attitude has now changed; its population has fallen dramatically and, perhaps, less soft fruit is grown in gardens anyway. Scientists have shown that the species' choice of food and even its winter distribution may be affected by the size of the crop of Ash seeds: years when Ash seeds are scarce correspond to reports of most 'damage' done to orchards by Bullfinches. Planting Ash trees may therefore help to attract this species to gardens, as will maintaining thick native bushes and traditional hedges that are not cut too frequently. Only rarely do Bullfinches visit bird feeders, although Nyjer seed may successfully attract them in some gardens.

GOLDFINCH *Carduelis carduelis*

Length 12 cm
Common resident in most of Britain and Ireland. Some leave in autumn, when a few migrants from Europe arrive in the east.

IDENTIFICATION

Small, active and colourful finch, although its bright plumage can be hard to see in some light. Adults have a sandy-brown body, white underparts, a red face (less on the female than on the male), black and white cheeks, and a black crown. The black wings have a brilliant golden-yellow bar and white spots, and the black tail also has white spots. Juveniles are greyer and more streaked, and they lack the bold head markings of the adults. The bill is quite long for a finch and is pale. The flight is light and bouncing. Its call is an attractive tinkling 'whit-a-whit', often heard from flocks in flight, while the song is a series of tinkling and twittering notes with trills.

HABITS

Goldfinches are usually seen in small flocks traditionally known as charms. Their longish bills allow them to reach inside spiky seed-heads, such as those of thistles and teasels, to extract the seeds. They are quite acrobatic, and a combination of bill shape and agility means they can exploit food sources that other finches find impossible to access.

Goldfinches often nest in loose colonies.

Juveniles lack the colourful facial pattern of the adults until their first moult.

Outside the nesting season they roam widely in search of food, and flocks will converge on a new supply, such as a field corner where thistles are seeding. At these places, flocks will often mix with other finches, especially Greenfinches, as well as sparrows and buntings.

FOOD

Feeds mainly on the seeds of tall plants such as teasels, thistles, ragworts, burdocks, and the smaller Common Groundsel and chickweeds. In summer it will also feed on insects and other invertebrates.

IN THE GARDEN

Allowing garden plants, especially native species, to go to seed will help many birds, especially Goldfinches. A wild area containing Common Groundsel, thistles and other 'weeds' may attract itinerant flocks of the species.

A recent development is that Goldfinches have adapted to using garden bird feeders, especially those containing Nyjer and black Sunflower seeds, so you may be able to attract them with a well-stocked feeding station.

Goldfinches will not use nest boxes, but they may sometimes build their tiny, neat nests in the branches of small trees or tall bushes in a quiet part of the garden.

CHAFFINCH *Fringilla coelebs*

Length 14.5 cm
One of the most numerous birds in Britain and Ireland. Resident, with additional migrants arriving for winter.

Male Chaffinches outnumber females in winter.

IDENTIFICATION

Sparrow-sized finch with a short, strong bill. The male has a pink breast and cheeks, a blue-grey head, a reddish-brown back, a greenish rump and two bold white wing-bars. Feathers on the crown may sometimes give a peaked appearance. The colours after the annual moult in late summer and autumn are subdued, but become brighter as the breeding season approaches. Females are brown versions of the males, and also have obvious white wing-bars. Both sexes have white outer-tail feathers that show in flight. The call is a loud 'pink, pink', and the song is a descending series of notes ending in a dry trill.

HABITS

Chaffinches are woodland birds and are at home wherever there are trees and bushes, although they regularly feed in open countryside, especially on agricultural land. They are frequent winter visitors to many gardens, where they may stay and nest. In autumn, many more arrive in Britain as migrants from northern Europe. These birds travel in flocks and congregate where food is plentiful. Before migration, the sexes separate, so it is not unusual to come across flocks of mostly males or mostly females (this habit gave rise to their scientific name of *coelebs*, meaning 'bachelor'). There is a tendency for females to winter further south than the males.

While not usually aerobatic, Chaffinches may sometimes be seen flying up to seize insects in the air. They may also become confused by reflections; individual males will sometimes display to their own reflections in windows or other shiny objects in late winter or spring.

FOOD

Feeds on seeds from grasses and other plants such as chickweeds. In summer, it also eats insects, and it feeds its young exclusively on insects and other invertebrates.

IN THE GARDEN

A supply of bird food containing Sunflower and other smaller seeds will attract this species to the garden. Chaffinches do not generally visit hanging bird feeders, and are more likely to take their food either on the ground or from a bird table. They will not usually use nest boxes, but they may stay and nest in thick shrubs or small trees, especially in dense plants that climb up the wall of a house or shed. Gardens with native shrubs and plenty of insect food are likely to prove most popular in summer.

Chaffinches build wonderfully camouflaged nests of moss and lichen.

BRAMBLING *Fringilla montifringilla*

Length 14 cm
Winter migrant to Britain and
Ireland, with variable numbers
arriving each autumn.

The bright spring plumage is hidden in winter below the buff feather tips of the male.

IDENTIFICATION

In winter, the Brambling may be mistaken for a Chaffinch, but it has an orange rather than a pink breast, orange shoulder patches and a mottled brown back. The underparts are white, and both sexes have an obvious white rump in flight but no white feathers in their tails. Males in spring become much more distinctive, with a blacker back and head, but when they arrive in autumn after moulting these brighter feathers are obscured by buff tips. As spring approaches, the buff tips wear away to reveal the bright colours underneath. The call is a rising nasal 'tchway', which may be given either when a bird is perched or in flight.

HABITS

Flocks of Bramblings cross the North Sea in September and October, returning in March. A few sometimes remain into the spring and some of these occasionally stay to breed, mainly in Scotland. Flocks remain together throughout winter, but some birds will join with flocks of Chaffinches at sites where food is plentiful.

Bramblings tend to be nomadic in their search for food. Beech mast is a real favourite and flocks will often home in on this harvest festival. Beech trees near roads and tracks tend to be particularly popular as the nuts are crushed by traffic and the birds find it easier to get at the soft kernel. In parts of Europe, vast flocks containing thousands or even millions of Bramblings will concentrate at places where Beech mast is plentiful. In years when mast is in short supply on the Continent, more Bramblings will migrate to Britain and Ireland.

FOOD

The Brambling feeds mainly on the ground in winter as it searches for fallen fruit and seeds from grasses and other plants. In summer, it becomes an insect-eater and is more likely to be seen feeding amongst the branches of trees.

IN THE GARDEN

This is a difficult bird to attract to gardens, although it will sometimes arrive if there are Chaffinches feeding, especially in cold weather or when its natural food is scarce. At these times, it takes commercial bird food containing plenty of seeds, but it usually prefers to feed on the ground. To cater for birds like the Brambling, some bird food should therefore always be put on a bird table and also on the ground, not just in hanging feeders.

Female Bramblings are distinguishable from female Chaffinches by their more orange plumage and white belly and rump.

GREENFINCH _Carduelis chloris_

Length 15 cm
Common resident in Britain and Ireland,
with some migrants arriving from the
Continent in autumn.

IDENTIFICATION

Rather stocky finch, olive-green in colour and darker on the back. It has bright yellow flashes on the wings and sides of its tail, and the rump can look surprisingly bright in flight. The bill is pale and heavy-looking, and the tail is slightly forked. Females are browner and more streaked than males, and juveniles are even more streaky. Its flight is undulating but less bouncy than that of the smaller finches. The call is a dry 'jup, jup, jup' and a repeated 'chi-chi-chi-chi', while the song is a series of wheezy notes with a long, drawn-out 'tzeeeeee' at the end.

HABITS

The Greenfinch has a distinctive song-flight, during which it flies with slow exaggerated wingbeats, rolling from side to side as it shows off its bright yellow feathers. It weaves a circular course back to a prominent perch, usually high up in a tall tree.

Greenfinches are social birds. While nesting they defend a very small territory, but they will flock where food is plentiful. While many species form feeding flocks in winter, Greenfinches do this in the breeding season as well. The reason being that they do not switch from eating

Females are stripy and slightly duller than males.

seeds to insects in summer, but continue to hunt seeds throughout the year. The male will even collect seeds and feed them to the female during courtship and incubation. Both adults feed the young with seeds regurgitated from their crops.

FOOD

Greenfinches mainly eat seeds, including those from chickweeds, Common Groundsel and Dandelion. They also eat grain on agricultural land and berries in autumn.

IN THE GARDEN

The Greenfinch comes readily to garden bird feeders, where it favours the larger seeds and is sufficiently agile to feed from hanging feeders. Peanuts (_see_ p14) and Sunflower seeds will attract small flocks. It is also dominant and will often keep others away while it is feeding. Greenfinches will sometimes nest in gardens in tall, thick shrubs and small trees although they will not use nest boxes.

TRICHMONOSIS

Greenfinches and some other birds sometimes suffer from a disease called trichomonosis which is caused by lesions in the throat that prevent feeding and result in death. If you see affected birds in your garden, temporarily stop feeding birds, clean feeders and leave bird baths dry until no further sick or dead birds are found in the garden.

SISKIN *Spinus spinus*

Length 12 cm
Breeds in conifer forests but roams more widely in winter; additional birds arrive in autumn from Europe.

IDENTIFICATION

Small, lively finch, similar in size to a Blue Tit. Has a dark green streaked back, a yellow-green breast and very pale, streaked underparts.

The male has a black cap and black bib in spring. The female

Female and juvenile Siskins are greyer than the males and more stripy.

is paler, greyer and more streaked than the male. Juveniles are similar to the female but are browner and even more streaky. All have obvious yellow bars on their wings and a deeply notched tip to their tail. The bill is more delicate and more pointed than in typical finches. The flight is light and 'bouncing'. Its call is a clear 'tsuu' or a ringing 'tsing', while the song is a sweet twittering and a drawn-out wheeze.

HABITS

The Siskin is an agile species that often feeds near the tips of branches and frequently hangs upside-down like a Blue Tit to reach food. It is also a sociable species, with flocks roaming the countryside in winter and sometimes visiting gardens; especially late in the winter. It nests almost exclusively in conifer woods and forests, and has benefited from the expansion of commercial forestry during the last 50 years.

The Siskins we see in our gardens in winter may be local, but more often they are visitors from elsewhere in Britain or Ireland, and some are migrants from Europe, as far away as Scandinavia, the Baltic region or even Ukraine. Movements appear to be triggered by a failure of the cone crop in pinewoods, resulting in a shortage of seeds.

FOOD

The seeds from cones are a vital food for this species, but it also takes seeds from other trees, especially birches and Alder, and from low-growing plants such as Dandelion and docks. In summer, it feeds on insects and other invertebrates.

IN THE GARDEN

A well-stocked bird table and bird feeders will attract Siskins if they are in the locality. Commercial bird food containing plenty of small seeds and peanuts (see p14) seems to work best. Silver Birch is a good tree to plant as its seeds provide food for Siskins, although they are unlikely to stay and nest.

LESSER REDPOLL *Acanthis caberet*

Length 11.5 cm
Breeds in northern Birch forests, young plantations and other woods and heaths. Moves to new areas for winter.

A small, brown, stripy finch with a red forehead and a small, black bib. It occasionally visits gardens to feed on seeds. In spring, males have a pink flush on the upper breast. May be attracted to birch trees.

HOUSE SPARROW *Passer domesticus*

Length 14–15 cm
Common resident across most of
Britain and Ireland.

IDENTIFICATION

Small and plump with a short, thick bill. Male has a brown head and neck with a grey cap, pale cheeks and a black bib. The rump is grey. The brown back is streaked with blackish marks, the underparts are off-white and it has a small white wing-bar. The female and juvenile have streaked backs and pale underparts, no black bib, and a light brown head with a distinctive pale streak behind the eye. The call is a familiar 'chip chip', and the song is a monotonous repetition of a single 'chirp'.

HABITS

House Sparrows have evolved to live close to humans, stealing our food, feeding off our scraps and even nesting in the roofs of our houses. In suburban areas, sparrow declines are thought to be due to a scarcity of food for chicks, while in rural areas, shortages of autumn food may be responsible, a problem likely caused by changes in agricultural practices.

Related to the weaver birds of Africa, House Sparrows build an untidy nest of straw, grass and other locally available materials, often in a shrub or cavity. In towns they regularly nest in buildings, perhaps under roof tiles or behind fascia boards. They are social birds, often nesting in loose groups and at other times gathering in small flocks to feed or dust-bathe. Occasionally, where food is plentiful, flocks may number 100 birds or more.

Female (right) House Sparrows sometimes pair up with several different males.

House Sparrows sometimes build a loose nest of straw in bushes, but more often they use holes in buildings or nest boxes.

FOOD

In summer, the House Sparrow takes a lot of insects and other invertebrates, which it feeds to its young, as well as nectar and seeds. In autumn and winter, it eats a variety of seeds and grain, and will take peanuts, other bird food and kitchen scraps, as well as generally scavenging in towns and cities. It will sometimes flutter up and seize insects in flight, and has even been seen picking flies out of a spider's web!

IN THE GARDEN

The House Sparrow's habit of hanging on bird feeders like a tit was apparently initially observed in Germany and was recorded for the first time in Britain in the 1950s. Now House Sparrows are quick to take advantage of any bird food. To encourage them to stay and nest in the garden, it is necessary to provide a suitable nest box, preferably placing several fairly close together to cater for the species' social nature.

REPTILES AND AMPHIBIANS

Grass Snake *Natrix natrix*

Length: male up to 80 cm;
female 120 cm or more
Widespread in England and Wales;
absent from Scotland and Ireland.

*The Grass Snake is usually seen singly, but
several will sometimes hibernate together.*

Identification

Our largest snake, with an extremely long, thin body, narrowing to a slight neck and distinct head. Eyes are round and lack lids. Body is covered in small scales. Usually green or olive, with small black spots along the back, and short black bars at intervals along the sides. Just behind the head on each side is a yellow or cream patch, almost forming a collar. Underside has broader scales and a chequered black and white pattern.

Habits

Usually found in or near wet habitats. Hibernates in holes in the ground between October and April, unless the weather is particularly mild. Once awake, it favours sunny, sheltered sites. Active during daytime when the temperature rises sufficiently.

The female lays 10–40 eggs in the summer. These have a leathery shell and are stuck together in clusters. Laying site must be warm

and moist, such as a compost or manure heap. Young emerge in late summer or early winter, and are 15–20 cm long and fully formed. Like other snakes, Grass Snakes shed their skin periodically. Newly moulted animals are particularly brightly coloured.

The Grass Snake is a good swimmer, often entering the water to hunt. It takes live animal food. The bones of the jaw are only loosely connected, allowing the mouth to open sufficiently to swallow prey that is much wider than the head. Although it is not venomous, it can bite if attacked or picked up. It also produces an evil-smelling liquid from the vent, which is an effective deterrent to predators.

Food

Feeds both in water and on land, taking frogs of all sizes, newts, small fish, young birds, mice, voles and shrews. Some individuals eat toads. The young eat tadpoles, and sometimes invertebrates such as worms and slugs.

In the garden

A pond is a vital part of the Grass Snake's habitat, and should preferably be surrounded by damp vegetation with good populations of frogs and newts. For breeding, Grass Snakes require heaps of rotting organic material such as manure, compost or leaf mould.

Slow-worm *Anguis fragilis*

Length up to 50 cm
A legless lizard, widespread throughout most of Britain, but not found in Ireland.

IDENTIFICATION

A long, thin body, snake-like in shape, but with a small head and without the narrowing at the neck. Eyes have lids. Scales are smooth, and those on the underside are similar in size to those above. Golden brown or bronze in colour, and very glossy. Young individuals and females have darker sides and a narrow dark line down the middle of the back. Some individuals – usually older males – have blue spots.

produced by live birth in August or September. These are 65–90 mm in length. Slow-worms may live for 30 years.

The outer skin is shed about 4 times in a year, after which the Slow-worm appears shinier and brighter. If attacked, it can break off its tail like other lizards as a means of defence, the predator left with the wriggling tail while the Slow-worm escapes. The tail usually regrows.

FOOD

Prey is fairly small, as evidenced by its small mouth and row of small teeth. It eats live prey, mainly slugs but also snails, spiders, insects and small earthworms.

The Slow-worm is a legless lizard, which gives birth to live young (bottom).

HABITS

Despite its very snake-like appearance, the Slow-worm is actually a species of legless lizard, the only one of its group in Britain. It lives in dry areas, especially where there are walls or banks, and is rather slow-moving. Mainly nocturnal. Spends only short periods basking in the sun, otherwise hidden by day in warm places under logs and flat stones, in thick grass or burrowing into the soil. Hunts both in the soil and above ground.

Hibernates underground from about mid-October, in a hollow or burrow, emerging again early in the spring. Females produce eggs, but these develop and hatch inside the body, so some 6–12 young are

IN THE GARDEN

Gardens can make a real contribution to the conservation of Slow-worms, which need areas of wild habitat and will benefit from compost heaps. In particular, they will use the underside of large, flat stones or similar materials as warm shelters. These can be carefully lifted for inspection occasionally, but should not be disturbed too often.

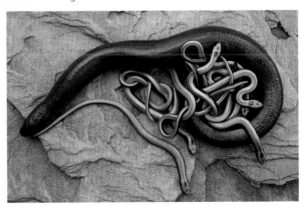

COMMON FROG *Rana temporaria*

Length up to 10 cm
Found in spring and summer
throughout Britain and Ireland.

IDENTIFICATION

Probably the most familiar of our amphibians (frogs, toads and newts). Lacks a tail, and has large jumping hind legs with big webbed feet. Variable in colour, from yellowish-green to reddish-brown, and marked with darker patches, especially across the legs and behind the eye. Moves in a series of hops, rather than walking. Skin is smooth, wet and shiny. Spawn is the familiar mass of jelly laid in water, with each small black egg surrounded by its own sphere of jelly.

HABITS

Common Frogs spend most of their time on land. They feed amongst damp vegetation, mostly at night. Like the other amphibians, they must return to water to breed. In water, they sit or float with their nose and prominent eyes just above the surface.

They breed in early spring. This may be February in the south, and March in the north, but there have been signs in recent years that breeding is starting earlier. Males gather in the pond first, and make a croaking call at night. When females arrive, a male clings to each one and they then move as one. They hibernate in damp soil beneath logs or rocks.

FOOD

Flies, caterpillars, beetles, spiders, woodlice, worms, slugs and snails are all commonly eaten by adults. Tadpoles initially feed on algae, scraping it off the surface of water plants

NOTE

Frogs and toads spend their young stage as black tadpoles, with round bodies and long, thin tails. As they grow, first the hind and then the front legs develop. The tail then disappears and they become miniature frogs or toads.

and stones. As they develop they become carnivores, eating small freshwater animals.

IN THE GARDEN

Common Frogs will breed in a garden pond. This should have shelving margins but preferably no fish, as these eat tadpoles. In addition, the adult frogs need a wild, damp area, rich in invertebrates, in which to feed. Good hibernation sites are log piles or stone rockeries near the pond. Care is needed on driveways on early spring nights when frogs are travelling to spawn.

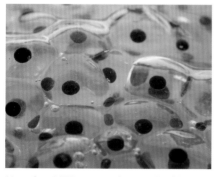

More than 1,000 eggs may be contained in one mass of spawn.

Tadpoles start out eating algae but soon become tiny predators.

COMMON TOAD *Bufo bufo*

Length male 6.5 cm, female 9 cm
Found in spring and summer
throughout most of mainland Britain,
but not in Ireland.

IDENTIFICATION

No tail. Hind legs and feet are longer than the forelimbs. Body colour is some shade of brown, although individuals vary from yellowish to reddish. Underside is whitish. Skin is dry and rough, and is covered with warty growths, the most prominent of which is a large raised patch behind the eye. Toads have shorter hind legs than frogs, and tend to crawl rather than jump.

Toads may use traditional migration routes to reach their breeding grounds.

HABITS

Common Toads are less dependent on damp places than other amphibians, and have been seen up to 3 km from a pond, although they must return to water to breed. They are active at night. By day they shelter under logs and stones, digging a small chamber in the soil in a place that is regularly used. Such chambers are also used for hibernation.

Breeding takes place in ponds and lakes. The toads arrive from mid-March and spawn between then and the end of April, although the timing will be earlier in the south and later further north. The males make a piping call, and unmated males can be seen floating at the surface of the water.

When pairing, the male grasps the female around the waist (a position called 'amplexus') while she lays her eggs. The spawn takes the form of long strings of jelly, unlike the clumps of frogspawn, and these are twined around water weeds. The eggs inside the jelly lie in double rows. They are black and hatch after about 10 days. The tadpoles develop into tiny toads and leave the water from the end of May.

FOOD

Catches its insect prey with the sticky tip of its tongue. Other prey include slugs and worms. At night, toads can sometimes be found beneath an outside light, feeding on fallen moths and other insects.

Females carry smaller males in amplexus before breeding.

IN THE GARDEN

Toads may breed in a garden pond, but not as commonly as frogs. They also need sites for daytime shelter and hibernation, such as logs and large stones resting on dry soil. They are popular with gardeners because they eat slugs and other invertebrates.

Tadpoles may be eaten by newts and birds amongst other predators.

Smooth Newt *Triturus vulgaris*

Length 8–9 cm
Widespread in the British Isles, but less common in Wales and Scotland.

Identification

Lizard-like, with a long, thin body and tail, and short legs. Skin is smooth. Dark green or brown with darker spots, especially in males during spring. Underside is yellow or orange with dark spots. In the breeding season, the male grows a frilly crest down the back and along the tail,

and a silvery-blue and orange stripe along the underside of the tail. He also grows fringes along the sides of the toes. On land when dry, the skin becomes velvety to the touch, and lacks the scales of a lizard.

Habits

Hibernates in dry soil, beneath stones or logs. In spring, returns to the water to breed. Before laying eggs, newts have an elaborate courtship display: the male swims in front of the female, blocking her path and displaying his crest. Then he lashes his tail, waving his scent towards her. Finally, he deposits a small sac of sperm, which the female swims over and picks up to fertilise her eggs. The eggs are white, enclosed in jelly and laid singly on the narrow leaves of water plants, which are then folded over, completely hiding the egg. This results in distinctly square-ended leaves, a clear sign that newts are breeding.

Around July, adults leave the pond and spend the rest of the year on land. The young take 5–6 months to develop and 3 years to grow to full size.

Food

On land, adult Smooth Newts eat invertebrates, especially slugs, small snails, earthworms and insects. In water, they eat insect larvae, crustaceans and snails. They also eat frogspawn and tadpoles.

In the garden

Commonly found in gardens and require a fish-free pond for breeding. Water Forget-me-not is an excellent plant for their egg-laying. A damp area is also important, as is a rockery or log pile for hibernation.

Newt Tadpoles

Identification

Small and slender body, looking a bit like tiny fish. Pale-coloured when young. Unlike frog and toad tadpoles, legs develop very early, looking rather spindly on the sides of the body. At the sides of the head are feathery gills, whose red colour may show.

Habits

By the end of the year, most newt tadpoles have grown stronger legs, lost their gills and

become small newts. Most leave the pond to hibernate.

Food

When very small, feed mostly on water fleas. Later can take a variety of slightly larger invertebrate prey.

GREAT CRESTED NEWT *Triturus cristatus*

(WARTY NEWT)
Body length 8–14 cm
Local but widespread through most of England and Central Scotland, but scarcer in the north of England, Wales, and the rest of Scotland. Not found in Ireland.

IDENTIFICATION
Large. Very dark, with round, black spots, giving an overall almost black effect. Underside is bright orange with black spots. In breeding season, male develops a tall, ragged-looking crest along the body, not continuous with the crest along the tail. He also has a broad, silvery stripe along the side of the tail. The tadpole is larger, darker and broader-bodied than those of the other species.

HABITS
Is able to find and colonise new ponds. Like the other newts, is found in the pond during spring, but may spend much of the rest of the year on land. Courtship display and egg-laying are similar to the Smooth Newt. Hibernation is usually on land, in the soil underneath suitable stones or logs.

FOOD
In water, many pond invertebrates including insects, water lice and snails. A predator of tadpoles, especially of frogs. On land, feeds on a large variety of invertebrates.

IN THE GARDEN
Requires a depth of up to 55 cm in at least part of the pond. Needs damp areas for land feeding, and suitable hibernation sites such as stones and logpiles.

Great Crested Newts and their habitat are strictly protected by law.

PALMATE NEWT *Triturus helveticus*

Length 8 cm
Common in western and northern Britain. Not found in Ireland.

IDENTIFICATION
Breeding male is greenish-olive with dark speckles, and a yellow underside with a few brown speckles. He develops a ridge along each side of the body, and a crest that is lower than that of the Smooth Newt and lacks a wavy edge. His hind toes are webbed and his tail tip appears cut off, but actually continues as a short, fine filament. After breeding, the crest, toe-webs and tail-filament are absorbed.

HABITS
Tends to spend more of the year in the water than the Smooth Newt, especially in hilly country, where it is usually the only newt.

FOOD
Similar to Smooth Newt, eating invertebrates on land and in the pond. Also eats frogspawn and tadpoles. Young feed on crustaceans, small insects and worms.

IN THE GARDEN
As for Smooth Newt.

COMMON LIZARD *Lacerta vivipara*

(VIVIPAROUS LIZARD)
*Body plus tail length up to 18 cm
Widespread in suitable habitat
throughout Britain and Ireland.*

IDENTIFICATION

A long, narrow body, with very long tail and short legs. Colour brown or yellowish, with a whitish throat. Female often has a darker central stripe, with dark sides. Male more variable with various stripes and spots. Very young lizards are much darker, almost black. Body covered with shiny, horny scales (unlike Newts), larger on the head.

Very young lizards (left) are much darker than adults. Approach quietly and you may observe lizards basking in warm sunny places (above).

HABITS

Very active and quick-moving, scuttling rapidly into cover when disturbed. Needs to warm up before active hunting, and does this by basking, often flattening the body to face the sun. Can hunt when its body temperature reaches 30°C.

Emerges from hibernation in March. In July, female produces 3–11 live young, which develop as eggs in her body but hatch on birth. (hence the species name of Viviparous Lizard). They are 4 cm long at birth, but grow rapidly to 7–8 cm by the winter. Hibernates in burrows underground. Mature at 2 or 3 years.

As with other reptiles, the outer skin is shed (sloughed) at intervals. Usually this is four times a year, although more while the lizard is still growing. Striking defensive behaviour means the lizard can shed its tail if attacked: there is a point of weakness at which the tail can be deliberately broken off. The detached tail wriggles violently, as an effective distraction to a predator. The stump heals and a new tail regenerates, although never as long as the original.

The forked tongue is much used in testing the environment. It is protruded to pick up scent particles, which are detected by the palate when the tongue is withdrawn.

Its predators include some birds, especially the Kestrel, and other larger animals including Hedgehogs and snakes.

FOOD

Can catch any invertebrate, even if quickly moving, which is small enough to swallow. Especially spiders, many beetles and other insects, and centipedes.

IN THE GARDEN

Needs a site with cover, and open sunny spots or logs for basking.

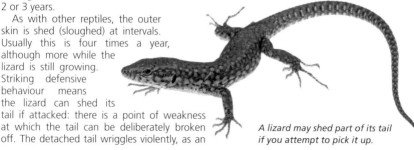

A lizard may shed part of its tail if you attempt to pick it up.

INVERTEBRATES

EARTHWORMS

Among the most familiar garden creatures. Found while digging, in soil or compost heaps, or detected from casts on the lawn. Several species occur in gardens.

IDENTIFICATION

A typical worm has a long, narrow body, no distinct head, is tapered at the front and usually flattened at the tail end. Body has segments along its length and a paler 'saddle' associated with reproduction.

HABITS

Worms move by pushing into loose soil, or eating through it. They crawl using pairs of tiny bristles on the underside of each segment. The skin is moist. They avoid light, as they will die if exposed to ultraviolet rays for long. In drought, they conserve water by curling in a ball in a cell below the surface. Eggs are laid in the soil, hatching as miniature worms.

FOOD

Most eat soil, digesting its organic contents. The waste passes out as 'casts'. Some also eat dead leaves and other plant remains.

IN THE GARDEN

Worms are an essential part of natural soil conditioning, incorporating humus and turning and draining it. They benefit if it contains a good supply of manure or compost. They are also food for much of the garden's wildlife.

NOTE

The large brownish worm mainly responsible for the 'casts' found on lawns is *Allolobophora longa*. The related *A. caliginosa* is smaller with a pale pink front end, and is one of the commonest species in cultivated areas.

The Cockspur Worm, *Dendrodrilus rubidus,* is 27–90 mm long and is widespread in Britain and Ireland. It is small, red and with a lighter saddle. Its body is rather flattened from top to bottom and it can be found in compost and manure heaps.

BRANDLING WORM
Eisenia foetida

Length 32–130 mm
Widespread in Britain and Ireland.

Has distinctive dark reddish and pale bands of colour. Lives in rich organic soil, and is also common in compost and manure.

LUMBRICUS TERRESTRIS

Length up to 300 mm
Widespread in Britain and Ireland,
especially on clay soil.

Very large earthworm, found in woods and pastures, and also in gardens. Reddish-brown above and yellowish below, with an orange-red saddle. Sometimes rather flattened at the tail end. Lives in very deep burrows, to a depth of 2 m.

(above) Lumbricus terrestris
(left) Brandling worm.

Slugs

Slugs are molluscs and are closely related to snails, although most lack the outer shell. Like snails, they are also very familiar to the gardener.

IDENTIFICATION

Slugs have tapering bodies that can contract into a short oval. They come in a variety of colours and have two pairs of tentacles, with eyes on the tips of the second pair. Most are shell-less. An oval area behind the head has an opening forming a breathing tube.

HABITS

They glide, on muscles under the body. Slime is discharged from behind the mouth, making a trail on which to crawl. Body slime protects them from drying out and from predators.

They emerge at night from under logs, stones, or from the soil. They feed with their tongue, which has several rows of scraping teeth. Some climb plants to feed. Eggs are round and pearly, laid in clumps in soil.

FOOD

Feed on dead and living plant material, especially leaves and shoots.

IN THE GARDEN

Slugs help the decomposition and recycling of plant material, as well as being food for a number of animals. Avoid chemical pellets as these can be very harmful to Song Thrushes and other wildlife.

NETTED SLUG

Deroceras reticulatum

(GREY FIELD SLUG)

Length 3.5–6 cm
Found throughout most of Britain and Ireland.

The most common slug. Has a short keel at the tail end. Body is rather soft, and is a mottled pale fawn or grey. Eats decaying plant material, but also tender shoots and seedlings. Organic gardeners use crushed eggshells or sand around plants, or trap slugs in dishes of stale beer.

GARDEN SLUGS

Arion hortensis agg.

Length 2.5–3 cm
Found throughout most of Britain and Ireland.

Small blackish or dark grey slugs with a dark line down each side. Underside of foot is orange or yellow. Feed on or below the soil, on roots and tubers of plants.

LARGE BLACK SLUG

Arion ater

Length up to 15 cm
Found throughout most of Britain and Ireland.

Very large. Usually black, although occasionally dark brown or reddish. Body is covered in rows of rough pimples. Contracts into a tall, compact hump when disturbed. Feeds mostly on decaying matter and fungi.

LAND SNAILS

Terrestrial snails are well-known molluscs whose body is enclosed in a shell. Several species occur in our gardens.

IDENTIFICATION

Snails can retract their elongated bodies into spiral or coiled shells. Shells vary in size, shape and pattern. Head has two pairs of tentacles, which protrude or contract. The second pair has eyes at the tip, while the front pair carries organs of smell.

HABITS

Glides on the muscular underside of the body. Mucus from a gland behind the mouth helps it move and leaves a shiny trail. Less susceptible to drying out than slugs, snails usually live in damp places, including cracks in walls, under logs and stones, or amongst vegetation. They emerge at night and in damp weather. In winter and in dry periods, they close the mouth of the shell with dried mucus. The tongue has rows of horny teeth that rasp the surface of food.

FOOD

Some snails help decomposition by feeding on dead vegetation. Others feed on live plant material, which is less welcome.

IN THE GARDEN

Food for the Song Thrush. Land snails benefit from long, rough vegetation, and from cover such as old walls and log piles. Avoid slug pellets, as these will also affect any predators that eat the snails.

GARDEN SNAIL

Cornu aspersum

Shell height up to 32 mm, shell diameter 25–40 mm
Common in England, Wales and Ireland. Scarcer in Scotland.

Well-known large snail of gardens, found around the base of walls, inside stored flowerpots, etc. Has a typical snail shape, with a bluntly pointed shell. Colour of shell is light brown, with several irregular darker bands and paler speckles running around the coils.

ROUNDED SNAIL

Discus rotundatus

Shell diameter 3–7 mm
Widespread in Britain and Ireland.

Very small. Shell is a flat coil, up to 2.5 mm thick, with an angled or ridged edge in profile; it has a rough surface, and is pale brown but with reddish-brown marks radiating across it. Found under dead wood, stones and moss.

WHITE-LIPPED SNAIL

Cepaea hortensis

Shell diameter up to 20 mm
Widespread in Britain and Ireland, although scarcer in the south and west.

Has a typical snail shape. Yellow or pale pink in colour, usually with several brown bands running around the coils and a white lip to the shell entrance. Occurs in grassland and hedges, and also sometimes in gardens.

WATER SNAILS

Water snails are molluscs whose body is enclosed in a coiled or spiral shell. Some larger water snails are often deliberately placed in a garden pond, while others may colonise accidentally, usually after being brought in on water plants.

IDENTIFICATION

Water snails have a shorter head than land snails, with only one pair of tentacles, and eyes on small bumps in front of the tentacles. They exhibit a variety of shell shapes.

HABITS

Like land snails, they produce slime, which helps them to crawl more easily. They too feed by rasping at surfaces with a tongue that is equipped with rows of small teeth. Larger species visit the surface to breathe air.

FOOD

Graze on the film of algae that grows on the surface of water plants and objects in the pond, often leaving visible trails. They also feed on dead material on the pond bottom.

IN THE GARDEN

Water snails are a valuable part of the pond ecosystem, eating algae and adding to sediment with their droppings. They benefit from a variety of water plants. Do not use chemicals to remove algae, as this will harm them.

GREAT RAMSHORN SNAIL

Planorbis corneus

Shell diameter 2.5 cm
Widespread in Britain and Ireland; more common in the south.

Shell is a large and distinctive, reddish-brown flattened coil. The tentacles are long and thin. These snails have red blood containing haemoglobin, which may allow them to make better use of oxygen in stagnant water. Eggs are laid in flat masses in jelly.

Ramshorn snails are named after the flat coils of their shells.

GREAT POND SNAIL

Lymnaea stagnalis

Shell length up to 5 cm
Widespread in Britain and Ireland.

Large brown shell with large last whorl and a thin spire. Shell of young is narrower. Head has flat, triangular tentacles. Often feeds on scum at the surface, as well as feeding in the usual way. Eggs are laid in a sausage-shaped mass of jelly.

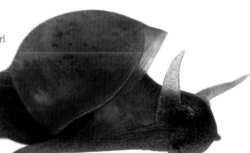

The Great Pond Snail often feeds upside-down at the surface, supported by surface tension.

WOODLICE

Woodlice are members of the class Crustacea. Most crustaceans, such as shrimps and crabs, are aquatic, but woodlice have adapted to the land, where they are mainly nocturnal and seek dark, damp situations in the day to prevent drying out.

IDENTIFICATION

Woodlice have rather flat, oval bodies that are divided into segments, with seven pairs of legs and conspicuous antennae. Under the abdomen are additional flattened legs, which in most species act as gills in respiration.

HABITS

Found under stones, logs, and the upper layers of compost heaps. Mostly nocturnal. Like all arthropods, they moult their exoskeleton as they grow. These 'shells' are often eaten by the woodlice as a source of calcium. The eggs and newly hatched, tiny young are carried by the female in a brood pouch formed by the flattened hind limbs.

FOOD

Woodlice eat mainly decaying vegetation such as dead leaves and rotting wood.

IN THE GARDEN

Woodlice are an important part of the decomposition process. By eating plant remains they speed up the process of recycling carried out by fungi and bacteria. They are also food for insectivorous birds and mammals. Woodlice can be encouraged by the provision of suitable dark, damp shelters.

COMMON SHINY WOODLOUSE

Oniscus asellus

Length up to 16 mm
Found throughout Britain and Ireland.

The most common garden woodlouse. Has a smooth, shiny shell. Body is rather broad with splayed edges, and is grey with rows of paler spots. Not well adapted to resist drying out, and so is found in damper habitats.

COMMON PILL WOODLOUSE

Armadillidium vulgare

Length up to 18 mm
Widespread in England and Ireland.

More common on lime-rich soils. Usually dark grey. Can roll up into a tight ball, which gives it its name. Able to tolerate drier conditions.

Rolling up in a tight ball by the Common Pill Woodlouse is a defence against drying out as well as against predators.

COMMON STRIPED WOODLOUSE

Philoscia muscorum

Length up to 11 mm
Widespread throughout Britain and Ireland.

A smaller woodlouse. Very smooth and shiny. The abdomen is noticeably narrower, contrasting with the rest of the body. Light brown and mottled, with a darker central stripe. Very active.

COMMON ROUGH WOODLOUSE

Porcellio scaber

Length up to 17 mm
Common throughout Britain and Ireland.

Has a dull shell with rows of tiny pimples. Dark grey, usually mottled. Better adapted to drier conditions. On the underside, two pairs of white patches on the hind limbs act as lungs. This species will often climb trees to feed on algae on the bark.

COMMON PYGMY WOODLOUSE

Trichoniscus pusillus

Length 4 mm
Found throughout Britain and Ireland.

Tiny and easily overlooked. Mottled, reddish-brown. Narrow, parallel-sided body, and narrow abdomen that should distinguish it from the young of larger woodlice. Found in compost heaps, dead wood and leaves.

ANT WOODLOUSE

Platyarthrus hoffmannseggi
(BLIND WOODLOUSE)

Length 4 mm
Occurs throughout Britain and Ireland.

Completely white. Always found in the nests of ants, e.g. under stones.

MILLIPEDES

This group of arthropods is characterised by having many identical body segments and many legs. Millipedes are found in damper situations and are most active at night. They are known to gardeners for the occasional damage they cause to plants.

IDENTIFICATION

Long, thin-bodied invertebrates, with a hard body covering, obvious antennae, numerous segments and many legs. Close inspection shows that each apparent segment carries two pairs of legs (centipedes have one).

HABITS

Basically soil animals, but more often found under stones, logs and bark, and in leaf litter. They also occur in the upper layers of compost heaps. Their bodies are very prone to drying out. Active at night.

Many species construct hollow 'nests' in the soil for their eggs. Female may stay with them until hatching. New hatchlings have only three pairs of legs and resemble primitive insects. Their outer case is moulted as the animal grows. This may take place in a special chamber, and often the cast skin is eaten.

FOOD

A wide range of plant foods, including dead and decaying material. Have also been recorded feeding on dead animal matter.

IN THE GARDEN

Millipedes play an important part in the decomposition cycle, breaking down plant remains and speeding the decay carried out by fungi and bacteria.

COMMON BLACK MILLIPEDE

Tachypodoiulus niger

Length up to 45 mm
Found throughout Britain and Ireland.

One of the 'snake' millipedes, with a long cylindrical body. When disturbed, can curl up into a coil. Dark brown or black.

FLAT MILLIPEDE

Polydesmus angustus

Length up to 45 mm
Found throughout Britain and Ireland.

Pale or dark brown, dull and rough textured. Back covered with flattened plates, so that superficially it resembles a centipede.

PILL MILLIPEDE

Glomeris marginata

Length 15–20 mm
Found throughout Britain and Ireland.

Shorter and wider than other millipedes, black or dark brown and shiny. Can curl into a tight ball. Like Pill Woodlouse (see p98), but no smaller segments in the abdomen.

(left) Common Black Millipedes will sometimes enter houses.

CENTIPEDES

Shiny brown centipedes are a familiar sight, scuttling away when a log or stone is removed. They are arthropods with many jointed legs, and while they resemble millipedes superficially, they are much more active.

IDENTIFICATION

Very long, thin invertebrates. Their bodies are clearly divided into segments, with one pair of legs per segment (cf. millipedes), and they have one pair of antennae.

HABITS

Centipedes are not well waterproofed, and so they are at risk of drying out. They are nocturnal and live in dark, damp places, under stones, logs, bark and leaves. Some thinner species live in crevices in the soil.

Like all arthropods, centipedes must moult their outer skin at intervals as they grow. They are active predators with large 'jaws' formed from the limbs on the first body segment. These are curved and sharp, and feature a poison gland that helps to kill prey, although British species are harmless to humans.

FOOD

Spiders, insects, woodlice, small earthworms and springtails.

IN THE GARDEN

Centipedes are important as small carnivores in the garden community. They can be encouraged by supplying plenty of suitable shelter.

WESTERN YELLOW CENTIPEDE

Halophilus subterraneus

Length up to 75 mm
Widespread in Britain
and Ireland, in woods and
gardens.

Very long and extremely thin. Pale yellow. Has 70 or more pairs of legs. Eggs are laid in batches and guarded by the female, without whose attention they may become infected with fungus and die. Young start with seven pairs of legs, adding segments and legs as they grow.

This is a 'burrowing centipede', adapted to tunnel in the soil and is often found by

A long thin body adapts this centipede to living in the soil.

gardeners while digging. In addition to small invertebrates, it includes plant material in its diet, such as the roots of vegetable crops.

COMMON LITHOBIUS

Lithobius forficatus

Length 18–32 mm
Widespread in Britain and Ireland,
particularly in gardens.

Shiny chestnut-brown centipede. Has 15 leg-bearing segments. The legs on the last segment are longer and trailing, and resemble tails. The young hatch with their full complement of legs.

An active species, running rapidly for cover when disturbed. Found under stones

and logs. Eggs are laid separately in the surface of the soil.

HARVESTMEN

Harvestmen (sometimes incorrectly called Harvest Spiders) are arachnids of the order Opiliones. Related to true spiders, they differ in body shape and by not producing silk.

IDENTIFICATION

Round body: head, thorax and abdomen appear to be a single unit. Has eight long, thin legs, the second pair longest. A pair of scent glands near the head look like eyes. The true eyes are on a small raised central hump.

HABITS

Nocturnal. Lives in rough vegetation. Prone to drying out, so usually shelters during the day. Movement is slow and appears fragile.

A predator that detects prey with the second pair of legs, catches it with a pair of pincers on the head and sucks out the body fluids.

Eggs are laid in soil, rotting wood or moss. Winters as eggs or immatures. Adults abundant in late summer; hence 'harvestmen'.

FOOD

Small insects and other invertebrates.

IN THE GARDEN

Benefits from uncultivated areas of longish vegetation.

> ### NOTE
>
> The most common species in gardens is usually *Phalangium opilio*. This is a large species, with a body length of about 8 mm. It is brown or grey, with a patterned back and white underside.

MITES AND TICKS

These small relatives of spiders are in the subclass Acari and are hard to see with the naked eye.

IDENTIFICATION

Mites usually have glossy black or brown round bodies. Adults have four pairs of legs and well-developed head and mouthparts.

HABITS

Hundreds of different mite species are abundant in gardens. Although little-known, they have a wide range of habits and ecology.

Free-living mites are found in soil, leaf litter, compost and moss. Most feed on decaying vegetation; they are important in decomposition and a few are predators.

Some mites are insect parasites. Some are harmless passengers on bumblebees or beetles. Ticks that feed on the blood of mammals and birds also belong to this group.

Some mites form galls on plants (*see* p127).

Most obvious are the bud galls found on Blackcurrant, and leaf galls (red pimples) found on Sycamore and Field Maple leaves.

FOOD

Varies with the habits of the species.

IN THE GARDEN

Many free-living mites are important agents of decomposition.

> ### NOTE
>
> Red Spider Mites *Tetranychus urticae* (pictured) feed on sap and may be pests in the garden. They can sometimes be seen running about in sunny weather on paving and walls. They are tiny, scarlet and active.

SPIDERS

WOODLOUSE SPIDER *Dysdera crocata*

Length up to 15 mm
Common in Britain and Ireland.

IDENTIFICATION
Medium-sized spider with elongated body and cylindrical abdomen. Shiny brown thorax, reddish-brown legs and the whitish abdomen, with spinning organs protruding. Large prominent fangs projecting forwards.

HABITS
Nocturnal. By day, shelters under logs, stones and in compost heaps in a cell made of silk. Rather slow-moving. Eggs are laid June–July, in a yellow silk mass beside the resting cell.

FOOD
A specialist hunter, killing its woodlouse prey by piercing its shell.

IN THE GARDEN
It benefits from the provision of good woodlouse habitat and compost heaps.

WOLF SPIDER *Pardosa amentata (Lycosa amentata)*

Length up to 7 mm
Widespread in Britain and Ireland; scarcer in northern Scotland.

IDENTIFICATION
Medium-sized with slightly elongated body, a medium-length oval abdomen that is only slightly longer than the thorax, stout legs. Grey-brown, with dark markings. Females often carry a round, white egg case.

HABITS
One of several wolf spiders. Active and fast-running, lives and hunts on the ground. Chases prey rather than using a web. Prefers sheltered sunny places with bare ground. Young may be carried on the female's back after hatching. Seen April–September.

FOOD
Insects and other invertebrates.

IN THE GARDEN
Prefers open sunny situations next to plant cover, and a varied insect community.

MONEY SPIDERS Family Linyphiidae

Average length 2.5 mm
Widespread in Britain and Ireland.

IDENTIFICATION
Tiny, with long, thin legs and usually a round, shiny black abdomen. Web is suspended horizontally and is obvious after heavy dew.

HABITS
A large family, which are tricky to identify. They produce gossamer, which floats in the air. This may anchor nearby or lift the spider and float for long distances of 100 m or more.

FOOD
Small insects, including flies and froghoppers.

IN THE GARDEN
Money spiders benefit from a variety of shrubs and other plants. They are food for many birds.

GARDEN SPIDER *Araneus diadematus*

*Body length female up to 12 mm,
male smaller
Common in Britain and Ireland.*

IDENTIFICATION

Large spider. Light brown, with lighter and darker markings, and a pattern of white dots and ovals forming a cross on the abdomen.

The abdomen is larger than the thorax and is wider towards the front. Striped legs. Produces a typical orb web that is circular with usually 25–35 spokes and a fine, neat spiral.

HABITS

The web is slung from a framework of straighter threads, and is suspended from shrubs, fences, walls, etc. Insects are trapped in sticky droplets on the spiral threads. The centre of the web is not sticky, and here the spider may sit and feel the vibrations caused by a struggling insect. Alternatively, the spider may hide at the end of a signal thread. Prey is paralysed with a venomous bite and is wrapped in silk until eaten.

Eggs are laid under shelter in a mass covered by yellow silk. Young are tiny, yellow with black marks, and mass together unless disturbed.

FOOD

Flying or jumping insects trapped in the web.

IN THE GARDEN

Benefits from a variety of shrubs as web sites, and from a rich insect population.

HOUSE SPIDERS *Tegenaria* species

*Body length up to 18 mm
Common and widespread throughout
Britain and Ireland.*

IDENTIFICATION

A group of several species, common in houses, often seen running across the floor or trapped in a bath. They are large spiders but appear even bigger because of their long, slightly hairy legs. Males are smaller, with thinner bodies. Both sexes are greyish brown, with mottled markings. The web is usually a large, sagging triangular sheet, suspended in a corner. At its corner is a funnel entrance leading to the tubular shelter where the spider hides.

HABITS

House spiders live in houses, sheds and out-buildings. Individuals found in bathtubs will not have entered through the plughole, but will have crawled or slipped in and then been unable to climb the smooth sides.

They prey on insects that fall onto the web, rushing out to capture them. Eggs are contained in a whitish silk sack hanging near the web. Females are found year-round, while males are most common in autumn.

FOOD

Flying insects, including moths, midges, mosquitoes, Common House-flies and Bluebottles.

IN THE GARDEN

Webs are not usually welcome indoors, but they may be tolerated in outbuildings and so should be left in such places.

Zebra Spider *Salticus scenicus*

Body length up to 7 mm
Common in Britain and Ireland, but
scarcer in the north.

Identification

Distinctive small spider, with a black and white zebra pattern and a habit of jumping. Has a slightly elongated body, and oval abdomen that is only just longer than the thorax. Has short, stubby legs and four pairs of eyes, the front pair visible to the naked eye.

Habits

Seen on sunny surfaces, such as walls and fences. Hunts prey rather than using a web. It watches, turning its head, then slowly stalks its prey and finally catches it with a jump that may be 20 times the length of its body. It jumps with the hind legs, while front legs help seize the prey. Silk is anchored before a jump and acts as a safety line. Eggs are laid May–June, and are guarded by the female in a cell made of silk inside a crevice. Adults are seen mostly in May–August.

Food

Small insects.

In the garden

Benefits from sunny areas of woodwork, such as fences. These should have crevices and should not be treated with chemical preservatives.

Daddy-long-legs Spider *Pholcus phalangioides*

Body length up to 11 mm
(including legs, may measure up
to 70 mm across)
Found in England, Wales and Ireland,
and spreading in range.

Identification

Has a tiny cylindrical body and extremely long, delicate, thin legs that are often held with a double bend. Often hangs close to a wall with hind legs bent back and front legs extended forward. Pale brown. It produces a loose web of fine threads, which is hard to see.

Habits

It was probably originally introduced to Britain. Found in houses, cellars and outbuildings. It apparently does not like central heating and extremes of cold. When disturbed, vibrates the web rapidly, so that its body becomes a blur.

Its long legs allow it to entangle its prey with silk while keeping out of the danger of bites from other spiders. After wrapping, the prey is bitten to paralyse and digest it. The bundle is discarded when it is finished with.

Eggs are laid in June, and are carried in the female's mouthparts as a small round bundle. The young hatch in 2–3 weeks and gradually disperse. Adults may be found at any time of year.

Food

Other spiders, mosquitoes, midges and clothes moths.

In the garden

Because the very fine webs catch insects and other spiders, it is a predator that might be welcome in the home, especially in sheds and outbuildings.

INSECTS

SPRINGTAILS AND BRISTLETAILS

These are wingless insects, usually very small. They resemble the primitive ancestors from which the winged insects are descended.

SPRINGTAILS

Collembola species

Body length up to 4 mm
Common in Britain and Ireland.

IDENTIFICATION

Springtails are tiny. Most have long narrow bodies; a few are short and fat. Usually pale brown or grey, with obvious antennae.

HABITS

Found in damp places, including dead leaves, and under stones and logs. A 'spring' in the tail helps it jump considerable distances.

FOOD

Mainly dead, decaying organic matter.

IN THE GARDEN

Aids decomposition and is food for other invertebrates. Keep dead leaves, logs, etc.

DIPLURA

***Campodea* species**

Body length up to 1 cm
Common in Britain and Ireland.

IDENTIFICATION

A group of small, wingless insects. They are white, with a very narrow body, short legs, conspicuous antennae and two tail appendages.

HABITS

They avoid light and seek damp places. In soil, decaying leaves, under logs and stones.

FOOD

Decaying plant remains and fungi.

IN THE GARDEN

Help decomposition, and are a food for small creatures. They are attracted by organic material in the soil, and compost heaps.

SILVERFISH

Lepisma saccharina

Body length up to 2 cm
Widespread in Britain and Ireland

IDENTIFICATION

Narrow, tapered, flattened silver body (covered in microscopic shiny scales) with three long tails. Antennae are long and waving.

HABITS

Silverfish usually live in small crevices inside the damp parts of the house. They have rapid movements, disappearing quickly when disturbed.

FOOD

Organic material, including paper and food remains (crumbs, flour, etc.).

IN THE GARDEN

Harmless, but not normally encouraged.

COMMON POND MAYFLY *Cloeon dipterum*

(POND OLIVE DUN)
Body length 15 mm
Widespread in ponds throughout
Britain and Ireland.

IDENTIFICATION
The thin, delicate body of the adult is curved at rest, with long legs and two very long, thin tails. Forewings are large and transparent but it lacks hindwings. A pre-adult stage has pale grey wings. Larva is thin, delicate and translucent, up to 10 mm long, with three tails.

HABITS
Eggs are laid in still water, and hatch into small swimming, gill-breathing larvae. They have a pre-adult stage instead of a pupa. This leaves the water, can fly weakly and comes to lighted windows at night. Adults fly May–October, but most live less than 24 hours.

FOOD
Adults do not feed. Larvae feed on the layer of microscopic algae in the pond.

IN THE GARDEN
A pond can be improved for mayflies by removing ornamental fish. Larvae will form an important part of the pond's food chain.

EARWIG *Forficula auricularia*

Length 15 mm
Common and widespread throughout
Britain and Ireland.

IDENTIFICATION
Body is long and rather flat, dark brown and shiny. Has a pair of short curved 'forceps' at the end of the body (straighter in the female). Has very short, pale wing covers, these reach only a small distance down the body and leave much of the abdomen exposed.

HABITS
Active at night. By day hides under logs and stones, in crevices and hollow stalks. Although the wings are fully formed, this species of earwig rarely flies.

Eggs are laid in a chamber in the soil and tended by the female, who keeps them clean and mould-free. Larvae look like small adults and are fed and looked after as a family group. Adults hibernate in winter.

FOOD
A general feeder, eating soft plant food such as flower petals, and also small invertebrates and carrion.

IN THE GARDEN
The Earwig is not always welcomed by gardeners, but is a part of the food web. Can be attracted by suitable shelter, such as flat stones and dead hollow stalks.

DAMSELFLIES

Related to dragonflies but smaller and more slender. Most often seen close to water.

IDENTIFICATION

The long, slender, bodies are mostly blue or red and males are usually brighter than females. They have a distinct dumbell-shaped head, prominent eyes and two pairs of long, transparent wings. At rest, wings are pressed together above the body.

Aquatic larvae are green or brown, have a slender body, long legs, and three leaf-shaped tails flattened sideways. A triangular head conceals jaws on an extendable 'mask'.

HABITS

Adults flutter above water and surrounding vegetation. When egg-laying, the male holds the female by the neck with claspers at the tip of his abdomen, so the two fly in tandem.

Eggs are laid in water. Larvae are predators. When fully grown, they climb a plant stem, stone, etc., for their final moult to adult form.

FOOD

Adults catch small insects in flight. Larvae eat aquatic invertebrates such as insect larvae, and small tadpoles.

IN THE GARDEN

Require a pond, with a good invertebrate population, no ornamental fish, emergent plants, plus flower-rich surroundings.

COMMON BLUE DAMSELFLY

Enallagma cyathigerum

Length 32 mm
Common throughout Britain and Ireland.

Often flies low over water. Male is sky-blue, with narrow black bands on the abdomen and broad blue stripes on the thorax. Female is a dull dark brown. Flies May–October.

Common Blue Damselfly egg-laying.

BLUE-TAILED DAMSELFLY

Ischnura elegans

Length 31 mm
Common throughout Britain and Ireland, but scarcer in the north.

Common damselfly; tolerates a range of pond conditions. Male mainly black with a bright turquoise-blue end to the abdomen. Sides of thorax also turquoise, as are narrow stripes on the upper side. Female is usually similar. Low-flying, often amongst marginal vegetation. Flies May–September.

Blue-tailed Damselflies pairing.

> ### NOTE
> The Azure Damselfly, Coenagrion puella, is another widespread damselfly that closely resembles the Common Blue.

DRAGONFLIES

The largest flying insects to be seen in the garden. Dragonflies are among the most ancient of insects, with a fossil record dating back 220 million years.

IDENTIFICATION

Large colourful body is longer and thicker than damselfly's. The two pairs of long, transparent, colourless wings have a network of veins, sometimes have dark spots and are always horizontal at rest. Compound eyes cover most of the round head.

Aquatic larvae are stout, brown or blackish, with a spidery appearance, and 3 spines on the end of the abdomen. The triangular head has large eyes and sharp jaws carried on an extendable 'mask' beneath the head.

HABITS

Rapid and darting flight, but also hovers. Males may be territorial and aggressive. When pairing, males hold females by the neck with claspers on the end of the abdomen. The female dips the tip of her abdomen into the water to lay eggs, or else inserts them into plant stems.

Larval stage lasts up to five years in some species. Mature larva leaves the water, where its skin splits and the winged adult emerges.

FOOD

Adults catch insects in flight. Larvae eat invertebrates, small fish and tadpoles.

IN THE GARDEN

They need a healthy pond with invertebrates, emergent plants, no ornamental fish, and flowering plants to provide insect food.

MIGRANT HAWKER

Aeshna mixta

Length 63 mm, wingspan 85 mm
Mainly in south and east Britain.

Male has a dark body with pairs of bright blue spots and smaller cream markings on each segment. Less territorial than other species, so several may be seen together in sheltered places. A migrant species, but now breeding in many areas. Flies July–October.

FOUR-SPOTTED CHASER

Libellula quadrimaculata

Length 43 mm, wingspan 75 mm
Found throughout most of England and Wales

Body rather flattened and tapered. Brown, with yellow edges to the abdomen. Wings each have two dark marks on the front edge, and hindwings also have a brown triangle at their base. Mainly seen close to water. Flies May–August. Aquatic larva is short and barrel-shaped, with a very spidery appearance.

> **NOTE**
> The Broad-bodied Chaser, *L. depressa*, is similar to the Four-spotted but has the mature male has a pale blue abdomen. It is found in southern Britain.

Dragonflies, like this Migrant Hawker, often perch in prominent positions.

Newly emerged Four-spotted Chasers may be seen around a garden pond.

Damselflies and Dragonflies

Identification

Photos and descriptions are males. Females are much duller.

Damselflies are smaller and slender, and their wings at rest can be folded together above the body.

Dragonflies are larger, with stouter bodies, and their wings at rest are held out to the sides.

These images are not to scale.

Azure Damselfly

Bright blue, with black bands on the abdomen. Two narrow blue stripes on the top of the thorax.

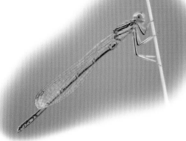

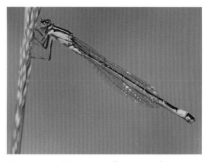

Blue-tailed Damselfly (page 110)

Body mostly dark, with one bright blue segment near the tail tip.

Common Blue Damselfly (page 110)

Bright blue, with black bands on the abdomen. Two broad blue stripes on the top of the thorax.

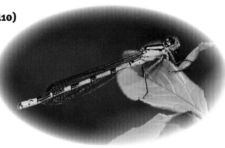

Large Red Damselfly

A large damselfly. Deep red abdomen and stripes on thorax, with darker bands near the tail. Red eyes.

Emperor Dragonfly

The largest dragonfly. Whole abdomen bright blue.

MIGRANT HAWKER (page 111)
Body dark, with pairs of bright blue spots along the abdomen.
(Common Hawker is similar but with bright yellow front edges to the wings)
(Southern Hawker is larger, with two blue bands at the end of the abdomen, and two large yellow' eye spots' on the front of the thorax.

BROWN HAWKER
Large. Brown body, with golden-brown tinged wings.

FOUR-SPOTTED CHASER (page 111)
Medium sized. Abdomen tapered, brown with dark tip. An extra four large dark spots on the wings.

COMMON DARTER
A smaller dragonfly. Abdomen bright red, or orange-red.

BROAD BODIED CHASER (page 111)
Medium sized. Abdomen short and broad, a pale powder blue.

COMMON FIELD GRASSHOPPER
Chorthippus brunneus

Body length 18–22 mm
Common in England, Wales, southern
Scotland and parts of Ireland.

IDENTIFICATION

Green or brown, mottled, or with stripes. A long body, short antennae, roughly a third of the length of body, and long hind legs, with the 'knees' often held upwards. Adults have hidden transparent hindwings. Forewings are folded over them and reach beyond the tip of the abdomen. It has marks on the thorax: each side has a pale line that bends inwards towards the middle.

HABITS

Active by day, especially in hot weather. When disturbed, moves in long leaps, often boosted by short flights. Adults seen June–October. Eggs laid below the surface of soil, where they hatch from May onwards. Nymphs resemble small wingless adults.

The grasshopper 'song', a series of short chirps, is produced by friction between the hind legs and the forewings.

FOOD

Leaves of plants, mainly grasses.

IN THE GARDEN

Prefers longer uncut grass with some bare patches, in dry, sunny areas of the garden.

SPECKLED BUSH CRICKET
Leptophyes punctatissima

Body length 10–17 mm
Widespread in England and Wales.

IDENTIFICATION

Body is bright green, covered with tiny dark spots and has a brown line down the back. Deeper-bodied and slightly shorter than a grasshopper, it has long legs, the hind pair extremely long and thin. Thin antennae are much longer than the body. Wing cases are short and brown. Female carries a broad, flattened and upward-curving ovipositor, 6–7 mm long, at the end of her abdomen.

HABITS

It is nocturnal and flightless, and climbs in shrubs and small trees. Eggs are laid in crevices and hatch May–June. Adults appear July–November. A faint chirp is produced by rubbing one forewing over the other.

FOOD

Occasionally small insects, but mainly leaves of Bramble and other shrubs and trees.

IN THE GARDEN

Crickets can be encouraged by native trees and shrubs, especially Bramble and Birch.

NOTE

The Oak Bush Cricket, *Meconema thalassinum*, often comes to lighted windows at night. It is pale green and slightly thinner than the Speckled Bush Cricket, with full-length wings folded over the body and reaching the end of the abdomen. The species is unusual in being mainly carnivorous, feeding on caterpillars and other insects.

GREEN SHIELD BUG *Palomena prasina*

Length 12.5 mm
Locally common; scarcer in the north.

IDENTIFICATION

Typical shield bug. Large, with a wide, flat body and protruding shoulders, giving it the shield shape. The protruding head has conspicuous antennae. Adult is green, turning brown in winter. Portion of forewings cross at the back (a bug characteristic), and the overlap is brown. Nymphs are green and wingless.

HABITS

Capable of flight, although normally the wings are hidden beneath the forewings. As in other bugs, the mouthparts are long, thin and pointed. This 'beak' is beneath the head, and used to pierce plants and suck their juices. Found among the leaves of shrubs.

FOOD

Feeds on the seeds of plants, while these are still green and soft, especially Bramble.

IN THE GARDEN

Native shrubs, especially Bramble and small trees, will provide a habitat for this species.

> ### NOTE
> The Hawthorn Shield Bug, *Acanthosoma haemorrhoidale*, is similar to the Green Shield Bug but even larger. It is green with diagonal brown markings.

THRIPS Thysanoptera

(THUNDERFLIES)
Length 2–3 mm
Widespread in Britain and Ireland.

IDENTIFICATION

Very small and black, with thin bodies. Magnification is needed to see the two pairs of very narrow wings with feathery fringes.

HABITS

Several similar species. Found in summer on flower heads, and amongst dead leaves. Flies weakly and cannot control its direction. Often in large numbers in thundery weather, hence their common name. They come into houses, and collect on windows or inside picture frames. Eggs are laid in plants, usually in spring, and adults hibernate in winter.

FOOD

Feeds mainly on soft plant tissues, whose surface they scrape to reach the sap.

IN THE GARDEN

Thrips are a food source for some invertebrates. They are also important as pollinators of flowers such as the composites, and benefit from Dandelion, Catsear, etc.

WATER BUGS

A number of 'true' bugs (Hemiptera) live on or beneath the water, and some are common in garden ponds.

POND SKATER

Gerris lacustris

Body length 8–10 mm
Widespread in Britain and Ireland.

IDENTIFICATION

Long, narrow black body. Narrow wings fold flat along abdomen. Legs are thin and long. Lives on the water surface and detects vibrations made by prey. Not all are able to fly.

FOOD

Small creatures trapped in the the water.

IN THE GARDEN

Needs a pond with unpolluted water.

GREATER WATER BOATMAN

Notonecta glauca
(BACKSWIMMER)

Length 1.5 cm
Abundant and widespread
throughout Britain and Ireland.

LESSER WATER BOATMEN

Corixa and *Sigara* species

Body length 6–12 mm
Abundant and widespread throughout Britain and Ireland.

IDENTIFICATION

Swims under water surface. Flattened, oval body is greenish-grey. Long back legs have paddle-shaped ends. Collects air, which is held as a bubble around the body. Flies well.

FOOD

Sucks up particles of detritus and algae.

IN THE GARDEN

Early colonist of new ponds. Important in decomposition, and food for carnivores.

IDENTIFICATION

Swims upside-down underwater. Long body is tapered towards the tail and not flattened. Long hind legs have paddle-shaped tips. Breaks the surface to collect air, which is carried as a bubble around the body. Flies to find new ponds.

FOOD

Seizes invertebrates, small fish and tadpoles and sucks them with sharp mouthparts.

IN THE GARDEN

Important pond predator that needs a clean pond with a healthy animal community.

COMMON FROGHOPPER   *Philaenus spumarius*

(Cuckoo Spit insect)
Length 8–9 mm
Abundant in Britain and Ireland.

IDENTIFICATION

Oval body, wider towards the front and tapered at the tail. Light brown, with variable darker markings. Head is wide with short antennae.

Front wings form hard wing cases, that do not cross as in other groups of bugs.

HABITS

Commonest of several species. Its back legs are not large, but it has a powerful jump when disturbed. Famous for producing white froth, or 'cuckoo spit', found on plants in summer. This froth is made by the soft-bodied nymph, which lives protected within it whilst feeding on the plant sap. Nymph is pale green. Adults occur June–September.

FOOD

Feeds on a wide range of plants by piercing the plant stem and sucking the juices.

IN THE GARDEN

Benefits from a variety of tall vegetation, including both wild and garden species.

LEAFHOPPERS   Family Cicadellidae

Length 4–8 mm
A number of common species are widespread in Britain and Ireland.

IDENTIFICATION

Most species are pale green or brown. Smaller than froghoppers, with narrower, delicate bodies. Forewings are folded over the back, meeting in the mid-line, and are less hard than those of froghoppers. Members of the family are characterised by a row of small spines along the long segment of the hind leg (needs magnification to be seen clearly).

HABITS

Leafhoppers live amongst all kinds of long vegetation, including herbaceous plants and grasses, and shrubs and trees. When disturbed, they can leap and may combine this with flying. They have sharp, piercing mouthparts hidden beneath the head. Adults are present throughout the summer.

FOOD

Most specialise in a narrow range of plants and pierce plant tissues to feed on the sap.

IN THE GARDEN

Leafhoppers benefit from long grasses and wild plants, and native shrubs and trees.

NOTE

The striking Rhododendron Leafhopper, *Graphocephala fennahi,* introduced from North America, can be found on rhododendrons in southern Britain. It is large (9 mm long) and vivid green with red stripes.

Rhododendron Leafhopper.

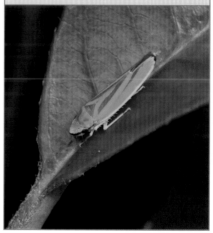

Aphids

Well-known as 'greenflies' or 'blackflies' that feed on the sap of both wild and garden plants. Rapid reproduction and large numbers means that they can seriously damage buds and shoots.

IDENTIFICATION

Even within a species, some individuals have wings while others are wingless. The abdomen is short and plump. At the rear there is usually a pair of tubes or horns (cornicles). Different species may be black, green, grey or pink.

HABITS

Wingless aphids are usually female, and give birth without fertilisation. Young are produced by live birth, and aphids reproduce rapidly. Later in the year winged individuals of both sexes disperse to other plants.

They live on growing shoots (a few on roots), which they pierce with sharp mouthparts. Any surplus sap is exuded from the cornicles as a sugary liquid (honeydew) and may drip to the ground, or is harvested by ants. In return, ants protect aphids from some of their predators.

FOOD

Feeds on different plant juices, depending on the particular aphid. Many use different plants later in the season.

IN THE GARDEN

Aphids are a vital part of the garden food web; chemical control should be avoided.

ROSE APHID *Macrosiphum rosae* (GREENFLY)

Length 2.5 mm
Abundant throughout Britain and Ireland.

A large aphid. Green, or sometimes pink. Cornicles are long and black (magnification may be needed to observe these). Found on buds and shooting tips of roses in spring and early summer. Also occurs, but less noticeably, on other garden plants later in summer. In May, Rose Aphids are an alternative food for Blue Tits feeding their young if other food is scarce.

BLACK BEAN APHID *Aphis fabae* (BLACKFLY)

Length 2 mm
Abundant throughout Britain and Ireland.

A stout-bodied aphid. Black or dark green. Cornicles are short and stubby. One of several similar species. Familiar on bean shoots, but also lives on other wild plants (e.g. dock). Eggs pass the winter on Spindle and other shrubs.

WOOLLY APHID *Eriosoma lanigerum*

Length 2 mm
Widespread in Britain and Ireland.

Hard to distinguish as an insect, as it is covered with a sticky fluff. Found on twigs and bark, and especially on apple trees, often where there has been some damage. These aphids are eaten by tits, particularly Long-tailed Tits.

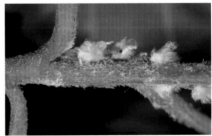

CABBAGE WHITEFLY *Aleyrodes proletella*

Length 2 mm, wingspan c. 3 mm
Widespread in Britain and Ireland.

IDENTIFICATION

Very small and white, with powdery white wings. Because the wings are not transparent, whitefly resemble tiny moths.

HABITS

Usually found on the underside of cabbage leaves. When disturbed, they fly off in a powdery

cloud. They use their sharp, pointed mouthparts to pierce plant cells and suck sap.

For most of their life, nymphs are attached to a single plant, feeding at the same place and surrounded by their cast skins as they grow. Adults can be seen in spring and summer.

FOOD

Cultivated and wild members of the cabbage family. Other whitefly species are specific to different plants.

IN THE GARDEN

Sometimes a pest on cultivated brassicas. Chemical insecticides should not be used.

> **NOTE**
> Similar to the Cabbage Whitefly is the Greenhouse Whitefly, *Trialeurodes vaporariorum,* an introduced species that infests greenhouse plants as well as indoor plants.

COMMON GREEN CAPSID *Lygocoris pabulinus*

Length 6 mm
Widespread in Britain and Ireland.

IDENTIFICATION

Has an elongated oval, flattened body, with a narrower head. Pale green, with a brown area at the tip of the abdomen where the wings overlap. Rather delicate, with thin legs and slender, medium-length antennae.

HABITS

This plant bug is commonly found in gardens. It lives among foliage on a variety of plants. Like other 'true bugs' it has sharp, pointed mouthparts, to pierce plant tissues and suck sap.

Lays eggs on woody plants to overwinter. Young feed on these plants in spring and then move to herbaceous plants as adults.

FOOD

A wide variety of wild and garden plants, including Potatoes and soft fruits.

IN THE GARDEN

A wide variety of plant bugs will be encouraged by a range of plants in the garden, and by long, uncut vegetation and shrubs.

GREEN LACEWING *Chrysoperla carnea*

Length adult 12–20 mm
Most common in southern Britain.

IDENTIFICATION

Pale green, but body may be pinkish before hibernation. Transparent wings fold along the body at rest. Flight is fluttering. Eyes are golden and the antennae are the same length as the body. Eggs are laid on slender stalks that are attached to plants, and the shaggy-looking grey-brown larvae have legs and jaws.

HABITS

Several green lacewing species are found in Britain and Ireland. Flies in the evening and at night, and is attracted to light. In autumn, adults attempt to hibernate in buildings. Several generations occur within a year and the adults disperse if there is a food shortage.

FOOD

Adults feed on nectar, pollen and honeydew from aphids. Larvae feed mainly on aphids, which they suck dry, often placing the remains on their backs, creating rudimentary camouflage.

IN THE GARDEN

A wild area containing native shrubs and even cultivated roses (with aphids!) attracts lacewings. Hibernation chambers can be made for them (*see* p248).

ROBBER FLY *Asilus crabroniformis*

Length 25 mm
Local in southern Britain.

IDENTIFICATION

A very large, striking fly. Has a long, tapered body, dark brown and black in colour, with a yellow tip to the abdomen. The long, thick legs have short hairs or bristles, and end in broad feet with two distinct pads. Has large eyes and a thick clump of hairs on the face. Proboscis (mouthpiece) is sharp and tapered, projecting forwards. Wings are held slightly open at rest. Larva is long, pale and maggot-like.

HABITS

An active hunter, chasing and catching other insects in flight. Often waits on a prominent leaf and makes a dash to catch its prey. The proboscis is sharp and hard, used to pierce prey and suck its juices, while facial bristles may give protection from struggling prey. Harmless to humans. Active July–October.

NOTE

The Snipe Fly, *Rhagio scolopaceus*, is similar in shape but has a narrower body, is not hairy and has narrow yellow bands on its abdomen.

FOOD

Flying insects, including midges and other flies. Larva eats decaying organic material.

IN THE GARDEN

Benefits from a variety of flowers and insects. The larva requires manure heaps.

Scorpion Fly *Panorpa communis*

Length 1.5 cm
Widespread but local in Britain
and Ireland.

IDENTIFICATION

Scary-looking, but harmless. Mainly brown body and long legs. Head protrudes downwards into a strong beak. The male's tail curves up, resembling a scorpion's. It is not a sting, but is actually connected with mating. Female has tapered abdomen. Long, transparent wings have black spots near the tip and are held flat, pointing backwards at rest.

HABITS

Lives among tall herbs and shrubs, especially in shady, damp places. Commonly seen on nettles. Flies well, but often found crawling. Eggs are laid in the soil. The caterpillar-like larvae are carnivores and scavengers. Pupates in soil. Adults seen May–August.

FOOD

A predator of spiders and small insects, and takes the juice of ripe fruit, but more often said to eat dead insects and carrion.

IN THE GARDEN

Prefers uncut wild plants, such as nettles.

Spotted Cranefly *Nephrotoma appendiculata*

(DADDY-LONG-LEGS)
Body length 2 cm
Common in Britain and Ireland.

IDENTIFICATION

Long, thin body. Abdomen yellowish-brown with dark, square markings. Has very long, delicate legs. Male's abdomen has a square end, while female's is pointed. Has one pair of long, narrow, transparent, shiny wings.

Larva is the legless leatherjacket found in soil. It is grey, long (up to 35 mm) and sausage-shaped. Tail end is star-shaped with two small, black breathing openings.

HABITS

Most common cranefly in gardens. Flies weakly with trailing legs. Comes to lights at night. Flies May–August, but mostly late summer. Female lays eggs in the soil, where the larvae burrow and feed before pupating.

FOOD

Adults hardly feed, occasionally taking nectar from open flower heads. Larvae feed on decaying plant matter, or on the underground roots and tubers of plants.

IN THE GARDEN

Adults are food for many birds, and the larvae are food for Starlings. Areas of short turf help the birds reach the larvae.

NOTE

Other common craneflies include members of the *Tipula* genus, which are larger than the Spotted Cranefly (up to 3 cm long), and have a grey body and often patterned wings.

MOSQUITO *Culex pipiens*

Body length 7 mm
Common in Britain and Ireland.

IDENTIFICATION

Slender and delicate. Hind pair of long, thin legs are held upwards at rest. Wings are long and transparent and held flat over the body. Abdomen is dark brown, with pale bands

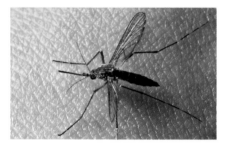

on each segment. Mouthparts are long and slender. Male has feathery antennae. Aquatic larva is long-bodied and legless, and frequently hangs by its tail from the surface.

HABITS

Female mouthparts are adapted for piercing skin and sucking blood. She needs a blood meal before she can develop eggs, and a nectar meal before hibernating. The eggs float as a raft on the water surface.

FOOD

The female sucks blood from birds (and, very occasionally, humans) and nectar from plants, especially Ivy. The male takes only nectar. Larvae feed by filtering particles of detritus and bacteria from water.

IN THE GARDEN

Breeds mainly in small water bodies such as rainwater butts. Hibernates in outhouses.

MIDGE *Chironomus plumosus*

Length 10 mm
Abundant in Britain and Ireland.

IDENTIFICATION

Long, slender fly, with thin, delicate legs. The abdomen projects beyond the wings, which are folded roof-like. Male has plume-like antennae; female's antennae are small and simple.

Aquatic larva is legless, thin, wormlike and bright red. Other species are brown or green.

HABITS

This is not a biting insect. Adults do not feed. Males swarm, especially at dusk. Larvae live in ponds or other water, such as water butts where they make thin, muddy tubes. Adults active April–September.

FOOD

Larvae filter particles of detritus from water.

IN THE GARDEN

Important in the pond community, as a filter-feeder and as a food for predators.

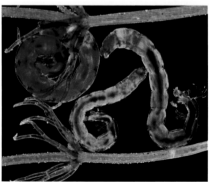

Aquatic larva.

> ### NOTE
>
> The Biting Midge, *Culicoides obsoletus*, is infamous for its annoying bite, especially at dusk. It is small (2 mm long) and elusive, with light brown markings on the wings.

Soldier Fly *Microchrysa polita*

Length 6 mm
Widespread in Britain and Ireland.

Identification
Medium-sized fly with rather square-ended abdomen. Bright, glossy dark green (soldier flies are named for their vivid metallic colours; other species in the group are black and yellow, or blue). Has a single pair of wings, held flat over the back at rest, and projecting beyond the end of the abdomen. Most of the wide head is occupied by large eyes. Antennae are short and form a 'V' between the eyes.

Habits
One of the most likely species of soldier fly to be found in gardens. Has a slow flight and is usually seen in sunny weather, visiting flowers or sunbathing. On the wing March–September. Breeds in manure or compost heaps, where the larva lives.

Food
Nectar. The larva feeds on decomposing organic matter.

In the garden
Benefits from a range of flowers through the whole season. Compost heaps or manure heaps are a vital habitat for breeding.

St Mark's Fly *Bibio marci*

(March Fly)
Body length 10–12 mm
Widespread in Britain and Ireland.

Identification
Large, narrow-bodied fly, black and hairy with glossy thorax. Flies with long legs dangling. Has a single pair of wings longer than its body. The short antennae are in front of large eyes, which occupy most of the head in the male.

Habits
Has a slow, clumsy-looking flight, and, with its dangling black legs, looks rather sinister but it is quite harmless. Flies on sunny days, over vegetation and amongst foliage, and is often seen pairing. Frequently settles. Adults fly from March onwards, and are named for St Mark's Day (25 April), which falls during the period when they are typically seen. The legless larva lives in soil and compost.

Food
Aphid honeydew from leaf surfaces, and nectar. Larva eats organic material and roots.

In the garden
May be an important source of insect food in spring for Swallows and other migrants. Benefits from compost heaps for breeding.

BEE FLY   *Bombylius major*

Length 10 mm, excluding proboscis
Common in southern Britain.

IDENTIFICATION

Pear-shaped body is broadest towards the tail. The small head is mostly taken up by the eyes. Densely furry with a golden tinge, and bumblebee-like; hence the common name. Mouthparts comprise a very long, thin proboscis,

roughly a third of the total length of the insect. This is held horizontally, pointing in front and unlike those of any of the other bee-like flies.

HABITS

Hovers motionless, making a faint high-pitched buzzing. Also vibrates its wings whilst holding onto flowers with its legs and probes with the long proboscis. Flies in spring.

The legless larva is parasitic on the larvae of solitary bees and wasps. The female lays eggs near the nesting cells of these insects, so that its larvae can enter and feed on the contents; the pollen and nectar placed there by the host, as well as the host's larva.

FOOD

Nectar, from early spring flowers. The larva parasitises solitary bees and wasps.

IN THE GARDEN

Flowers such as Primrose, violets and Lungwort attract this species.

DRONE-FLY   *Eristalis tenax*

Length 14 mm
Widespread in Britain and Ireland.
One of several similar species.

IDENTIFICATION

Large, stout hoverfly. A true fly with a single pair of wings. Blackish body with orange-brown stripes on the abdomen, and a broad head with

Larva (below) is known as the 'rat-tailed maggot'.

large eyes. It closely mimics the male or drone Honey Bee.

The larva is legless and lives in stagnant pools. The soft, pale grey, sausage-shaped body has a long extensible breathing tube at the tail; hence its name, 'rat-tailed maggot'.

HABITS

Frequently hovers, emitting a continuous buzz or whine. Often seen in sunny, sheltered clearings. Territorial, chasing off other individuals. Despite its appearance, it is harmless and does not sting. The sucking mouthparts are longer and more slender than those of most hoverflies, making it better adapted to feeding on nectar when visiting flowers.

FOOD

Mainly nectar (and a little pollen) from flat or open flowers, where this food is fairly accessible. The aquatic larva feeds on decaying organic matter in the mud.

IN THE GARDEN

Favours sheltered, sunny glades in the garden. As with other hoverflies, requires a variety of flowers with easily obtainable nectar. Larvae need a shallow, muddy part of the pond.

HOVERFLIES

A large group of flies of the Syrphidae family. Over 60 different species have been recorded in gardens.

IDENTIFICATION

Hoverflies have a single pair of wings with a distinctive vein running as a border along the hind edge. Bodies vary from oval to slender. Heads and eyes are large, and antennae are small. Many are wasp or bee mimics, and others use black and yellow warning colours, but all are harmless to humans.

HABITS

Very active flight; hovering in one place and rapid darting. They visit flowers to feed. The sucking mouthparts may be long and slender, adapted to taking nectar, or short with a spongy tip, adapted to taking pollen.

FOOD

Pollen and nectar. Some larvae scavenge on organic matter, and many prey on aphids.

IN THE GARDEN

Adults need accessible open flowers – both wild and garden varieties – all through the season. Umbellifers and composites are particularly favoured, as is Ivy in the autumn. Aphids are an important source of food to many hoverfly larvae, so chemical control of aphids should be avoided. Instead, try interplanting susceptible plants with flowers that attract adult hoverflies, such as African Marigold.

SYRPHUS RIBESII

Length 13 mm
Throughout Britain and Ireland.

Medium to large, broad-bodied hoverfly. Wasp-like yellow bands on a black abdomen. Visits flowers for pollen and nectar. Adults are active April–November, and large numbers are often seen together. Larva is greyish-white, slug-like, broad behind and narrow at the front end. Feeds on aphids.

EPISYRPHUS BALTEATUS

Length 12 mm
Throughout Britain and Ireland.

Medium-sized hoverfly. Typical of the group, but with a rather narrow, parallel-sided body with broad yellow bands on the abdomen divided by an additional narrow band of black. Seen March–November and sometimes appear in large swarms of migrating individuals. Larva feeds on aphids.

MELANOSTOMA SCALARE

Length 9–10 mm
Throughout Britain and Ireland.

A smaller hoverfly. Very narrow-bodied, the abdomen with parallel sides. The yellow marks on the abdomen are not complete bands – a black line runs down the middle of the back. Present April–November, but most common in spring. Larva feeds on aphids.

House Flies

Abundant and widespread group of flies from the Calliphoridae and Muscidae families, found throughout Britain and Ireland.

IDENTIFICATION

These 'typical' flies have short, broad bodies that are shiny and slightly hairy. At rest the single pair of flat and delta-shaped wings is held backwards. Eyes are large and antennae short. Legless larvae (maggots) are whitish, moving by wriggling and crawling.

HABITS

Numerous June–September. Often seen at windows, or around food. Mouthparts have a fleshy pad that is extended during feeding, and digestive juices exuded. It then sucks the partly digested liquid.

FOOD

House flies are attracted by decaying materials, but also visit human food. Hygiene problems arise if bacteria are transferred to food by the flies.

IN THE GARDEN

Important in the process of decay of animal bodies. Also a food for insectivorous animals.

BLUEBOTTLE *Calliphora vomitoria*
(BLOW-FLY)

Length 10–12 mm
Widely distributed in Britain and Ireland.

Large, glossy, blue-black fly that makes a loud buzzing. Females often seen indoors. Males in particular visit flowers for nectar.

Attracted to meat or dead animals. Lays clusters of yellowish eggs on potential food. Larvae hatch in less than a day, and can be fully grown in a week. Larva is the typical maggot, whitish with a tapered front end and square tail. It creeps away to pupate, adults emerging 8–10 days later.

GREENBOTTLE

Lucilia caesar

Length c. 9 mm
Widespread in Britain and Ireland.

Smaller than the Bluebottle. Bright, glossy green. Eyes are reddish and cover most of the head. Larva is a typical maggot.

Rarely comes indoors. Seen in the garden in sunny weather. Visits manure and dead animals, and flowers for nectar. Eggs are laid on carrion, where the larvae feed and develop.

COMMON HOUSE-FLY

Musca domestica

Length 7–8 mm
Widespread in Britain and Ireland.

Smaller than both the Green- and Bluebottle. Black, with orange patches on sides of abdomen, prominent head and reddish eyes.

Often indoors. Seeks food around rubbish bins. Outdoors, is found around compost and manure. Eggs are laid in organic refuse and can develop to the adult stage within seven days.

GALLS AND GALL WASPS

Galls are growths on plants, caused by a parasite that encourages plant cells to grow in an unusual way; the resulting structure provides it with food and shelter. Each pairing of parasite and host produces a distinct gall. Many are caused by gall wasps (family Cynipidae), although other galls are provoked by midges, moths, mites, nematode worms and fungi.

IDENTIFICATION
Gall wasps are tiny. They have wasp-shaped bodies with a narrow waist, an abdomen that is usually rather flattened sideways and small wings with a simple pattern of veins.

HABITS
Many species have two generations a year, producing different galls in spring and summer.

FOOD
Larvae feed on plant tissues within the gall.

IN THE GARDEN
Appropriate hosts are needed by each species. Larvae and pupae are food for birds such as tits, which peck them out.

COMMON SPANGLE GALL
Neuroterus quercusbaccarum

Wasp length 4 mm
Abundant in Britain and Ireland.

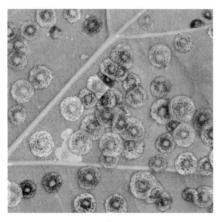

Tiny black wasp. Spangle galls form on the underside of oak leaves in autumn, each containing a single developing wasp. Galls are circular, up to 5 mm across, almost flat but with a raised centre. They are reddish, turning brown in autumn, and attached by a narrow stalk.

Two generations a year. Adult females emerge from old spangle galls in late winter. They lay eggs on the buds of oak trees, and these produce small, spherical, translucent green 'currant galls' on oak catkins, where the larvae grow. Males and females emerge from these currant galls in summer. The female then lays eggs on the underside of oak leaves, where the spangle galls form. Larvae pass the winter in the fallen leaf litter.

ROBIN'S PINCUSHION GALL
Diplolepis rosae
(BEDEGUAR GALL)

Wasp length 4–5 mm
Common in Britain and Ireland.

Black wasp with a yellow abdomen. The large shapeless gall (diameter 60 mm or more) is found on Dog Rose. It is covered by long branched filaments or hairs. Green at first, turning red later, and brown in winter. Inside are the chambers of up to 60 larvae.

One generation a year. Adults emerge in May and lay eggs in buds. Larvae develop through the summer, and winter in the gall.

NOTE
Maple and Sycamore Galls are red pimples on the upper side of the leaves. They are caused by mites of the Eriophyidae family.

Ants

Ants are well known in gardens for the large colonies they form under stones or in lawns. They are small members of the order Hymenoptera, a group that includes the bees and wasps.

Identification
Small, usually wingless with a short, almost round abdomen, connected to the thorax by a slender 'waist'. Antennae bend forwards.

Habits
Ants live in colonies. The individuals normally seen are workers, which are non-breeding females. They collect food, care for the eggs, larvae and pupae, and defend the colony, although some species have a specialised soldier caste that does the latter. The queen is larger and stays in the nest, laying eggs.

The nest is an excavated network of galleries and chambers, underground or under a large stone etc. Workers ensure the right conditions by moving the eggs, larvae and pupae as the temperature changes.

Mating takes place when the colony produces a swarm of winged individuals (flying ants). These are either young queens or males, which are smaller. Swarming usually occurs in humid conditions, and nearby nests swarm at the same time. Swarms often attract insect-eating birds. Mated females descend to the ground, shed their wings and seek a place to lay eggs, produce workers and start a new colony. The males simply die after mating.

Food
Both plant food (mainly high-value foods such as seeds) and animal food (small invertebrates) are taken to the nest. Some ants collect honeydew from aphids (see p118).

In the garden
Important in the ecology of gardens as predators of invertebrates and protectors of aphids. Also become prey for birds when swarming and green Woodpeckers from the ground.

Black Garden Ant
Lasius niger

Length worker 3–5 mm
Abundant in Britain and Ireland.

Black or dark brown. Colonies may contain 4,000–7,000 workers. These are often under paving stones or around house foundations. Small heaps of fine soil may be seen around the nest, and regular trails to feeding areas.

Omnivorous. Eats seeds, small invertebrates and takes honeydew from aphids. Cannot sting, but will bite. Swarms July–September.

Black Garden Ant drinking honeydew.

Red Ant
Myrmica rubra

Length worker 4–5 mm
Common in Britain and Ireland.

Acid from Red Ants can sting humans.

Light red-brown. Nests are mainly in the soil, sometimes under stones, logs, etc. Colonies are smaller than those of the Black Ant. Eats mainly small invertebrates and milks honeydew from aphids. Will sting, injecting acid into the victim. Swarms July–October.

ICHNEUMON *Netelia testaceus*

Body length 16 mm
Common in Britain and Ireland.

IDENTIFICATION

Most familiar of many ichneumon species. Despite often being called the 'Ichneumon Fly', it is not a true fly but related to ants and wasps. A large, slender insect, with a long, thin waist and narrow abdomen. Thorax looks 'hunched', with the waist curved upwards. Body is light orange-brown with a dark tip to the abdomen, long antennae, and long thin legs. A short ovipositor is hidden in the abdomen. Wings are large and transparent with small brown spot at the front edge.

HABITS

Mainly nocturnal. Attracted to light and often seen at windows at night, where it looks rather alarming. If handled it can puncture the skin, but the sting is not poisonous. Like most ichneumons, its larva is a parasite of other insects. The female penetrates the host with her ovipositor and lays a single egg. The larva feeds on the internal tissues of the prey, although the host remains alive for some time and even pupates. Adults therefore emerge from their host's pupa.

FOOD

Adults visit flowers for nectar. The larvae are parasitic on moth caterpillars.

IN THE GARDEN

A diversity of plants, including native species, will encourage good populations of the moths that provide hosts for the larvae.

RUBY-TAILED WASP *Chrysis ignita* agg.

Length 10–11 mm
Common throughout Britain
and Ireland.

IDENTIFICATION

Small to medium-sized insect. Head and thorax are green or blue with a bright metallic sheen. Ruby-red abdomen is also shiny and metallic-looking. Abdomen shows only three segments, and has four small teeth at the tip.

HABITS

One of several brightly coloured members of the Chrysididae family, sometimes called the cuckoo wasps. Lays eggs in the cells of solitary wasps or bees, where its larva feeds on the host's larva. Adult lacks a sting but has a strong cuticle as a defence against being stung. Adults active April–September. Runs around on walls and log piles as it searches for the nests of hosts.

FOOD

Adults feed on nectar. Larvae feed on the larvae of other solitary wasps and bees.

IN THE GARDEN

Adults need nectar-bearing flowers. Breeding is helped by providing nesting habitats for solitary bees, including walls with weak mortar, log piles, artificial bees' nests, etc.

GOOSEBERRY SAWFLY *Nematus ribesii*

Length female 7–9 mm, male smaller
Widespread in Britain and Ireland.

IDENTIFICATION

Has a short, wide head, medium-length antennae and a dull orange body; the male's with dark marks. Larva is long, thin and greenish with dark spots and a shiny black head, and easily mistaken for a caterpillar. Has three pairs of short legs on the thorax, like a caterpillar, but seven pairs of stumpy false legs on the abdomen.

HABITS

Several sawfly species visit gardens. The female has a toothed ovipositor, with which she cuts slits in leaves to lay eggs. Larvae often stay close together; signs of their feeding on leaves are obvious.

FOOD

Adults feed on pollen, especially from umbellifers. Larvae eat the leaves of Gooseberry, *Ribes uva-crispa*, and currant plants.

IN THE GARDEN

Larvae can strip a Gooseberry bush. A garden with rich insect fauna attracts more predators and reduces the risk of this.

SOLITARY WASPS *Passaloecus* species

Length 6–7 mm
Common in Britain and Ireland,
especially in the south.

IDENTIFICATION

Shiny black, with a narrow oval, pointed abdomen and a short, wasp-like waist. Has a relatively wide head, with backwards-curving antennae. The wings are held outwards at rest.

HABITS

Adults emerge and mate in midsummer. Male then dies and female searches for a hole in a dead branch, fencepost or old woodwork, usually made by a wood-boring beetle.

The nest is stocked with aphids, which the female catches and immobilises. After each batch of 20–30 aphids, she lays an egg on one, closes off the cell and starts another. There are usually 3–5 cells. Inside, the larvae feed on the aphids, pupate and emerge as adults the following spring.

FOOD

Adults feed on nectar. Larvae feed on aphids.

IN THE GARDEN

These wasps depend on nest sites made by wood-boring beetles, and so are helped when old wood or log piles are left in sunny locations.

Social Wasps

Social wasps live in colonies, in nests they construct themselves. They are known for their warning colours, and their painful and unpleasant stings.

IDENTIFICATION

These familiar wasps have well-known black and yellow markings. Queens are large, while workers are smaller and less hairy than bees. The thorax is black with small yellow marks, and the abdomen is yellow with black bands and spots. These and the facial markings help to distinguish the species.

HABITS

Social wasps live in a colony. A papery nest is produced from wood they scrape from dead trees, fenceposts, etc. with their jaws. Nests may be in a hole in a tree, a roof space, a cavity in a wall or underground. In spring, a queen builds a layer of cells enclosed by an outer shell.

In the cells she lays eggs, which become the first workers. Workers enlarge the nest and feed new larvae. Later, males are produced, as well as new queens that leave to find mates. In autumn, males and workers die and young queens hibernate.

FOOD

Wasps feed on nectar and ripe fruit. They also eat other insects and carrion on which the larvae are also fed.

IN THE GARDEN

Wasps are important predators. Hibernating queens rely on late flowers such as ivy.

COMMON WASP

Vespula vulgaris

Length c. 16 mm, queen c. 22 mm
Common in Britain and Ireland.

Black bands on the abdomen have a broader middle section, projecting backwards at the mid-line in a short point, and there is a black spot on each side of this. The front of the face, between the eyes, has a black anchor-shaped mark, with the cross-piece between the eyes. Nest is yellowish in colour.

HORNET

Vespa crabro

Length c. 27 mm, queen 30 mm
Southern Britain, but apparently increasing in range and numbers.

Much larger than other wasps. Abdomen is orange-yellow, while the thorax and abdominal stripes and spots are golden brown.

GERMAN WASP

Vespula germanica

Length c. 16 mm, queen c. 22 mm
Common in Britain and Ireland.

Black bands on the abdomen each have a long backwards-pointing projection down the mid-line, almost joining to form a line down the back and with a black spot on each side. Face has three small black spots arranged in a triangle, and a further black mark higher up between the eyes. Nest is grey.

HONEY BEE *Apis mellifera*

Length 12–14 mm
Widespread in Britain and Ireland.

IDENTIFICATION

Workers, with dark and lighter brown bands on the abdomen, are our most familar bees.

HABITS

Kept in hives, but colonies also live in natural hollows. Colonies have a queen and as many as 50,000 workers. Workers gather food for themselves and the larvae, and they build honeycombs

of wax to store food and provide brood cells. They tend the eggs, larvae and pupae, and have a sting as a defence. Queen's eggs normally hatch as workers. Drones hatch from unfertilised eggs, and new queens develop frm larvae given special food. New queens may lead a swarm of workers to start a new colony.

FOOD

Nectar and pollen.

IN THE GARDEN

Honey Bees rely on a variety of flowers for the whole season, and are important pollinating agents.

SOLITARY BEES

Solitary bees do not form colonies.

IDENTIFICATION

Variable in size. These species lack pollen baskets and instead trap pollen amongst the dense hairs on their hind legs.

HABITS

Female excavates a nest burrow, makes a small number of cells, fills them with pollen and nectar, and lays a single egg in each. The larvae hatch, develop and pupate with no further maternal visits.

FOOD

Nectar and pollen.

IN THE GARDEN

These important pollinators can be encouraged by variety and sequence of flowers, by dead wood and homemade wild bee nests.

TAWNY MINING BEE

Andrena fulva
(LAWN BEE)

Length 14 mm
Widespread in southern Britain.

Size of Honey Bee. Hairy with flattened abdomen. Body is bright ginger, although male is blackish. Nest is a tunnel dug in light soil, including lawns, with excavated soil often showing as a small, shallow mound. Needs easy access to nectar.

LEAFCUTTER BEE

Megachile centuncularis

Length 13–14 mm
Widespread in Britain and Ireland.

Resembles a Honey Bee. Female has dense hairs under the abdomen to trap pollen. Nest is a tunnel in dead wood or a plant stem, and is lined with semicircular pieces cut from the edges of leaves, usually rose. The resulting holes are a clue that this species is present.

BUMBLEBEES

Members of the genus *Bombus*, bumblebees are widespread throughout Britain and Ireland.

IDENTIFICATION

Large, fat, furry bodies, with wings that look rather too small. Body usually black, with bands or tail segments of yellow, fawn, white or red. A few have ginger or fawn thoraxes, with pale abdomens. Slow, heavy flight, with a loud droning noise.

HABITS

Large queens emerge from hibernation in early spring, seeking flowers. They make a nest, often just below the ground surface, covered with moss, or in a tunnel underground, often an old mouse hole. Sometimes they take over bird nest boxes.

Queen forms a colony, laying eggs and feeding larvae in wax cells. Larvae then make their own silk chambers, and emerge as workers to feed the next batch of larvae. Workers resemble the queens but are noticeably smaller. Larvae are fed on collected pollen and nectar,

but these are not stored as in Honey Bees. Later in the summer, males and new queens are produced. In autumn, the rest of the colony dies and the queens hibernate in a burrow or similar site.

Bumblebees can sting, although they are not usually aggressive.

FOOD

Pollen and nectar from flowers. Pollen gathered by combing into 'pollen baskets', formed on the hind legs from groups of special stiff hairs.

IN THE GARDEN

Gardens are very important to bumblebees, as they are declining in many of their countryside habitats. A sequence of nectar-bearing flowers throughout the season, especially in early spring, is vital. Unfortunately, nest boxes have been found to be ineffective, so plant bee-friendly flowers to attract them.

RED-TAILED BUMBLEBEE

Bombus lapidarius

Length queen c. 23 mm
Widespread in Britain and Ireland.

Large bee with a relatively long abdomen. Black, with a red tip to the tail. Short-tongued, taking nectar especially from flowers with clustered heads, such as composites.

BUFF-TAILED BUMBLEBEE

Bombus terrestris

Length queen c. 24 mm
Widespread throughout Britain and Ireland.

Very large. Has a band of yellow at the front of the thorax and around the abdomen, and a white or buff tip to the tail. A short-tongued species, taking nectar from flowers with accessible nectaries, but also 'robs' nectar from flowers by biting a hole in the back.

EARLY BUMBLEBEE
Bombus pratorum

Length Queen c. 18 mm
Widespread in Britain and Ireland.

Small, with yellow bands across the front of the thorax and middle of the abdomen, and an orange tip to the tail. A medium-tongued species, although its narrow head allows it to reach nectar from fairly deep flowers.

WHITE-TAILED BUMBLEBEE
Bombus lucorum

Length: Queen 22 mm;
worker 13 mm
Widespread in England, Wales and Scotland.

IDENTIFICATION
Large. A pale yellow band at front of thorax, and one near front of abdomen. Tail white.

HABITS
One of the first Bumblebees to emerge in spring. Feeds on shorter-tubed flowers. Will often rob nectar from longer flowers such as Honeysuckle, or Runner Beans, by biting a hole at the bottom of the tube or the flower spur. Workers can forage far from the nest, so can reach even urban sites.

Nest is made below ground, lined with finely shredded grass, moss, or leaf litter.

GARDEN BUMBLEBEE
Bombus hortorum

Length: Queen 22 mm; worker 14 mm
Common and widespread in Britain and Ireland

IDENTIFICATION
Broad, bright yellow bands on collar, hind edge of thorax and front of abdomen. Tail white.

HABITS
A long-tongued bee, able to reach nectar in deep long-tubed flowers, including many garden flowers. An important pollinator of bean crops.

Nest often under ground, in sunny sites.

CUCKOO BEES
Cuckoo bees closely resemble Bumblebees. They can be distinguished by their shinier and less hairy bodies, often darker wings, and by their lack of pollen baskets. They do not make their own nests or produce a colony with workers. Instead, as their name implies, the females enter the nests of bumblebees and lay eggs there, and the larvae are reared as their own by the bumblebee host's workers.

There are several species. Most of them resemble very closely the bumblebee species whose nest they use.

COMMON CARDER BEE

Bombus pascuorum

Length: Queen 17 mm; worker 12 mm
Widespread in Britain and Ireland. One of
several species of Carder Bees.

IDENTIFICATION

Rather small. Whole thorax is ginger. Abdomen
is pale ginger, with faint dark rings.

HABITS

A long-tongued bee, taking nectar from deep
flowers. White Dead-nettle is particularly
favoured by emerging queens. Also important
as fruit tree pollinators. The nest is built at

ground level or just below, usually among grass
tussocks. Like the other carders, the nest is
woven from moss, dry grass or other fine plant
matter which the bees collect.

TREE BUMBLEBEE

Bombus hypnorum

Length: Queen 20 mm; worker 12 mm

A recent colonist from Europe. First recorded
in 2001, and has since spread throughout the
south of England. Will almost certainly spread
further.

IDENTIFICATION

Easy to recognise. A plain ginger thorax.
Abdomen black with white tail.

HABITS

Strongly associated with parks and gardens.
Feeds from a wide range of cultivated flowers.
    Nest sites are usually above ground, often
in holes in trees (hence the common name),
and frequently in bird nestboxes. Colonies are
often quite large.

FLOWER BEE *Anthophora plumipes*

(HAIRY-FOOTED FLOWER BEE OR SPRING FLOWER BEE).

Length 16 mm
Fairly common in southern parts of Britain.
Not a true bumblebee, with a different
structure for collecting pollen on the
hind leg.

IDENTIFICATION

Female is a large, entirely black bee, except for
fringes of yellow hairs on the hind legs, which
look rather like pollen baskets. Male is brown,
with tufts of long hairs on the middle legs.

HABITS

Very rapid in flight, with a higher pitched noise
than bumblebees. Also hovers well.
    Often seen in gardens early in the year,
visiting spring flowers such as Lungwort. This is
not a social bee, and so does not have colonies
with workers. The female excavates a nest,
usually in a bank. Here in stores of collected
pollen, she lays eggs which hatch into new
females and males.

GROUND BEETLES

These members of the family Carabidae are typical beetles. They are predators, with large curved jaws that are used to catch and eat smaller invertebrates. Immature stages are active and mobile larvae, which look unlike adult beetles.

BLACK GROUND BEETLE
Pterostichus madidus

Length c. 15 mm
Widespread in Britain and Ireland.

IDENTIFICATION
Perhaps the most common of the black ground beetles found in gardens. Body is fairly flat and wing cases have narrow parallel grooves. Shiny black, but legs usually brown.

HABITS
Flightless. Fast-running. Feeds at night. Shelters under stones, logs and old leaves by day.

FOOD
Eats small invertebrates, especially caterpillars. Unusually, this species also eats seeds.

IN THE GARDEN
Ground beetles are predators on other invertebrates and they are prey for insectivorous birds and mammals. They can be encouraged by a diverse habitat, particularly if it provides cover, such as stones, tiles and log piles.

SMALL GROUND BEETLE
Amara aenea

Length 7–8 mm
Widespread in Britain and Ireland.

IDENTIFICATION
Small, with a neater, more oval body outline than the Black Ground Beetle. Shiny, with a brassy or copper sheen.

HABITS
Fast-running. Often seen on open ground, especially in hot, sunny weather. Able to fly.

FOOD
Small invertebrates.

IN THE GARDEN
Similar to Black Ground Beetle.

VIOLET GROUND BEETLE
Carabus violaceus

Length up to 30 mm
Widespread in Britain and Ireland.

IDENTIFICATION
A very large beetle with smooth wing cases. Black, but with a violet colour around the edges of the wing cases and thorax.

HABITS
Nocturnal, hides under logs or stones by day.

FOOD
Invertebrates, including slugs.

IN THE GARDEN
Similar to Black Ground Beetle.

FLEA BEETLE · Phyllotreta nigripes

Length 2–3 mm
Widespread in Britain and Ireland.

IDENTIFICATION

Very small, with a short, deep, oval body, and a hard cuticle and wing cases. Shiny and dark blue-black. Upper section of the hind leg is large and thick.

HABITS

Found on the leaves of its food plants, where it makes numerous small holes in the leaves. Adults emerge in spring. They can fly, but usually just jump if disturbed.

FOOD

Seedlings and young leaves of plants, especially brassicas. Larvae feed on the roots.

IN THE GARDEN

Important in the garden food web. Any control should avoid the use of insecticides.

SOLDIER BEETLE · Rhagonycha fulva

Length 10 mm
Common in Britain and Ireland.

tip of the abdomen protrudes. Shiny orange-brown, with black marks at the tips of the wing cases. Antennae are long.

HABITS

Visits umbellifers and other flower heads in summer. Flies slowly. Larva hunts amongst leaf litter. Adults occur June–September.

FOOD

Eats insects found in flower heads. Larvae hunt invertebrates, including snails.

IDENTIFICATION

Medium-sized beetle with a long, narrow body and rather soft wing cases, from which the

IN THE GARDEN

Encouraged by umbelliferous flowers, and contributes to their pollination.

ROSEMARY BEETLE · Chrysolina americana

Length 8 mm.
Newly arrived colonist from eastern Europe or the Mediterranean. First recorded in England in 1994, and spreading rapidly. Already widespread in England, and recorded in Wales, Scotland and Ireland.

IDENTIFICATION

One of the family of leaf beetles. Oval shaped, highly metallic-looking with green and purple stripes. Larvae are slug-like, and grey with darker stripes.

HABITS

Often found in small clusters on the food plant, eating leaves down to the base. Can be found throughout the winter and much of the year. Larvae feed on the undersides of leaves. They leave the plant to pupate in the soil.

FOOD

Rosemary, and other related herbs such as Lavender, Thyme and Sage.

IN THE GARDEN

Can be removed if necessary by hand picking.

BEETLE IDENTIFICATION

STAG BEETLE *Lucanus cervus*

Length: Male up to 75 mm, female 30–45 mm.
Local and scarce in South and East England. Decreasing and threatened.

IDENTIFICATION

Very large. Head and thorax black, wing cases reddish-brown. Male has enormous jaws, resembling antlers, which give the beetle its name. Female has much smaller, but more powerful, jaws. The larva is a fat curved grub, with yellow head.

HABITS

Adults emerge in summer. Flight is slow and heavy, with a deep droning sound. May sometimes be found stranded on the ground. Larva lives and feeds in decaying wood, e.g. large logs and tree stumps. Takes up to four years to mature.

FOOD

Adult feeds on nectar and tree sap. Larva on rotting wood.

IN THE GARDEN

Rare in gardens, but may occasionally be found in the south in wooded areas. Needs large rotting trees.

LESSER STAG BEETLE

Dorcus parallelipipedus

Length 20–30 mm.
Local but widespread in Southern and Central England, and Wales.

IDENTIFICATION

Blackish. Body parallel-sided, with head almost as wide as thorax. Jaws prominent but do not form 'antlers'.

HABITS

On the wing in summer. Larvae feed in decaying deciduous wood.

IN THE GARDEN

Depends on very rotten tree stumps and other dead wood.

COCKCHAFER

Melolontha melolontha
(MAYBUG)

Length 20–30 mm
Locally common in southern Britain.

IDENTIFICATION

Large, distinctive beetle with deep, stout body and a small head. Black thorax and chestnut-brown wing cases with deep grooves. Black abdomen protrudes beyond the wing cases. Short antennae have fan-shaped ends. Larva is a fat, white grub, with brown head, short legs, and lives in the soil.

HABITS

Flight is slow and heavy, accompanied by a droning noise. Active in the evening and at night. Flies around trees and shrubs, and is attracted to light. Eggs are laid in the soil, where the larva lives and grows for 3–5 years. Adults emerge for a short period, in May–June.

FOOD

Adults feed on tree leaves. Larvae eat humus in the soil, but mostly plant roots.

IN THE GARDEN

Encouraged by the presence of trees.

FURNITURE BEETLE *Anobium punctatum*

Length 2.5–5 mm
Abundant throughout Britain
and Ireland.

IDENTIFICATION

A small beetle usually located by the neat round exit holes, 1.5–2 mm across, it makes in wood. Narrow cylindrical body, with the thorax tilted so that the head is hidden. Antennae have a club-shaped tip. Larva is a thin, white grub.

HABITS

One of the most common wood-boring beetles. Found outside and indoors in woodwork. Indoors, it is known for its depredations on furniture and building timbers. In a garden, it inhabits dead wood, tree trunks and branches, untreated fences and sheds.

Eggs are laid in crevices in wood. On hatching, larvae eat their way into the wood, forming a widening tunnel as they grow. The emerging adult leaves the typical 'woodworm' hole. Adults fly May–July.

FOOD

Larva obtains nutrition from the dead wood.

IN THE GARDEN

Furniture Beetles are important in the breakdown of dead wood, and in producing holes and tunnels, which other insects use as nests. They are also food for woodpeckers. They, and other wood-boring beetles, can be encouraged in the garden by leaving dead branches on trees, or by making a stack of logs in a suitable dry place.

SCARLET LILY BEETLE *Lilioceris lilii*

Length 6–8 mm
Local, common in southern Britain
and spreading.

IDENTIFICATION

A small to medium-sized beetle. Very striking, with a scarlet body and a black head and legs. Wing cases form a rectangular shape, wider than the thorax and head. The larva appears brown or black and slug-like, but this is an outer covering; larval excreta collects around the body, hiding it in a gelatinous mass that is most unpleasant to handle (it is thought that it mimics a bird dropping).

HABITS

An introduced species, arriving in the UK in the early 1940s, and a member of the large leaf beetle family. Noticeable on the leaves of its food plants from late spring. Also emits a faint squeak. Pairs are often found mating, and if disturbed will drop to the ground. Larvae feed on the undersides of leaves, around the edges. Adults are found April–August and the species overwinters as pupae.

FOOD

The leaves of lilies and other members of the lily family, such as fritillaries.

IN THE GARDEN

An unwelcome garden pest. Best controlled by hand-picking or other methods that do not involve the use of chemical insecticides.

LADYBIRDS

Ladybirds are a family of beetles (Coleoptera). Among the best known of all the insects, they are also popular with gardeners as predators on aphids.

IDENTIFICATION

Ladybirds are known for their red wing cases and black spots, although some are black, yellow and brown with spots of red, black and white. All are rounded with a flat underside. Short antennae have club-shaped ends, and short legs can be hidden under the body. They fly well.

The larvae resemble short caterpillars, but with prominent segments, a tapered abdomen and longer legs. Common larvae are grey with black spots and yellow marks. Pupae are similar in colour at first, then turn black and attach themselves firmly to a stem or leaf.

HABITS

Most ladybirds are predators. They walk and climb to hunt aphids. When startled, they withdraw their legs and either clamp to the surface or drop to the ground. Bright colours warn that they are distasteful, and they exude drops of a staining and bitter-tasting fluid. Adults hibernate from autumn until spring. Eggs are laid near a colony of aphids.

FOOD

Both adults and larvae eat aphids. Adults also eat pollen and nectar if animal food is short.

IN THE GARDEN

Populations of many native ladybirds are declining. Gardens are important for food and hibernation sites such as plant stems and log piles. Chemicals should not be used to control aphids.

SEVEN-SPOT LADYBIRD

Coccinella 7-punctata

Length 5.5–7.5 mm
Widespread in Britain and Ireland.

Large ladybird, common in gardens. Has bright red wing cases, each with three black spots, plus a seventh spot spanning the wing cases. Black thorax with white front corners.

Adults emerge from hibernation in March, lay eggs in May–June, and new adults emerge in August or September.

TWO-SPOT LADYBIRD

Adalia 2-punctata

Length 3.5–5 mm
Widespread in Britain and Ireland.

Small ladybird, typically has bright red wing cases, with two black spots, and white edges to the thorax, but there are many colour varieties. The next most common variety is black with four red spots. Will often hibernate in buildings, around window frames, etc.

NOTE

The Harlequin Ladybird, *Harmonia axyridis*, arrived from Asia in 2004, and has spread through most of England and Wales. It competes with native species for food and also eats other ladybirds. It is large (7–8 mm long), and although variable in colour and pattern, is most often red with up to 21 spots.

LADYBIRD IDENTIFICATION

SEVEN-SPOT LADYBIRD

Large. Bright red with three black spots on each wingcase, and one extra, centrally just behind the thorax.

The Seven-spot's larva has a tapered, grey body with yellow spots and six legs.

TWO-SPOT LADYBIRD

Small. Bright red, with one black spot on each wingcase.

TEN-SPOT LADYBIRD

Very small, round. Red with ten black spots. (sometimes black with red spots).

FOURTEEN-SPOT LADYBIRD

Very small, round. Yellow, with rather square black spots. Sometimes more black than yellow.

HARLEQUIN LADYBIRD

Very large. Many colour varieties. Most common is bright red with a large number of black spots. Other varieties may be black with two red spots, black spots ringed with white, completely red and others.

LINED CLICK BEETLE *Agriotes lineatus*

Length 7.5–10.5 mm
Common and widespread in Britain and Ireland.

IDENTIFICATION

Medium-sized beetle. Neat, with a long body, a head that merges into the thorax, and round-ended wing cases. Thorax projects backwards at the hind corners, and antennae are conspicuously jointed. Brown with a darker head and thorax, and fine parallel stripes on the wing cases. The larva is the so-called 'wireworm', with a thin, yellow, worm-like body, a hard head and three pairs of small legs, adapted to life in the soil.

HABITS

Commonest of several click beetles, found in gardens, grassland and agricultural land. When on its back, the adult gives a sudden jump, accompanied by a sharp click. When disturbed, it drops to the ground to escape. Visits flower heads, especially umbellifers. Adults are most often seen in May–July. The larvae live in the soil, often under lawns.

FOOD

Adults feed on pollen and nectar, and may eat the soft parts of flowers. Larvae eat roots, especially of grasses, but also of other plants.

IN THE GARDEN

Click beetles are an important food for birds that feed on lawns and on the soil, but are not welcomed by all gardeners because of the damage they cause to the roots of plants.

NETTLE WEEVIL *Phyllobius pomaceus*

Length 9 mm
Common throughout most of Britain and Ireland.

IDENTIFICATION

Weevils are small to medium-sized beetles with hard bodies and wing cases, a rather rounded appearance and a long 'snout' (rostrum) with jaws at the tip. The antennae are elbowed at a right angle. This species is bright golden or bluish-green, and it has a shorter snout than many weevils, with the antennae located close to the tip. The larvae are dark and plump.

HABITS

One of several weevils found in gardens. Almost entirely confined to Stinging Nettles, feeding around the edges of the leaves and creating a ragged effect. Adults are often found pairing and only appear May–June, after which they die. The species spends most of the year, including winter, as a larva. It lives and pupates in the soil, and new adults emerge in May.

FOOD

Adult eats the leaves of Stinging Nettle, and the larvae feed on its roots.

IN THE GARDEN

It benefits from a patch of Stinging Nettles, while other weevils require a variety of plants, especially native shrubs and trees.

ROVE BEETLES

The Staphylinidae family is a large group of beetles containing several species that occur in gardens. All have long, thin bodies, with very short wing cases that leave most of the abdomen exposed. As a result, they resemble earwigs, but without that group's pair of pincers. Although the wing cases are short, most species have fully developed wings and can fly.

DEVIL'S COACH-HORSE

Staphylinus olens (Ocypus olens)

Length 25 mm
Found throughout Britain
and Ireland.

IDENTIFICATION

The largest rove beetle. Completely black, including the wing cases, and has fine hairs that create a velvety texture. Has a large, square head with prominent jaws, giving it a rather alarming appearance.

HABITS

Active at night, hunting invertebrates, which are seized and eaten with the large jaws. May also give humans a painful but harmless nip. In daytime, hides under stones, logs, bark, etc. When disturbed, performs a threat display with the abdomen curved upwards, tail held high, and jaws opened wide and snapped together. Accompanies this display by secreting a foul-smelling fluid from its abdomen

FOOD

Feeds on a range of invertebrates, including slugs. The larva also preys on invertebrates.

IN THE GARDEN

An important predator of garden invertebrates. Can be encouraged by providing a good supply of logs and bark as shelter.

Although vaguely scorpion-like, the Devil's Coach-horse is usually harmless to humans.

TACHYPORUS HYPNORUM

Length 4 mm
Common and widespread throughout Britain and Ireland.

IDENTIFICATION

A very small rove beetle. Abdomen is strongly tapered, almost to a point. Wing cases and sides of thorax are orange-brown, contrasting with the black head and abdomen.

HABITS

Found under stones and logs, but also in dead leaves, compost heaps and moss. A predator, hunting small invertebrates. Found any month, but particularly in winter and spring.

FOOD

Catches small invertebrates, including springtails, mites, etc.

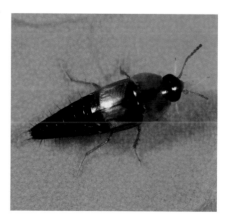

IN THE GARDEN

Encouraged by shelter in the form of logs, stones, etc., and also by compost heaps and ground cover of dead leaves and moss.

Water Beetles

The two main families of water beetles, Dytiscidae and Hydrophilidae, are both represented in garden ponds. Both have aquatic larval stages.

Great Diving Beetle
Dytiscus marginalis

Length 30 mm or more
Widespread but local in Britain and Ireland.

IDENTIFICATION
Very large, with streamlined oval body and head slightly sunk into the thorax. Hind legs are flattened, with a dense row of swimming hairs. Dark brown with a greenish sheen, and yellow border around the thorax and wing cases. Male has smooth, glossy wing cases and a pair of obvious suckers on its front legs. Female's wing cases are furrowed with fine parallel grooves. Larva grows large, is pale brown, has a large head, long curved jaws and a tapering body with two short tails.

HABITS
A strong swimmer. When not swimming, must hold onto something underwater or float to the surface. Its air supply is drawn from the surface and carried under the wing cases. Flies well enough to colonise new ponds.

FOOD
Both the adults and larvae eat many aquatic invertebrates, as well as tadpoles.

IN THE GARDEN
Garden ponds can make an important contribution to the conservation of water beetles. They need a community of freshwater creatures, excluding ornamental fish.

Hydrophilid Water Beetle
Hydrobius fuscipes

Length 8–9 mm
Widespread in Britain and Ireland.

> **NOTE**
> There are many other species of diving beetle, all smaller than the Great Diving Beetle and some very small indeed. All are carnivorous.

IDENTIFICATION
Smaller and not as stream-lined as the Great Diving Beetle, although it has a smooth outline and a flat underside. Glossy black with rusty-coloured legs. Larva is long and maggot-like, widest in the middle. It has three pairs of small legs, and long, curved, toothed jaws.

beneath the wing cases, and as a silver bubble on the underside. It flies when necessary. Eggs laid in a cocoon, which floats on the surface until hatching.

FOOD
Adult feeds on water plants. The larva is a predator of soft-bodied pond invertebrates.

IN THE GARDEN
See Great Diving Beetle.

HABITS
Swims weakly, or climbs on submerged plants. Holds air

Leaf Miners

Small insects from several unrelated groups feed on leaves from the inside and are known as leaf miners. Larvae eat the soft tissue between the upper and lower skin of the leaf and the result is a pattern on the surface. Most leaf miners are specific to a particular plant. In gardens, Holly, oaks, Bramble, roses, lilacs, Honeysuckle and sowthistles may be used. Small birds, especially tits, peck the larvae and pupae out of the leaves.

Holly Leaf Miner

Phytomyza ilicis

Length adult 2.5 mm
Widespread in Britain and Ireland.

IDENTIFICATION

Common on Holly, sometimes affecting a high proportion of leaves. This is a very small fly that resembles a tiny Common House-fly, but its wings have a simpler pattern of veins. Produces an irregular mine: a large blotch with extensions and short galleries around it, pale with brown central areas.

HABITS

The larva is active from early spring. Minute black hooks at the mouth allow it to scrape away and eat the plant cells. When fully grown, it pupates inside the mine, and the hatching adult leaves through an exit hole. Mined evergreen leaves are found year-round, although many will be empty. Adults fly April–July, but mainly in midsummer.

FOOD

Larvae feed exclusively on the soft tissue inside Holly leaves.

IN THE GARDEN

Needs the presence of Holly.

Blackberry Leaf Miner

Stigmella aurella (Nepticula aurella)

Length adult 3–4 mm
Widespread in Britain and Ireland.

IDENTIFICATION

This leaf miner is among the smallest of moths, with narrow wings that fold along its back. Forewings are brown, with a contrasting yellow band towards the tip. Hind wings have feathery margins, although these are seldom visible. The mine, in a Bramble leaf, is a long and usually meandering gallery that starts narrow and becomes wider as the larva grows. Gallery is pale fawn with a dark line down the middle formed from droppings.

HABITS

Has two generations a year. In late spring and summer, adults lay eggs on a leaf. Caterpillars feed on the leaf tissue and, when fully developed, they leave through an exit hole and pupate on the ground. The autumn generation hibernates as larvae within the leaf.

FOOD

The larvae feed exclusively on the soft tissue on the inside of Bramble leaves.

IN THE GARDEN

Needs overgrown Bramble plants as food.

WATER FLEAS *Daphnia* species

Length 2 mm
Abundant in Britain and Ireland.

garden ponds. All are very small, requiring magnification to examine their features. Often used as fish food in the aquarium trade.

The visible body is in a transparent outer shell. On it there are several pairs of branched, feathery limbs, which beat to create a current of water through the shell. This allows the animal to receive oxygen and also filters food particles. The antennae beat downwards and act as swimming organs, so that water fleas appear to jerk up and down in the water.

Numerous eggs are carried in a space at the back of the shell. To survive winter or drying out, this darkens and hardens to retain only two very resistant eggs. Eggs hatch into miniature water fleas.

IDENTIFICATION
Has a tiny oval body with narrow tail spine. Translucent or pink. The head is at the top, and has a single black compound eye in the centre and a pair of long, forked antennae.

HABITS
These are not fleas, or even insects. They are in fact a group of crustaceans, related to shrimps and woodlice, that live in fresh water, including

FOOD
Filters microscopic algae and particles of other detritus from the water.

IN THE GARDEN
Daphnia are a very important part of the pond community, filtering the water for food and in turn becoming prey for many small carnivores. They require a well-balanced pond, preferably without fish.

COPEPODS *Cyclops* species

Length 2–3 mm
Abundant and widespread in Britain and Ireland.

IDENTIFICATION
Very small, green or greyish in colour with two long antennae and a second smaller pair. Have a single simple eye. Body is pear-shaped: wider at the front, and tapered at the abdomen. Females carry an oval egg sac on each side of the abdomen, easily seen with the naked eye. The body ends with a pair of thin tails, each with bristles.

HABITS
Found in still, fresh water, including ponds, usually amongst vegetation or near the bottom. Swim in a series of rapid darting movements. Mouthparts grasp food rather than filtering it from the water. Females carry eggs until they hatch, when they each produce a small triangular larva.

FOOD
Algae, detritus and small invertebrates, especially small Midge larvae.

IN THE GARDEN
By eating small food particles, and in turn becoming prey for small predators, copepods contribute to a healthy pond food web. They will occur naturally in a well-balanced pond.

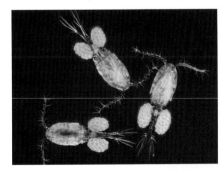

BUTTERFLIES

THE WHITES

It is tempting to dismiss all white butterflies as 'cabbage whites', but close observation reveals several distinct species.

IDENTIFICATION
Mostly white or pale yellow. Males and females have differing black marks.

HABITS
Smaller species generally appear in March, with the Large White flying in April. There are further generations during the year.

FOOD
Caterpillars of Large and Small Whites feed on brassicas, nasturtiums and Wild Mignonette. Green-veineds feed on Garlic and Hedge Mustards, Cuckooflower and Charlock.

IN THE GARDEN
With fewer vegetable gardens, Large and Small Whites are scarcer than they once were. Garlic Mustard can be introduced to the wild areas to attract Green-veined Whites, and nasturtiums added to flower borders. Nectar-rich flowers attract all three species.

LARGE WHITE
Pieris brassicae

Adult wingspan 56–66 mm, caterpillar length up to 40 mm
Widespread in lowland Britain and Ireland, scarce in the far north.

Noticeably larger than the other two species, with black tips to the wings. Female has two black spots on the upper forewings. Undersides in both sexes are often yellowish-green. Caterpillar is green with large black spots, a yellow line along the back, short dark hairs and also gives off an unpleasant smell

SMALL WHITE
Pieris rapae

Adult wingspan 46–54 mm, caterpillar length up to 25 mm
Widespread in the south. Migrants arrive from the continent in spring.

Smaller than Large White, with less or no black on the wingtips. Males have a single small black spot in the centre of the forewings, females have two. Undersides similar but yellowish. Green caterpillar has small black dots and a yellow stripe on its back, and yellow marks along its sides.

GREEN-VEINED WHITE
Pieris napi

Adult wingspan 40–52 mm, caterpillar length up to 25 mm
Widespread in lowland Britain and Ireland, but scarce in the far north.

Slightly smaller than Small White and more variable. Forewings have black tips: one spot on the males and two spots on the females. Underside yellowish-cream with grey-green veins. Caterpillar is pale green flecked with black.

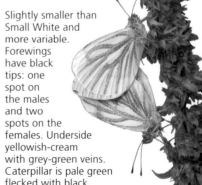

BRIMSTONE *Gonepteryx rhamni*

Adult wingspan 52–60 mm,
caterpillar length up to 33 mm
Common in southern England, Wales
and Ireland, but not in Scotland.

The adult is leaf-shaped for camouflage.

IDENTIFICATION

Large yellow butterfly that has a leaf-shaped profile when resting with its wings closed. Male is bright butter-yellow, while the female is more washed out and greenish. The wing undersides tend to be paler and greener. Both sexes have an orange spot in the centre of each wing.

Egg starts greenish, and gradually turns to yellow and then grey. Caterpillar is green flecked with black, and has a white line along the sides of the body. Above this line it tends to be bluish, while below it is more yellowish-green. The green head is finely spotted with black. Pupa is bluish-green and resembles a curled leaf as it hangs from a plant.

HABITS

The Brimstone is a resident of countryside and open woodland, and is perhaps one of the longest-lived of all adult butterflies. There is just one generation each year. Adults hibernate in winter, usually within an evergreen bush, and may sometimes be seen flying on warm, sunny winter days. They mate in spring, after hibernation, and lay their eggs singly on the undersides of leaves during May.

The caterpillars hatch after about ten days and pupate around a month later. When not feeding, they rest along the central rib of a leaf for maximum camouflage. The pupal stage lasts about ten days, after which the new generation of Brimstone adults flies in late summer; these will then hibernate during the approaching

Caterpillars rely on camouflage for protection from birds who prey on them.

winter and, all being well, may live to see the following spring.

FOOD

The main food plants used by Brimstone caterpillars are Buckthorn and Alder Buckthorn. Adults feed on nectar from a wide variety of plants both in the countryside and in gardens but have a particular fondness for thistles.

IN THE GARDEN

Introducing Buckthorn into a garden hedge or wild area would be beneficial for the caterpillars, and retaining thick evergreens such as Holly or clumps of Ivy will provide possible wintering sites for adults. It is important that autumn pruning takes account of these places and that gardens are not kept over-tidy. A good herbaceous border in summer will attract adult Brimstones, but so too will wild areas containing clovers, Dandelion, scabious and other countryside flowers.

PEACOCK *Anglais io*

*Adult wingspan 54–58 mm,
caterpillar length up to 42 mm
Commonly seen in spring and summer
in Britain and Ireland, except in the far
north of Scotland.*

IDENTIFICATION

Unmistakable butterfly when seen at rest, with large eye-spots on all four of its wings, although the front two look blurred compared to those on the hindwings. Ground colour is a velvety reddish-brown with blackish marks and a grey-brown border to the forewings.

Eye-spot pattern is black, yellow and blue on the forewing, and mainly blue and black on the hindwings. Often rests with its wings closed, showing the dark camouflaged underside. Sexes are similar, although females are slightly larger.

Eggs are green and laid in batches under leaves. Caterpillar is grey-green at first, but soon becomes velvety-black with fine white spots and with black spines on each segment of the body. Its head is shiny and black, and the 'suckers' are tipped yellow. Pupa is green when attached to nettles, but blackish when found elsewhere.

Caterpillars may travel away from their nettles to pupate.

HABITS

There is one generation each year. Adults hibernate in hollow trees, outhouses or crevices, and may be seen on the wing in mild weather from February onwards. They then mate and lay their eggs on the underside of nettle leaves, near the top of the plant. Eggs hatch after about two weeks and at first the small caterpillars live together in a communal web, before leaving and living independently until they pupate about four weeks after hatching. The caterpillar may travel some way from its food plant and climb a plant (often a tree) to pupate, hanging head-down from a leaf or stem. The adult emerges from the pupa after about two weeks. It is this stage that forms the late-summer population and those that survive will hibernate in the autumn.

The false 'eyes' may distract predators, and thus protect the butterfly from attack.

FOOD

The caterpillars feed on Stinging Nettle leaves and occasionally other plants. Adults visit flowering plants such as clovers, Bramble and Teasel, and feed on rotting windfall fruits.

IN THE GARDEN

Allowing adults to hibernate in outbuildings, log piles and other unheated, enclosed spaces will ensure they survive the winter (they can be hard to spot at this time, as the wings are held closed and show no colour except black). Nettles will provide the species with a place to lay its eggs and feed the caterpillars. Planting nectar-rich, cultivated plants such as stonecrops, Lavender and verbenas, and introducing native species such as Teasel and Bramble will attract the species to a garden and provide it with the food it requires.

COMMA   *Polygonia c-album*

Adult wingspan 44–48 mm,
caterpillar length up to 35 mm
Widespread resident of southern
England and Wales; scarce elsewhere.

Colour may vary between
broods – and even individuals
from the same brood.

IDENTIFICATION

Butterfly with a most distinctive and unusual shape. The ragged wing edges are symmetrical, so that at rest, with wings raised over the back, the shape resembles a dead leaf. When open, the wings are bright orange-brown with a scattering of dark marks and a dark outer margin. Underside is dark with a pale comma-like mark, which gives the species its name. Of the two generations a year, those of the summer brood tend to be less bright than autumn broods.

Eggs, laid singly or in small groups, start green but become yellowish towards the time of hatching. Caterpillar is blackish, with orange-brown bands and yellow or white spines. The rear half of the top of its body is off-white with dark marks and is said to resemble a bird dropping to prevent it being eaten! Pupa is brown tinged with pink.

HABITS

There are two generations a year. Adults hibernate in autumn and are often seen flying on warm days in late winter or early spring. Eggs are laid singly or in small groups on the upper side of leaves from May onwards and hatch after two or three weeks. Caterpillars tend to live singly on the underside of leaves and pupate by hanging head-down from their food plant. The adult emerges after another two or three weeks. These fresh butterflies produce another generation, and it is these offspring that will eventually hibernate on a shed wall, a branch in a bush or amongst a bunch of dead leaves.

FOOD

Caterpillars feed on Stinging Nettle, Hop, elms and willows. Adults take nectar from a variety of flowering plants, including burdocks and Bramble.

IN THE GARDEN

Shrubs should not be overpruned in autumn, so that some thick areas are retained in which the Comma may hibernate. Adult butterflies may find their way into sheds and outhouses in autumn and should always be left alone to complete their hibernation. A nettle patch may encourage this species to breed, and nectar-producing plants such as Bramble will provide food for adults in summer.

PAINTED LADY *Vanessa cardui*

*Adult wingspan 54–58 mm,
caterpillar length up to 28 mm
Migrant to Britain and Ireland,
arriving in varying numbers each year.
Scarcer in the north and west.*

IDENTIFICATION

Large orange-brown or sometimes pinkish butterfly with black marks, and with black wingtips that contain white marks. Underside is pale and marbled with a small eye-spot on the lower portion of the hindwing.

Eggs are laid singly and start off green, becoming darker before hatching. Caterpillar is blackish with fine white speckling, black or yellowish spines and a yellow line running along the sides of the body; below this it is reddish-brown. Pupa is greenish-grey and may look metallic.

HABITS

This is a remarkable long-distance migrant, starting its journey in north Africa. It arrives here mainly in May or June and is noticeably more numerous in some years than others. On arrival it may initially be observed moving through the countryside, while later it may patrol an area almost territorially. It is unable to survive our winters.

FOOD

The food plants of the caterpillars are thistles, mallows, burdocks, Viper's Bugloss and nettles. Adults will feed on nectar from burdocks, Bramble and many other summer-flowering plants.

IN THE GARDEN

This butterfly is a frequent visitor to gardens in years when it is plentiful. A wild area containing thistles, mallows and burdocks may provide a breeding area for this attractive but unpredictable visitor from Africa, and a selection of summer-flowering plants, will also attract adults. Stone paving in a sheltered spot facing the sun sometimes provides a suitable area for these insects to 'sunbathe'.

Migrating Painted Ladies may be seen moving through the countryside in some years.

RED ADMIRAL *Vanessa atalanta*

*Adult wingspan 56–62 mm,
caterpillar length 35 mm
Familiar summer migrant to most
parts of Britain and Ireland; increasingly
overwintering here.*

IDENTIFICATION

Striking black butterfly with bands of red on its fore- and hindwings, white spots near the tips of the forewings and some tiny blue spots on the hindwings. Underside is mainly dark but repeats an obscure version of the upperwing pattern. Sexes are alike.

Eggs start green and become darker with age. Caterpillars are variable, although they always have a black head. The most usual form is blackish with a freckling of white spots, black or yellow spines on each segment that have a red ring at the base, and a series of yellow marks down each side forming a wavy line. A paler version has a greenish or yellowish body and pale spines. Pupa is grey with some gold marks.

HABITS

Most Red Admirals arrive here as migrants from southern Europe and north Africa in early summer. These lay eggs singly on the upper sides of leaves, which hatch after a week. The solitary caterpillar lives in a tent of curled leaves and is ready to pupate after a month, often wandering some distance from its food plant to do so. The pupa hangs head-down, sometimes in a leaf tent, and the adult butterfly emerges two or three weeks later.

The Red Admiral was once just a summer migrant to Britain, but can survive our winters and is doing so in increasing numbers. There is also evidence that some move south in Autumn, and individuals seen arriving along the French coast in October are assumed to be migrants from Britain.

FOOD

The main food plant of the caterpillar is Stinging Nettle, as well as other members of the nettle family and the Hop. Adults feed on the nectar of many wild and garden flowers, and are particularly attracted to rotten fruit in autumn.

IN THE GARDEN

A nettle bed can act as a breeding site for this species. Nectar-rich flowers such as stonecrops and Ivy will attract adults, and some windfall apples and other fruit should always be left on the ground as these can be a magnet for Red Admirals.

The Red Admiral is both a resident and an annual migrant to Britain from the Continent.

SMALL TORTOISESHELL *Aglais urticae*

*Adult wingspan 45–50 mm,
caterpillar length up to 22 mm
Widespread in Britain and Ireland,
with some additional migrants
arriving from Europe.*

IDENTIFICATION

Orange-red butterfly with black marks on the wings. Has delicate blue crescents on the narrow blackish border of both the fore- and hindwings. Underwing is blackish. Females are slightly larger than males.

Eggs are laid in clusters and are green at first but soon become yellowish. Caterpillars may be variable, but they generally have a black head and a black body with tiny white spots and two broken bands of yellow along each side. Each segment of the body has a series of black or yellowish spines. Pupa is grey or sometimes pinkish, or may be black when not connected to its food plant.

HABITS

The Small Tortoiseshell is often seen 'sunbathing' in a sheltered spot with wings spread. There are two generations in a year. Adults hibernate for the winter and start flying on warm days in February–April. They mate after hibernation and batches of eggs are laid on the underside of young leaves during April and May. The caterpillars hatch after ten days and at first live together in a communal web.

The caterpillars feed almost exclusively on Stinging Nettles.

Later, they become solitary before pupating. The pupae hang from the leaves and stems of nettles and other local plants, and the adult butterflies emerge after about two weeks. These adults lay their eggs in July, and it is the young from this second generation that will hibernate the following winter. While many do survive the winter, some migrant Small Tortoiseshells from the Continent augment the British population in summer.

FOOD

The main food plant for the caterpillars is Stinging Nettle. The adults take nectar from wild plants such as Bramble, Dandelion and Ivy in autumn, and also from cultivated plants such as Michaelmas Daisy and stonecrops.

IN THE GARDEN

This is one of the few butterflies in our region that hibernates as an adult and mates in the spring. It will enter buildings, including houses and garden sheds, in autumn in its search for suitable hibernation crevices (behind pictures is popular). The hibernating insect's survival depends on it remaining undisturbed until the first warm days of spring. A good nettle bed will help this species to breed, and nectar-rich plants will help to feed the adults.

Small Tortoiseshells commonly 'sunbathe' in open sunny spots in the garden.

THE BROWNS

The 'brown' butterflies are sun-loving species that sometimes visit gardens, especially if there are areas of long grass.

IDENTIFICATION

As the group name suggests, these are predominantly brown, and have small eye-like marks on their wings. Male Gatekeepers and Meadow Browns are smaller than females, and have dark patches on their upperwings that are formed by scales. These scales release a scent to attract females.

HABITS

All three species winter as caterpillars and pupate in spring. Wall has two broods a year, while the others have one. Eggs are laid singly on the blades or stems of grasses. Caterpillars feed at night, and Meadow Brown caterpillars continue to feed on mild winter days.

FOOD

The food of all three species is grasses. Adults are attracted to a variety of flowering plants, with Bramble being especially popular.

IN THE GARDEN

A wild area with rough grass may provide a breeding site, but most visitors to the garden will be adults attracted to flowering plants.

MEADOW BROWN
Maniola jurtina

*Adult wingspan 42–54 mm,
caterpillar up to 25 mm
Common in Britain and Ireland.*

Larger than Gatekeeper, and usually settles with wings closed over its back. Upper side is dusky brown with some orange and a small eye-spot near the front edge. Underwing pattern is more orange, also with an eye-spot. Caterpillar is bright green with a dark line down its back and a broken line along its sides. Its body ends in two points with white tips.

GATEKEEPER
Pyronia tithonus

*Adult wingspan 34–38 mm,
caterpillar length up to 23 mm
Common in summer in southern
England, Wales and Ireland.*

Smaller than the other two species. Likely to settle with wings open, showing a dusky brown border and bright orange-brown centre. One eye-spot near the front of the wing and a similar spot on the underside. Caterpillar is yellowish-brown with brown freckling, a dark line down its back and lines along its sides.

WALL BROWN
Lasiommata megera

*Adult wingspan 36–50 mm,
caterpillar length up to 25 mm
Declining species in England, Wales
and southern Scotland.*

Larger than the Gatekeeper. Also settles with wings open. Orange-brown with dark lines and one eye-spot on the forewing and several on the hindwing. Underwing pattern similar except hindwing is mottled. Caterpillar is green with pale dots and three pale lines along its back; the points on its tail are also pale.

SMALL COPPER *Lycaena phlaeas*

*Adult wingspan 22–27 mm,
caterpillar length up to 15 mm
Found April–October widespread
except in northern Scotland.*

IDENTIFICATION

Small, bright orange-red butterfly with dusky borders to its forewings, and brownish hindwings with a bright orange stripe near the rear border. There are dark spots on the bright areas. Underside is pale grey with black spots and sometimes a suggestion of orange. Second-generation adults are brighter than the first, and hindwings sometimes have a pronounced tail.

Eggs are yellowish-white, turning grey. Small, plump caterpillar has small head that retracts into the body. It is green with a pink-purple line along the centre of its back, and also a pinkish line along each side. Pupa is brown or greenish with black spots and a line down its back.

Although still common, the Small Copper declined during the 20th century.

they are brilliantly camouflaged. Caterpillars from the first hatching are fully grown after a month, while those hatching in autumn delay pupating until the following spring. The pupa is suspended under a leaf.

FOOD

Caterpillar feeds on docks, Common Sorrel, Sheep's Sorrel and Common Knot-grass. Adult is attracted to verbenas, scabious and Ox-eye Daisy.

HABITS

Often settles in patches of warm sunlight with wings spread. It is very active, chasing off rivals.

There are two or three generations in a year. Eggs are laid singly at the base of leaves and the caterpillars feed on the leaf undersides, where

IN THE GARDEN

A butterfly of many habitats, it will sometimes visit gardens, especially in rural areas, and may breed if its food plants are present.

SPECKLED WOOD *Pararge aegeria*

*Adult wingspan 47–50 mm,
caterpillar length up to 27 mm
Widespread in spring and again in
summer in England (except high
ground in the north), Wales, Ireland
and northern Scotland.*

IDENTIFICATION

Blackish-brown with yellowish marks and an eye-spot on the forewing and three more along each hindwing.

Eggs are pale green and become less shiny as they get close to hatching. The bright green caterpillar has fine hairs, a large head and its body tapers off at the rear. Pupa hangs head down and starts green, often turning purple or brown.

Found in woods and shady places but likes to rest with wings spread in sunlight. Males are very territorial and chase rivals in dancing flights.

FOOD

Caterpillar feeds on grasses, especially Couch, Cock's Foot and Annual Meadow Grass. Adults feed on honeydew from aphids and nectar from a variety of plants such as Bramble.

HABITS

This species is becoming more common and appears to be expanding its range in the British Isles. Adults have two or three generations and may be seen between March and October.

IN THE GARDEN

A wild area with uncut grass may provide a suitable breeding and feeding area for caterpillars, and aphids may provide food for adults.

HOLLY BLUE   *Celastrina argiolus*

Adult wingspan 23–30 mm, caterpillar length up to 13 mm Widespread in spring and again in summer in England, Wales and Ireland; absent from Scotland.

IDENTIFICATION

Pale lilac-blue butterfly with dusky edges and a narrow, whitish margin to the forewings. Underside is pale silvery-blue with black spots. Female is more heavily marked than the male, and the later generation of the year tends also to have stronger marks.

Eggs are whitish and are laid singly. Caterpillar is rather stout and woodlouse-shaped. It is a velvety, yellow-green with a pale line along its side and two small humps on its back, which sometimes appear pinkish. The black head may be withdrawn into the body. Pupa is dark brown, blotched, with a dark mark down the back.

HABITS

There are two broods a year. It overwinters as a pupa and emerges in April or May, when it may be seen in open woods, hedgerows and gardens. Eggs are laid on the underside of the

flower buds of Holly, and caterpillars hatch after a week. They are well camouflaged as they feed on the buds, flowers and newly growing berries. The pupa is attached to the leaves and a new generation of adults is on the wing three weeks later in July and August. This generation often selects Ivy for its eggs, and it is the pupae from this second hatching that overwinter. Numbers may vary considerably from year to year, probably as a reflection of winter weather and parasitic wasp populations.

FOOD

The food plants of the caterpillar are mainly Holly and Ivy, but also include some other shrubs such as Dogwood, snowberries and gorses. The adults are attracted to flowering plants, including Garlic Mustard in spring and Bramble in summer.

IN THE GARDEN

This butterfly is appearing more commonly in gardens. It lives up to its name, and Holly bushes, especially tall ones with lots of new growth, will encourage it to breed. Ivy is used by the later generation and to be most beneficial it needs to grow tall so that it flowers prolifically, providing food for the caterpillars. Adults require nectar from flowering plants in spring, and Bramble will attract the second flight later in the year. A pond with a muddy edge may also attract this butterfly down to drink.

COMMON BLUE *Polyommatus icarus*

Adult wingspan 25–30 mm,
caterpillar length up to 13 mm
Common except for the highest hills
and northern islands.

IDENTIFICATION

Small butterfly. Male is bright violet-blue, bordered by a fine black line and a white margin. Underside is visible at rest, and is

silvery-grey (browner females) with white-ringed black spots and some orange crescents near the wing edges (Holly Blue has no orange crescents). Female is dusky brown, sometimes with a blue flush near the body, and has orange crescents around the edges of the wings.

Dumpy caterpillar is pointed at the head and tail. It is green with a dark green line down the centre of its body and pale whitish-green lines along its sides. Pupa is also green.

HABITS

Produces two generations a year, and sometimes a third in the south. Caterpillars of the second or third generation overwinter, and pupate in spring. Several adults will sometimes gather to drink in damp places.

FOOD

Caterpillars feed on bird's-foot trefoils and clovers. Adults visit various flowering plants.

IN THE GARDEN

A butterfly of downs and meadows, but sometimes visits gardens and occasionally breeds there if its food plants are present.

SMALL SKIPPER *Thymelicus sylvestris*

Adult wingspan 24–27 mm,
caterpillar length up to 21 mm
Common in England and Wales.

IDENTIFICATION

Small golden-brown, moth-like butterfly. At rest, it adopts a typical 'skipper position' with wings half-closed and forewing over hindwing. Wings are generally plain with a dusky border, but males have a narrow, black scent-brand along the centre of each forewing. Green caterpillar is stout, tapering towards each end. It has a dark green line along its back and a pale stripe along the sides of its body. The green head is large and round.

HABITS

Territorial and chases intruders. Fast-flying but is often seen sunning itself with wings half-open. One generation a year. Eggs are laid in July and the caterpillar lives in a sheath of grass leaves, which it spins together. It remains inside during the winter, pupates in June and emerges as a butterfly in July.

FOOD

The caterpillars feed mostly on grasses, especially Yorkshire Fog, but also Timothy and Creeping Soft Grass. Adults are attracted to thistles and clover flowers.

IN THE GARDEN

Visits country gardens and sometimes those in suburbs where there are suitable flowers.

Moths

Micro Moths

A large group of more than 2,000 species. Pages 160–3 provide details of some of the more identifiable micro moths that may visit homes or gardens.

Case-bearing Clothes Moth
Tinea pellionella

Adult wingspan 10–20 mm
Found across Britain and Ireland.

Identification
Small, plain brown moth with darker hindwings and rather long antennae. Its pale-coloured larva lives its short life inside a tubular case of spun silk and collected fibres. It carries the case around and retreats inside if threatened. It also pupates in the case.

Habits
Outdoors, adults fly June–October; indoors, they may be seen any time. They may be attracted by bright lights, but more often they live in dark places and retreat into dark corners if disturbed. Larvae live in birds' nests and indoors in clothes' cupboards.

Food
Adults do not feed, but larvae eat clothes and carpets and damage items made mainly from natural fibres. Reputedly, they are more likely to feed on fabric soiled with sweat or food stains. Outside, the species' natural food is detritus found in birds' nests.

In the garden
Case-bearing and Common Clothes Moths are two of the few creatures to feed on keratin (the substance that makes hair, wool, feathers and other structures that grow from the skin), and have an important role in recycling natural waste products, especially feathers and fur. In the home, both are regarded as pests, although eradication should use the least damaging chemical solutions.

Common Clothes Moth
Tineola bisselliella

Adult wingspan 10–20 mm
Common in Britain and Ireland.

Identification
Small, plain, pale brown moth with a slight sheen on the wings and pale hindwings. Antennae are rather long. Larva is whitish with a brown head, and it builds a shelter of fibres that is not portable.

Characteristics
Larva lives in dark and often slightly damp places. Adults flee into dark corners if disturbed.

Food
The adults do not feed, but their larvae cause considerable damage to fabrics in the home. However, the species has become less of a pest than it was in the past, as clothes are cleaned more frequently and are more often made of synthetic materials, and the home atmosphere is drier owing to central heating.

In the garden
See Case-bearing Clothes Moth.

Green Longhorn
Adela reaumurella

Adult wingspan 14–18 mm
Widespread in England, Wales and
southern Scotland.

IDENTIFICATION
Has metallic bronze-green forewings close along the body, purple-brown hindwings, a black furry head and extremely long forward-facing white antennae. Female has shorter antennae and fewer hairs on its head.

HABITS
Males often swarm in spring sunshine, sometimes dancing like midges, while females remain in undergrowth. Eggs laid April–June. It remains a caterpillar for the summer and winter, pupates the following spring and adults emerge April–June.

FOOD
Larvae live in portable cases made from dead leaves, in leaf litter under oak and birch trees.

IN THE GARDEN
Leave fallen leaves so that this and other invertebrates can shelter there in winter.

Leaf-Roller Tortrix
Croesia bergmanniana

Adult wingspan 10–15 mm,
caterpillar length up to 10 mm
Flies in summer in Britain and Ireland.

IDENTIFICATION
Small, bright yellow-orange with brownish marks and small pale patches. At rest, the wings lie flat and the general shape tends to be triangular. Caterpillar is yellow-green with a large black or dark brown head.

HABITS
A frequent visitor to rural gardens. Adult lays eggs on plant stems June–July, and these hatch in the following spring. The caterpillar lives and pupates in the rolled edges of a rose leaf, and adults are flying again in June.

FOOD
Eats rose leaves.

IN THE GARDEN
Leaving domestic varieties of roses unsprayed and reintroducing native Dog Roses to a small garden will attract this species and help to increase biodiversity generally.

Epiblema cynosbatella

Adult wingspan 15–20 mm
Common in hedgerows and gardens.

IDENTIFICATION
Small, distinctive moth. Forewing is grey with darker and lighter markings, and hindwing is white with some blotching. At rest, the wings almost encase the body.

HABITS
At rest, with wings folded along the body, the pattern breaks up its shape and it also has added protection owing to its remarkable resemblance to a bird dropping. Adults fly May–June.

FOOD
Caterpillars feed on rose buds and shoots.

IN THE GARDEN
Wild areas, especially if planted with Dog Roses, will help attract this and other species.

Micro Moths

Garden Grass-veneer
Chrysoteuchia culmella

Adult wingspan 24 mm
Found in Britain and Ireland.

Identification
Small, whitish moth with dark streaks on its narrow, pale forewings, slightly orange tips and a pale angled line near the end. Wings slightly shorter than other grass moths.

Habits
Rests head-down with wings wrapped around its body, giving a long, thin appearance. One of several grass moths that visit gardens. It is attracted to light and is easily disturbed from long grass. Sometimes occurs in large numbers,

which may be migrants from mainland Europe. It flies May–September and there is one generation a year.

Food
The larvae feed low down on grass stems.

In the garden
An area of long grass left uncut during the summer will help this and other species.

Mint Moth
Pyrausta aurata

Adult wingspan 18–20 mm, caterpillar length up to 13 mm
Locally common in Britain and Ireland, except northern Scotland.

Identification
Small, colourful moth with purple forewings and golden spots. Dark hindwing has a yellow bar that is not always visible. Caterpillar's shape tapers towards head and tail. It is green or brown with a dark stripe along its back and black spots on each body segment.

Habits
Flies during both day and night. Produces two generations a year, the first in May–June and the second in July–September. Caterpillars of the second generation winter in a spun cocoon.

Food
Caterpillar feeds on mints and Marjoram.

In the garden
Mint, especially Catmint, may attract this pretty species to the garden.

Small Magpie
Eurrhypara hortulata

Adult wingspan 24–28 mm
Common in southern Britain and Ireland.

Identification
White wings are heavily spotted with blackish marks. Forewings are bordered with black, and the body is yellow and black.

Habits
Active at dusk. One generation a year. Caterpillars feed inside a rolled-up leaf or two leaves spun together. They hibernate in a cocoon in the leaf and the pupa forms there in spring. Adults fly June–September.

Food
Caterpillar eats nettle, mint and bindweed.

In the garden
Nettles and mints help this and other species.

MOTHER OF PEARL
Pleuroptya ruralis

Adult wingspan 26–40 mm,
caterpillar length up to 25 mm
Widespread in Britain and Ireland.

IDENTIFICATION

Delicately marked moth that settles with its wings spread, showing most of its hindwing. Appears almost translucent, with 'washed-out' markings and, in certain lights, a slight iridescence, especially on fresh specimens, hence its common name. Caterpillar is largely hairless, green with some darker spotting along the back.

HABITS

Flight is rather slow and 'ghost-like'. Although it belongs to the group known as micro moths, this species is larger than many so-called macro moths. It flies at night and frequently comes to lighted windows.

One generation a year. Caterpillar feeds inside a rolled-up leaf from September to the next summer, although it hibernates in winter in a cocoon on the ground.

FOOD

Caterpillar feeds mainly on nettles, but also on goosefoots, oraches and Meadowsweet.

IN THE GARDEN

This attractive and harmless moth benefits from a wild area containing nettles.

WHITE PLUME MOTH
Pterophorus pentadactyla

Adult wingspan 26–34 mm
Relatively common over much of Britain
and Ireland.

IDENTIFICATION

One of the largest of the plume moths, a group that belongs to the micro moths. Has a long, thin, white body and long feather-shaped wings. At rest, the wings close over one another and the insect appears T-shaped. The legs are long and white. Caterpillar is pale green with tufts of hairs and yellow spots on each segment, and has a thin, dark green line down its back.

CHARACTERISTICS

Found along hedgerows, on wasteland and, frequently, in gardens, where it is attracted to lighted windows. The adult flies June–July, and the species some-times produces a second generation in late summer. It overwinters as a caterpillar inside a rolled-up leaf.

FOOD

Caterpillar's food plant is Hedge Bindweed.

IN THE GARDEN

Bindweed is not popular with gardeners, but this attractive moth is a welcome addition to the garden fauna.

MACRO MOTHS

Pages 164–180 cover species known as Macro Moths. They are generally larger than the Micro Moths and easier to identify. Some are very colourful and, while most are night-flying, a few species can be seen during the day.

BUFF ARCHES

Flies June–Aug.

Found in gardens close to woodlands and grasslands. Larvae feed on Bramble and Dewberry. Rare in Scotland.

SNOUT

Two generations in the south fly: June–Aug and Aug–Oct.

Gardens near rivers, woods and overgrown areas. Abundant in mainland Britain. Larvae feed on Stinging Nettle.

BLOOD VEIN

Two generations fly:
May–July and July–Sept.

Found in gardens, often near damp and overgrown areas and hedgerows. Scarce in Scotland but spreading north. Larvae feed on docks, Common Sorrel and Knotgrass.

GARDEN TIGER

Flies July–Aug.

A declining species. Gardens near fairly open areas including rivers and woods. The furry 'wooly bear' caterpillars feed on nettles, docks and Burdock.

Early Thorn

Flies Feb–May and July–Sept.

Widespread in Britain and Ireland. Comes to gardens from woods, hedges and scrub. Larvae feed on Blackthorn, hawthorn and many other plants.

Lunar Underwing

Flies late Aug–Oct.

Often abundant in most of the British Isles but decreases in northern Scotland. Larvae feed on Annual Meadow Grass and other grasses.

Spectacle

Flies mainly May–July.

There may be a second generation in July–September. Common throughout most of mainland Britain. Larva eats Stinging Nettle.

Macro Moths

Common Swift *Hepialus lupulinus*

Adult wingspan 25–35 mm,
caterpillar length up to 38 mm
Common in most of Britain, scarcer in
northern Scotland, local in Ireland.

Identification

Very variable species that holds its wings tent-
like along its body when at rest. Male is usually
dark brown with distinctive marks that may
be white and obvious, or darker and blending
in with the rest of the wing. Female has paler
marks or often plain grey wings. Caterpillar
is waxy yellowish- or greenish-white with a
brown head and small brown spots.

Habits

Produces one generation a year, the adults
flying May–July. Found on grassland, verges and
disturbed land, and often in gardens. Comes
to lighted windows. The eggs are dropped at
random by the female in flight, and the species
overwinters as a caterpillar.

Food

Caterpillar lives underground, eating the roots of
various grasses and other plants. It is considered
a pest in agricultural areas.

In the garden

A possible inhabitant of a garden's wild area,
but more often seen as an adult at dusk.

Currant Clearwing *Synanthedon tipuliformis*

Adult wingspan 20 mm,
caterpillar length up to 18 mm
Widespread but decreasing in England,
local in Wales, Scotland and Ireland.

Identification

One of the clearwing family of moths, which
resemble flies, and have transparent wings with
bronze marks and dark veins that radiate out
from the body. This species has a black body
with a fine yellow collar, yellow lines on the
thorax, and three (female) or four (male) yellow
bands on the abdomen.

Habits

Day-flying species with one generation a year.
Adults fly June–July. Maggot-like caterpillar
lives inside the stem of its food plant, where
it overwinters. Adults settle on leaves in sunny
locations, and many males may be attracted to
the scent of a single female.

Food

The caterpillar eats Red Currant and Black
Currant. Adults also visit Ground Elder.

In the garden

This is a declining species, probably owing to
the fact that fewer currant bushes are now
grown in gardens. The introduction of these
plants may help its return, especially in southern
Britain. Larva is hard to spot inside a plant stem,
but brown dust may issue from holes in the
stem and the adult leaves an exit hole when it
breaks out from the pupa.

CHINESE CHARACTER *Cilix glaucata*

Adult wingspan 18–22 mm, caterpillar length up to 12 mm Widespread in Britain and Ireland except high ground and the far north of Scotland.

IDENTIFICATION

At rest, it holds its wings steeply over its back and the grey and white pattern merges so that the whole adult insect resembles a bird dropping. Caterpillar is reddish-brown and its body tapers at both ends, the tail terminating in a small spike. It has a dark brown line along its back, dark speckling and a wart-like swelling on its body.

HABITS

If disturbed, it is more likely to fall to the ground than fly, relying on its similarity to a bird dropping as a defence against being eaten. Two generations a year: First flies April–June and second in July–September. Overwinters as a pupa attached to leaves or bark.

FOOD

The caterpillars feed on a variety of shrubs and trees, including Hawthorn, Blackthorn, Pear, Rowan and Bramble.

IN THE GARDEN

May be found during the summer on the top of a leaf as it mimics a dropping. It sometimes comes to a lighted window. A garden hedge of native plants may attract this moth.

GARDEN CARPET *Xanthorhoe fluctuata*

Adult wingspan 18–25 mm, caterpillar length up to 25 mm Widespread in Britain and Ireland.

IDENTIFICATION

Pale grey or white moth that rests with wings spread. Has distinctive dark patches of grey or dark brown on the forewing, these often separate or sometimes extend across the two forewings to form a dark band. Caterpillar varies from brown to grey to green; it is darker along the back, with darker blotches that are sometimes tinged pink.

HABITS

Produces one generation a year in the north and up to three in the south, so adults may be seen flying at dusk May–October. Caterpillars feed at night. It winters as a pupa.

FOOD

Caterpillars feed mainly on plants belonging to the cabbage family, including Garlic Mustard, Horseradish and Shepherd's Purse, as well as cultivated plants such as nasturtiums.

IN THE GARDEN

Often attracted to lighted windows and can sometimes be found on walls during the day. It may be helped by developing a vegetable garden or wild area.

YELLOW SHELL *Camptogramma bilineata*

*Adult wingspan 20–25 mm,
caterpillar length up to 25 mm
Widespread in Britain and Ireland
except uplands and northern islands.*

IDENTIFICATION
Pretty yellow or yellowish-brown
moth, with fine, pale, wavy lines
running across the wings, and
with a different shade of yellow
between the lines. The small
caterpillar is green, brown or
grey, with one dark and two pale
lines along its back and a pale
line along its sides. Varies in both
colour and size across Britain.

HABITS
There is one generation each year and the
adults fly June–August. Caterpillar feeds by
night and hides by day, sometimes under
a stone, curling into the shape of a question
mark. It overwinters as a caterpillar and pupates
in the spring below the surface of the soil.

FOOD
Caterpillar feeds on low-growing plants such as
Dandelion, chickweeds and grasses.

IN THE GARDEN
Adults visit garden flowers at night but are not
common at lighted windows. A wild area and
herbaceous border will attract this species.

BRIMSTONE MOTH *Opisthograptis luteolata*

*Adult wingspan 32–37 mm,
caterpillar length up to 33 mm
Widely distributed throughout
Britain and Ireland.*

IDENTIFICATION
Butter-yellow moth with several reddish-
brown blotches on each wing. Caterpillar is
remarkably twig-like: it is greyish- or reddish-
brown with a double-pointed hump halfway
along its body.

HABITS
Produces two or three overlapping generations
a year, so adult moths are in flight any time
between April and October. It overwinters
either as a caterpillar or as a pupa in a cocoon
on the food plant, on the ground or in a
crevice. Caterpillars are one of a group known
as 'stick caterpillars' because
of their excellent camouflage,
and their colour may change
depending on their food plant.

FOOD
Eats the leaves of a variety
of shrubs and trees, including
Hawthorn, Blackthorn and Plum.

IN THE GARDEN
Adults may visit gardens and
are attracted to lighted widows
at night. Planting native trees
and shrubs will assist this and
other species.

WINTER MOTH *Operophtera brumata*

*Adult male wingspan 22–28 mm
Common and widespread in Britain
and Ireland.*

IDENTIFICATION
Small, drab moth, the male of which flies weakly after dark. There is some variation among males, but most have indistinct dark lines crossing grey-brown wings and an obscure central band. Hindwing is brown. Female is smaller and flightless, with a small, plump, dark body and rudimentary wings. Caterpillar

is known as a 'looper', owing to the way it moves. It is green with a darker stripe on its back and pale marks along its sides.

HABITS
Males may be seen in car headlights from October–January (there are also Autumn Moths, which are more distinctly marked). Females attract males with a strong scent. Eggs are laid in winter and caterpillars are active in spring. Caterpillars join leaves with silk to form a shelter; sometimes they become numerous and defoliate trees or shrubs.

FOOD
The caterpillars feed on the fresh leaves of many species of tree, including fruit trees.

IN THE GARDEN
Fruit growers use sticky bands around trees to catch females as they climb a tree before mating. However, the caterpillars are important food for many small birds, especially tits, which synchronise their broods to coincide with the maximum numbers of loopers.

WILLOW BEAUTY *Peribatodes rhomboidaria*

*Adult wingspan 30–38 mm,
caterpillar length up to 40 mm
Widespread in England, Wales, Ireland
and lowland Scotland.*

IDENTIFICATION
Medium-sized grey or brown moth that rests with its wings fully spread. Its pattern is delicate, with a darker ragged line running across the wings and another fine diagonal line merging with it. There are also almost black forms. The stick-like caterpillar is long and thin, and occurs in various shades of brown; sometimes it has dark, diamond-shaped marks along its back.

HABITS
Adults of first generation fly June–August. A second generation sometimes flies August–October in southern England. Nocturnal, but may be found resting during the day. An almost black form was once common in industrial areas, where it blended with the sooty environment.

It overwinters as a caterpillar and pupates the following summer.

FOOD
Caterpillars feed on trees and shrubs, including Hawthorn, Silver Birch, Ivy and Wild Privet. Adults take nectar at night from plants such as Creeping Thistle and Ragwort.

IN THE GARDEN
A thick mixed hedge and some native trees will increase the chances of it breeding.

SWALLOW-TAILED MOTH   *Ourapteryx sambucaria*

*Adult wingspan 40–50 mm,
caterpillar length up to 50 mm
Common in much of England, Wales
and southern Scotland.*

IDENTIFICATION

Delicate and beautiful moth that is lemon-yellow with fine brown lines running across its wings. Hindwings end in a small point with two dark spots. Older specimens tend to be paler and some are almost white. The reddish- or yellowish-brown caterpillar is a master of camouflage: resembling a twig, it rests holding onto a branch at its rear end and with the body projecting at an angle.

HABITS

Usually one generation a year. Adults fly June–August, but if a second generation is produced these fly in October. Nocturnal, but flies in daylight if disturbed. Woods and hedgerows are its usual habitat, although it also visits gardens. Overwinters as a caterpillar, which hides in a crevice in bark.

FOOD

The caterpillar feeds on the leaves of Hawthorn, Blackthorn, Wild Privet and Ivy.

IN THE GARDEN

Adults are sometimes attracted to lighted windows. Many of the species' food plants may be present in a wildlife garden.

PEPPERED MOTH   *Biston betularia*

*Adult wingspan 35–60 mm,
caterpillar length up to 60 mm
Widespread in Britain and Ireland.*

IDENTIFICATION

The most common form in rural areas is white with black lines and marks, but in some places, especially towns and cities, there is a black form with white spots where the wings join the body. There is also an intermediate form that is almost equally patterned grey and black. The caterpillar can look remarkably like a twig, is purplish- or greenish-brown with the suggestion of a purple line down its back and a pair of prominent swellings towards the rear of its body.

HABITS

A much studied species owing to the rapid expansion of the black form in industrial areas in the late 19th and early 20th centuries, where it was, presumably, better camouflaged in sooty locations. There is one generation. Adults fly at night in May–August and the pupa winters just below ground.

FOOD

Caterpillars feed on trees and shrubs, including Hawthorn, Blackthorn, Silver Birch and Bramble.

IN THE GARDEN

It may be attracted to lighted windows. The introduction of native shrubs to a garden will benefit this and other species.

HAWKMOTHS

Our largest moths. Strictly nocturnal, but can sometimes be found resting on walls or tree-trunks during the day.

POPLAR HAWKMOTH
Laothoe populi

Adult wingspan 70–100 mm, caterpillar length up to 65 mm Widespread and relatively common throughout Britain and Ireland.

Large grey and brown moth with bright chestnut markings on its hind wings. At rest, the hind wings often bulge in front of the front wings. Caterpillar is plump, green flecked with white, and has seven greenish-white diagonal lines on each side, and sometimes also red spots. It has a 'horn' on its rear end.

Adults fly mainly May–August and do not feed. Caterpillar feeds on Poplars and also sallows and willows. Winters underground as a pupa. Will come to gardens close to its food plants and is often attracted by light.

PRIVET HAWKMOTH
Sphinx ligustri

Adult wingspan 90–120 mm, caterpillar length up to 100 mm Widespread in the south and east, scarce in north and west.

Our largest resident hawkmoth. Camouflaged grey-brown wings with pink and black striped body and pink and black striped hindwings that are hidden when resting. Caterpillar is usually bright green with seven white and purple diagonal stripes along its sides and a curved 'horn' at its rear.

Overwinters as a pupa underground. Flies June and July. A woodland moth that will visit gardens. Larvae feed on Privet, Ash, guelders, Lilac and some other shrubs. It leaves distinctive cylindrical droppings under its food plants.

ELEPHANT HAWKMOTH
Deilephila elpenor

Adult wingspan 58–70 mm, caterpillar length up to 80 mm. Widespread in England and Wales, scarcer in Scotland and local in Ireland.

Beautiful moth with pink and olive-green marks on its forewing, a pink hindwing and pink lines on its chunky body. Caterpillar starts green and often turns brown. It has large eye-spots on the fourth and fifth body segment and a curved 'horn' at the rear.

The caterpillar's eye-spots can swell up when alarmed to frighten predators. Adults fly May–August.
Caterpillar feeds on willowherbs and, sometimes, garden fuchsias. Adults may be attracted by Honeysuckle.

HUMMINGBIRD HAWKMOTH

Macroglossum stellatarum

*Adult wingspan 40–50 mm,
caterpillar length up to 45 mm
Mainly a summer migrant; seen
throughout Britain and Ireland.*

IDENTIFICATION

Usually seen hovering. Has grey-brown forewings with darker wavy marks, and orange hindwings. Body is brown and there are obvious white spots on the sides of the black

tail. Caterpillar is green with a yellow-tipped 'horn' on its tail, white speckles and two white stripes along its back and a yellow stripe along each side.

HABITS

Resembles a hummingbird as it hovers and feeds from flowers with its long, curved proboscis. Active in daylight, especially in sunny spots, and also after dark. Arrives in variable numbers in summer from Europe and north Africa. Sometimes overwinters in the south and may fly on warm winter days.

FOOD

Caterpillar feeds on Lady's and Hedge Bedstraw, and Wild Madder. Adults feed on nectar.

IN THE GARDEN

A delightful and unpredictable addition to the garden that can be encouraged by nectar-producing herbaceous border plants such as Red Valerian.

SILVER Y

Autographa gamma

*Adult wingspan 35–43 mm,
caterpillar length up to 25 mm
Migrant to Britain and Ireland,
especially in the south and east.*

IDENTIFICATION

Marbled grey-brown forewings have a conspicuous pale inverted 'Y' mark. Hindwings are paler. Rests with wings alongside its body, when two prominent tufts of hairs on its back are most visible. Caterpillar is bluish- or yellowish-green, with a dark green line on its back and a white line along the sides of its body. There are often black marks on the 'cheeks' of its green head.

HABITS

In some years, large numbers of Silver Ys invade from the Continent, mainly in early summer. They breed then move south, and do not overwinter. The moth may be seen hovering in front of flowers day or night, but especially at dusk. The caterpillar, which 'loops' as it walks, is sometimes very numerous.

FOOD

Caterpillars feed on a variety of low-growing plants, including nettles, clovers and bedstraws, as well as cultivated plants such as Pea, Cabbage and Runner Bean.

IN THE GARDEN

Plants rich in nectar, such as valerians, will attract these moths to a garden at dusk.

Buff-tip   *Phalera bucephala*

*Adult wingspan 50–65 mm,
caterpillar length up to 60 mm
Widespread in England, Wales and
southern Ireland; local in Northern
Ireland and Scotland.*

Identification

At rest, the wings are held along the body, giving it a remarkable similarity to a small twig or cigarette end. Its colour is that of Silver Birch, with a prominent buff or creamy-white patch at the wingtips. The caterpillar is yellow-orange with broken black lines running along the back and sides, and orange-brown rings across the body at each segment. It has a fine covering of white hairs.

Habits

Beautifully camouflaged at rest – especially on a Silver Birch. One generation a year. Adults fly May–July, sometimes coming to lighted windows. Overwinters as a pupa in the soil. Caterpillars tend to stay together and can strip all the leaves from a branch or small tree. In some years they are particularly numerous and defoliate many trees in a locality.

Food

Adults do not feed. Caterpillar feeds on leaves of various small trees and shrubs, especially those of Sallow and birches, but also others such as flowering cherries.

In the garden

Adults will be attracted to light. Breeding depends on the presence of suitable shrubs or trees, and gardeners being tolerant.

Figure of Eight   *Diloba caeruleocephala*

*Adult wingspan 40 mm,
caterpillar length up to 40 mm
Common in England and southern
Scotland; scarce elsewhere.*

Habits

Adults fly September–November and often come to lighted windows. Eggs are laid in autumn and hatch the following spring. Pupa forms in June–July in a cocoon on or below the surface of the soil or in leaf litter.

Food

Caterpillars feed on leaves on a variety of trees, including Hawthorn, Blackthorn, Dog Rose, and fruit trees such as Plum and Pear.

In the garden

A mixed hedge or a shrubbery of native plants may attract this moth and leaves should be left to decompose naturally. It is, however, at home on garden fruit trees, so gardeners should resist the temptation to spray these with insecticides.

Identification

Rests with wings folded along its body. Forewing is brown and grey with two grey-centred white marks that are joined at one point, the lower one of which resembles the figure 8. Caterpillar is blue-grey with broken yellow lines down its back and sides, and a series of raised black spots.

WHITE ERMINE *Spilosoma lubricipeda*

*Adult wingspan 30–42 mm,
caterpillar length up to 40 mm
Common in most of Britain and
Ireland, except northern Scotland.*

IDENTIFICATION

Snowy white with large furry head, fine
black spotting on the wings and one slightly
larger black spot. The number and size of the
spots vary, and some individuals, especially in
the north, are cream-coloured or buff. At rest,
the wings lie along the body, but in flight the
yellow body with black spots may be seen.
Caterpillar is grey with a red stripe along its
back and covered with black hairs.

HABITS

Nocturnal. Flies mainly May–July and overwinters as a pupa in a cocoon of silk among
leaf litter and other plant debris. Produces one
generation a year, although occasionally a
second brood of adults fly in autumn.

FOOD

Feeds on a variety of low-growing herbaceous
plants, including docks.

IN THE GARDEN

A well-vegetated garden may attract this
lovely moth, and even if it does not breed it
may come to lighted windows after dark.
The caterpillar's hairs help protect it from
insectivorous birds.

CINNABAR *Tyria jacobaeae*

*Adult wingspan 32–42 mm,
caterpillar length up to 30 mm
Widespread in England and Wales,
scarce in the north.*

IDENTIFICATION

Scarlet (or deep pink) and velvety black.
Forewings are broad with a red line and two red
spots, hindwings are red and black. Caterpillar
has yellow and black hoops along its body.

HABITS

Nocturnal. May be attracted to light. It
also flies weakly in daylight, usually having
been disturbed. Bright colours of adult and
caterpillar indicate they are distasteful and
a warning to predators. Only Cuckoos have
overcome the problem and eat the caterpillars.
Adults emerge May–August. The species
overwinters as a pupa.

FOOD

Caterpillars feed mainly on Common Ragwort
and sometimes Common Groundsel, and are
relatively obvious on these plants. They eat
flowers and leaves, often leaving only a slender
stem before moving to another plant.

IN THE GARDEN

Windblown seed of Common Ragwort and
Groundsel will sometimes find its way into
gardens. Otherwise, the adult is an occasional
visitor to gardens.

COMMON FOOTMAN *Eilema lurideola*

*Adult wingspan 28–35 mm,
caterpillar length up to 22 mm
Widespread, mostly in England
and Wales.*

IDENTIFICATION

Rests with wings folded flat over the back, giving it a long, thin appearance. Wings are greenish-grey with a yellow stripe along each side that does not quite extend to the wingtip. Underwing is straw-coloured, often with a dusky border. Black caterpillar is grey underneath, has a red stripe along each side, and is covered in black and grey hairs.

HABITS

One of a group of similar-looking moths. One generation a year, with adults flying mainly July–August. Caterpillars hatch in autumn, hibernate in winter and continue developing in spring. Adults come to lighted windows.

FOOD

Caterpillar feeds on lichens and algae growing on trees and fences, as well as on plants such as Hawthorn and Bramble.

IN THE GARDEN

A 'soft' boundary of native hedging plants and mature trees may provide a home for this common but often overlooked moth.

SETACEOUS HEBREW CHARACTER *Xestia c-nigrum*

*Adult wingspan 35–42 mm,
caterpillar length up to 37 mm
Common in lowland Britain and Ireland.
Migration from Continent is suspected.*

FOOD

Caterpillars feed on docks, Common Chickweed and Common Groundsel, as well as other herbaceous plants, especially nettles.

IN THE GARDEN

Nocturnal visitor to gardens; may stay if enough herbaceous plants are present.

IDENTIFICATION

Pale, straw-coloured, triangular mark on the centre of the leading edge of each wing contrasts with an adjoining blackish block, said to resemble a letter of the Hebrew alphabet. Ground colour varies from light to dark grey-brown or sometimes reddish. Caterpillar is grey-brown or green with a double row of black dashes along its back, becoming larger towards the tail. There is also a yellow line along each side of its body.

HABITS

Two generations a year in the south. Suspected immigrants from the Continent may swell the numbers in summer. Nocturnal. Adults fly May–July and August–October, and come to lighted windows. Scatters eggs near food plants. Caterpillars hibernate in winter and pupate in spring.

GARDEN DART *Euxoa nigricans*

Adult wingspan 28–35 mm,
caterpillar length up to 40 mm
Common throughout England, Wales,
Ireland and lowland Scotland.

IDENTIFICATION

Drab moth with pale straw underwings. Most have sooty-brown forewings, but in some individuals they are lighter or reddish-brown. Close inspection shows a delicate patterning with a kidney-shaped mark that is sometimes lighter than the rest. At rest, one wing mostly overlies the other. Caterpillar is yellowish-brown above, greenish with a grey stripe on the sides. It has black spots with short hairs.

HABITS

Caterpillars belong to a group known as 'cutworms', from their habit of biting through the stems of small plants at ground level and felling them. They feed on leaves. One generation a year, which survives the winter as an egg. Adults fly June–October.

FOOD

Caterpillars eat clovers, docks and plantains, as well as cultivated herbaceous plants.

IN THE GARDEN

Comes to lighted windows at night. Leaving uncut grass with mixture of clover and plantains might help attract it to breed.

HEART AND DART *Agrotis exclamationis*

Adult wingspan 30–40 mm,
caterpillar length up to 38 mm
Widespread in Britain and Ireland,
although localised in north Scotland.

IDENTIFICATION

Close inspection reveals a black line on the body, just behind the eyes. Forewings have a blackish dart and a rough, heart-shaped pattern on a background that varies from sooty to light brown. Hindwings are paler. Caterpillar is reddish-brown above, greyish underneath, three reddish lines on its back and numerous black spots from which hairs grow.

HABITS

The caterpillar is one of a group known as 'cutworms', which eat through the stems of plants. It burrows into the underground roots of the plant or feeds on its leaves and shoots at night. During the day it hides in the soil. Two generations a year, the first flying May–August and the second (mainly in the south) in the autumn. Full grown caterpillars overwinter in cocoons and pupate in spring.

FOOD

Caterpillars feed on low-growing plants such as Common Chickweed, plantains, Fat Hen and goosefoots, and on vegetables such as Lettuce and Turnip.

IN THE GARDEN

Comes to lighted windows after dark and is attracted to herbaceous plants in the garden.

LARGE YELLOW UNDERWING *Noctua pronuba*

Adult wingspan 45–55 mm,
caterpillar length up to 50 mm
Widespread in Britain and Ireland, plus
some immigrants from Europe.

IDENTIFICATION

Forewings are mottled brown with dark spot near each wingtip, and wings overlap when at rest, giving the moth a long, thin appearance. Hindwings are bright yellow with a dark border. Caterpillar is yellowish, brown or even green, but it always has a double row of black bars along its back and another broken dark line along the sides of its body.

HABITS

Nocturnal and usually well camouflaged during the day, but if disturbed it may fly about flashing its bright underwings as it makes for cover. It is a long-lived moth that flies June–October, with most seen August–September. Adults come to light and to nectar-producing flowers. It overwinters as a caterpillar.

FOOD

Caterpillars eat a wide range of herbaceous plants, including Dandelion, docks, grasses and cultivated plants.

IN THE GARDEN

A mixed herbaceous border or a wild area may provide a home for this moth.

LESSER YELLOW UNDERWING *Noctua comes*

Adult wingspan 37–45 mm,
caterpillar length up to 50 mm
Widespread in Britain and Ireland.

IDENTIFICATION

Smaller than the Large Yellow Underwing and lacks the dark spot near the wingtip. Forewing colour is variable but has a dark crescent in the centre of the yellow underwing. Wings are proportionately a little broader and the shape at rest is less elongated than its relative. Caterpillar is grey, brown or green, with a yellowish-brown band along each side and a double row of black dashes on the hind segments.

HABITS

Nocturnal. Adults may be attracted in large numbers to lighted windows. One generation a year, the adults flying June–October. Eggs laid in August and the caterpillars hatch in September, hibernate in winter and feed on new buds and leaves the following spring.

FOOD

Caterpillars eat a variety of low-growing herbaceous plants such as docks, chickweed, Foxglove and nettles. They also climb the branches of shrubs such as Hawthorn.

IN THE GARDEN

A regular visitor to gardens that feeds on nectar-rich plants at night. It also comes to lighted windows. Herbaceous plants and shrubs will provide a habitat for this moth.

Cabbage Moth *Mamestra brassicae*

*Adult wingspan 40–47 mm,
caterpillar length up to 45 mm
Widespread in Britain and Ireland,
but less common in the north.*

Identification

Large grey and brown mottled moth with few obvious characteristics except an often obscure kidney-shaped mark on each forewing. Hindwings are also grey. Caterpillars start green with yellow rings between the segments of their bodies; later they vary from brown to greyish green, with two lines of black dashes along their back that join near the tail, and also a band of yellow, orange or green along each side.

Habits

Nocturnal. Two or three generations a year. Adults fly May–September. Can be numerous and is regarded as a pest in agricultural areas. Eggs are laid on the underside of leaves and hatch in about eight days. Caterpillars feed at night and hide on or under the ground by day.

Food

The caterpillars feed on a wide variety of herbaceous plants, including brassicas and other low-growing species.

In the garden

Visits lighted windows. May sometimes breed where Cabbages are being grown.

Sycamore Moth *Acronicta aceris*

*Adult wingspan 35–45 mm,
caterpillar length up to 40 mm
Common mainly in southern England
and south-west Wales.*

Identification

Variably grey-shaded moth, often pale with delicate dark grey, black or brown mottling. Outer edges of wings are slightly paler. Gentle 'S' shape pattern of dark marks when at rest. Hindwing is dusky or greyish white. Caterpillar looks like a tuft from a bright yellow fluffy carpet. It has long, yellow hairs plus four pairs of reddish tufts and several black-bordered white marks on its back.

Habits

Single generation. Adults fly June–August and may come to lighted windows. Distinctive caterpillars are usually seen in late summer, and often adopt a 'U' shape at rest. The species overwinters as a pupa.

Food

Sycamore is the species' main food plant, but it also eats Field Maple and Horse Chestnut, and some apparently eat the leaves of oaks and Plum. Adults take nectar from flowers.

In the garden

Caterpillars may be found feeding on their usual food plants or on ornamental maples that are introduced to some gardens.

ANGLE SHADES *Phlogophora meticulosa*

Adult wingspan 45–50 mm, caterpillar length up to 40 mm Both resident and an immigrant in most parts of Britain and Ireland.

IDENTIFICATION
Distinctive moth with wings that may look crumpled and with a well-defined triangular mark on each forewing. Wings are held alongside the body when at rest. Olive-green and pinkish-brown when newly emerged. Caterpillar varies from green to reddish-brown, and has a pale stripe along its back and another along each side. It also has a series of small diagonal marks on either side of its back.

HABITS
Nocturnal. Probably two generations a year, but adults have been seen in every month. Fewer seen May–June, and most August–October, when large numbers of immigrants arrive. Unusual shape is wonderful camouflage, as it may be mistaken for a dead flower.

FOOD
The caterpillars eat a variety of plants, including nettles, Hop, docks and Bramble.

IN THE GARDEN
May be attracted to lighted windows at night. The adults are commonly seen in gardens and may sometimes stay to breed.

RED UNDERWING *Catocala nupta*

Adult wingspan 70–80 mm, caterpillar length up to 70 mm Common in central and south-east England and in parts of Wales.

IDENTIFICATION
Large moth with mottled grey-brown upperwings that have delicate, but rather obscure, jagged line markings. Hindwings are crimson-red with black edges. Caterpillar is large and brown, with darker marks on the back and suggestions of paler marks on each body segment. It tapers off slightly at the rear, and has two rounded projections towards the end.

HABITS
Produces one generation a year, the adults flying August–October. Well camouflaged when resting on tree bark. Its natural habitat is woodland, parkland and riverbanks. The caterpillars feed at night and hide in cracks in bark during the day. It overwinters as an egg.

FOOD
The caterpillars feed on the leaves of poplars and willows.

IN THE GARDEN
While this moth is unlikely to breed in gardens, it may visit flowering plants at night and can sometimes be found resting on walls during the day.

Dark Arches *Apamea monoglypha*

**Adult wingspan 45–55 mm,
caterpillar length up to 45 mm
Abundant in Britain and Ireland.**

an oval and a large kidney-shaped mark. Rather shiny caterpillar is greyish with black spots and a shiny black head.

Habits

Usually one generation, with adults flying June–August. May be a second generation in the south, with adults flying September–November. Caterpillar hibernates among grass roots. Caterpillars eat the bottoms of grass stems and spend the day in small chambers among the roots. They pupate below ground.

A dark form of this moth is found in greater proportions in industrial areas. It has been speculated that this variation ensures better camouflage, and hence better survival, in more smoky, sooty places.

Food

Caterpillar feeds on grasses, including Couch Grass and Cocksfoot. Adults visit flowers for nectar after dark.

Identification

Wings appear rather pointed at rest. Variable colour, ranging from light grey-brown to black. The pattern, however, is consistent and includes

In the garden

Common visitor to gardens. Areas of long grass may encourage breeding.

Burnished Brass *Diachrysia chrysitis*

**Adult wingspan 35–42 mm,
caterpillar length up to 35 mm
Widespread in Britain and Ireland.**

Identification

When fresh, the moth's iridescent yellow-green really does shine like brass! This colour is broken up by patches or bands of brown.

The body is hairy, the hairs rising to a tuft on the back. Caterpillar is pale green with darker green along its back and an irregular white line and black marks along its sides.

Habits

Nocturnal. Attracted to lighted windows and sometimes found in sunny positions in the day. Adults fly June–July, but there may be later generations, especially in the south. Some of these are noticeably smaller as the caterpillars have less time to feed. During the day, caterpillars hide in a folded leaf.

Food

The caterpillars eat nettles, Spear Thistle and other herbaceous plants. Adults often feed on nectar from garden plants.

In the garden

Adults are attracted by species such as Red Valerian, whose nectar they feed on at night. Caterpillars pupate in leaf litter near their food plants, so leaving some leaves where they fall in autumn will help this and other species.

WILD FLOWERS

CREEPING BUTTERCUP *Ranunculus repens*

Height 15–60 cm
Common throughout Britain
and Ireland.

IDENTIFICATION

Typical buttercup. Flower 20–30 mm across, usually with five bright yellow and glossy petals. Sepals are not turned downwards, and flowering stem has grooves or furrows down its length. These features distinguish it from the Meadow Buttercup (no grooves on stem) and Bulbous Buttercup (sepals turned downwards). Leaves have three large lobes, divided into further lobes with toothed edges. Flowers May–August.

CHARACTERISTICS

Common buttercup of meadows, pastures and verges, especially damp soils, and the one occurring most often in gardens. Perennial, with leaves found year-round. Produces small seeds on a round seed head. Has thick clumps of roots. Spreads by runners, which produce new plants at the nodes. Grows quickly from seed and difficult to remove.

IN THE GARDEN

A useful lawn flower, if not cut too frequently. Visited by a wide range of insects, including Honey Bees, for pollen and nectar. Seeds are eaten by House Sparrow, finches and Dunnock, and the plant itself is eaten by a number of generalist caterpillars.

COMMON POPPY *Papaver rhoeas*

(FIELD POPPY, CORN POPPY)

Height 20–60 cm
Common throughout most of Britain
and Ireland; scarcer in Scotland.

CHARACTERISTICS

Flowers May–August. Annual, found in gardens and in the wild (the familiar poppy of arable fields and roadsides), although much reduced by herbicides. Ripe seed capsule develops small holes around the rim, and minute black seeds are scattered when the tall stem sways in the wind. Seeds survive in the soil for years, germinating when exposed to light by cultivation or disturbance.

IN THE GARDEN

The flowers are visited by bees and other insects, for the blue pollen. The tiny seeds are useful as food only to slender-billed birds such as Dunnock. Poppies are easily grown from seed, either planted or self-sown, but they are not meadow flowers and will germinate the next year only in bare ground.

> ### NOTE
> The Long-headed Poppy, *P. dubium*, is more common in the north. Its flowers are smaller than those of the Common Poppy (3–7 cm across) and paler.

IDENTIFICATION

Single tall stalks carry bright scarlet flowers 7–10 cm across. Has large 'pepper-pot' seed capsule in the centre. Leaves long and narrow with several narrow side branches.

SHEPHERD'S PURSE *Capsella bursa-pastoris*

Height 3–40 cm
Common throughout the British Isles.

IDENTIFICATION

Small to medium-sized upright plant. Very small flowers (2–3 mm across) are white with four petals and in a small group at the tip of the stem. Seed pods are on stalks up the stem, and are a flattened triangular or heart shape. Stems lengthen as more pods are produced. Leaves are usually a neat rosette at the base of the stem. These basal leaves have an elongated oval shape, narrowed at the base, and usually indented edges. A few small, pointed leaves grow on the stem.

CHARACTERISTICS

A familiar plant of bare soil. Annual, growing and flowering rapidly from seed in any month of the year. The heart-shaped pod contains several small, round seeds. These have been likened to coins in a purse, giving the plant its common name. The flower is self-pollinated, or self-fertile. This gives it an advantage in setting seed during the winter months.

IN THE GARDEN

Although self-pollinated, flowers produce nectar, and are visited by small insects. The seeds are an important food for sparrows and finches, and are also eaten by Dunnocks.

HAIRY BITTER-CRESS *Cardamine hirsuta*

Height up to 30 cm
Common and widespread throughout the British Isles.

IDENTIFICATION

Has a small erect stem; at its top is a group of very small flowers (3–4 mm across), white with four petals. The seed pods are long (18–25 mm) and thin, and are held erect, parallel to the stem. As they develop they grow higher than the remaining flowers at the tip. Leaves are slightly hairy; there are few on the stem, and a rosette on the ground, from which the flower stalk grows. Basal leaves have stalks and short, rounded leaflets along each side.

CHARACTERISTICS

A member of the cabbage family (Brassicaceae). An annual and abundant garden weed, growing in bare ground, paths, etc. Often found in with potted plants at garden centres. Germinates early and grows quickly and short lived. Flowers April–August, but usually dies down in summer. A large number of seeds are produced quickly, and these are dispersed when the pod dries and splits, scattering up to 75 cm from the plant. The hairs on the leaves give this plant its common name, although it is not quite as hairy as you might suppose.

IN THE GARDEN

The flowers are visited by very small insects and the leaves are eaten by some general herbivorous invertebrates. The seeds are eaten by sparrows, finches and Dunnock.

HEDGE MUSTARD   *Sisymbrium officinale*

Height 25–70 cm
Common in most of Britain and Ireland.

IDENTIFICATION

Upright, very stiff, rough-feeling stem. Yellow flowers with four petals, very small (3 mm across) and borne in a group at the tip of the stem. Stem elongates as more fruits are formed. Fruits are thin, elongated pods (15×1 mm), held upright and close to the stem. Lower leaves form a rosette at the base of the plant and are deeply divided, with 4–5 side lobes. Small leaves grow up the stem.

CHARACTERISTICS

A member of the cabbage family (Brassicaceae). Annual, sometimes surviving through the winter. Found on wasteland, arable fields, hedgerows and verges. Flowers in June–July. Found in neglected areas of the garden, along boundary hedges, etc.

IN THE GARDEN

Flowers visited by very small insects, and seeds taken by House Sparrows, finches and Dunnocks. A food plant of some butterflies, especially Green-veined White and Orange-tip, as well as general plant-feeders such as the Garden Carpet Moth.

COMMON VIOLET   *Viola riviniana*

(DOG VIOLET)
Height 14–22 cm
Widespread in Britain and Ireland.

IDENTIFICATION

Flowers are a violet-blue colour, 14–22 mm across, with five petals, two at each side and one centrally at the front. This front petal forms a tube or spur that projects behind the flower. In this species the spur is paler than the rest of the flower (usually whitish), which is a distinguishing feature. Leaves are heart-shaped, borne on stalks, and have slightly toothed edges. Fruit is an oval capsule, roughly 10 mm long, divided into three chambers of seeds.

CHARACTERISTICS

Wild relative of violas and pansies that occurs naturally in gardens or is introduced. A small, low-growing perennial. Flowers April–June. Leaves mostly in a loose rosette, with the flowers borne on side shoots.

IN THE GARDEN

Flowers provide nectar for spring insects, including bees, hoverflies and the Bee Fly. It is food of some butterfly and moth caterpillars.

> **NOTE**
> Another species of violet, the Sweet Violet, *V. odorata*, is often grown in gardens. It has darker petals than the Common Violet, including the spur, and a strong scent. The leaves are larger and downy.

COMMON MOUSE-EAR   *Cerastium fontanum*

(MOUSE-EAR CHICKWEED)

Trailing shoots up to 15 cm long.
Common in Britain and Ireland.

IDENTIFICATION

Resembles Common Chickweed, although its trailing shoots are tougher than those of that species. Small white flowers, usually with five petals, deeply notched and 5–8 mm long; they are borne on more erect shoots, up to 45 cm tall. The fruit is a small, curved cylindrical capsule. The leaves are small, dark green and hairy (thicker than those of Common Chickweed). They vary in shape on flowering and non-flowering stems, some resembling a mouse's ear (hence common name), while others are longer and more pointed.

CHARACTERISTICS

Perennial. Grows on bare ground like Common Chickweed, but because it lives longer and has a creeping habit, it is also very often found on lawns, grassland and in other habitats with short vegetation. Flowers mainly in April–September. Self-pollinated.

IN THE GARDEN

The flowers are visited by very small insects, mostly flies. The seed capsules are always close to the ground, and are eaten by sparrows, finches and Dunnocks.

COMMON CHICKWEED   *Stellaria media*

Trailing stems up to 50 cm long
Widespread and abundant in Britain
and Ireland.

IDENTIFICATION

A low-growing plant with thin, weak stems. White flowers are small (petals 4.5 mm long) and are borne towards the tip of the stem. There are actually five petals, but each is so deeply divided as to give the impression of ten, and pointed green sepals show in between. Leaves are soft and pale green, pointed oval in shape, on short, broad stalks near the plant's tip, and longer stalks further down. Two rows of fine hairs grow along the stem, although a lens may be needed to see these clearly.

CHARACTERISTICS

One of our most familiar garden weeds, on bare and disturbed ground, especially in gardens. An annual, growing in flower-beds and vegetable gardens. Has thin roots and thin stalks that are easily broken. Flowers January–December. Flowers are self-pollinated, allowing seeds to be set year-round.

IN THE GARDEN

The flowers are visited by small bees and flies, and are important as an early food source for these insects. The seeds are food source for House Sparrows and Dunnocks. The leaves are eaten by many general plant-feeding moths, including Setaceous Hebrew Character, Angle Shades and others.

PROCUMBENT PEARLWORT *Sagina procumbens*

Low-growing; trailing side-shoots may spread 20 cm and 5 cm high
Widespread in Britain and Ireland.

IDENTIFICATION

Small tuft of a plant that looks similar to a moss. Flowers are minute, appearing green. Petals are white but are scarcely visible and sometimes actually absent, so the flower is made up of sepals (usually four). Has very thin stems bearing small whorls of narrow leaves. Tends to form a central rosette with no flowers, sending out side shoots that trail at first and then turn upwards when flowering.

CHARACTERISTICS

Flowers May–September. The most common pearlwort in gardens in bare habitats. Perennial.

NOTE

The other common pearlwort often found in gardens is the Annual or Common Pearlwort, *S. apetela*. This has erect stems that lack the trailing side shoots, and it dies down in autumn.

Grows on lawns, but more conspicuous on paths, especially cracks in paving. Self-pollinating.

IN THE GARDEN

Colonises bare places, providing a micro habitat for microscopic invertebrates.

GOOD KING HENRY *Chenopodium bonus-henricus*

Height 30–50 cm
Widespread but local in England, Wales and southern Scotland.

IDENTIFICATION

A medium-height erect plant. Green flowers on thin, leafless spikes at the tip of the stem. Individual flowers are very small, with protruding stamens. Has triangular or spearhead-shaped leaves, up to 10 cm long, the young ones with a mealy surface. Stems may have a reddish tinge.

CHARACTERISTICS

Perennial in farmyards, fields with rich soil and wasteland. In gardens, grows around compost heaps and in very

rich soil. Introduced and once cultivated as a green vegetable. Flowers May–July. Seeds are roughly 2 mm long, brown and exposed in the seed heads.

IN THE GARDEN

Flowers visited by small insects. Seeds eaten by sparrows, finches and Dunnocks, and by mice and voles. Food for a few moth caterpillars, including Dark Spinach and Nutmeg.

NOTE

Originally called 'Good Henry' to distinguish it from 'Bad Henry', the similar-looking Dog's Mercury, *Mercurialis perennis*, which is not edible.

Fat Hen *Chenopodium album*

Height up to 100 cm
Common throughout most of Britain and Ireland (local in Scotland).

IDENTIFICATION
Green flowers, on erect side branches. Individual flowers are small and round, arranged in spikes up the stiff, erect stem. Leaves are diamond-shaped. Plant may have a whitish powdery look. Stem often has a reddish tinge.

CHARACTERISTICS
Found in arable ground, wasteland, gardens and rubbish tips. Flowers June–October and pollinated partly by wind, partly by insects. Seeds are small (1.5 mm long). In gardens it grows in cultivated areas, particularly

in manured soil. Once it was cultivated for its seeds, which were added to flour or used separately, or even eaten as a vegetable.

IN THE GARDEN
The flowers are visited by small insects for pollen. The seeds are eaten by sparrows, finches and Dunnocks, and by mice and voles. It is a food plant of a number of moth caterpillars.

Common Orache *Atriplex patula*

Height 30–90 cm
Common in most of Britain and Ireland.

IDENTIFICATION
Medium-height plant. Flowers are grey-green, on narrow spikes and forming a loose flower head. Each flowering spike is on a stalk arising from a leaf axil. Individual flowers are very small. Lower leaves are diamond-shaped or almost spearhead-shaped with a few teeth, those at the lower corners pointing forwards (this is a distinguishing feature). Upper leaves are narrower. The plant may have a slightly mealy appearance.

CHARACTERISTICS
An annual weed of arable land, gardens and wasteland. In agriculture, it is a major weed of beet crops, requiring special methods of control owing to its close relationship to beet. It is a variable plant. The stem has spreading branches, sometimes straggling on the ground. Like many arable weeds, the seeds are long-lived and may survive in the soil for up to 30 years. Flowers July–October.

IN THE GARDEN
Flowers are visited by small insects. Seeds are eaten by sparrows, finches and Dunnocks, and also by mice and voles. A food plant of the caterpillars of several moths, including Dark Spinach, Plain Pug, Nutmeg and Orache.

Common Mallow *Malva sylvestris*

Height up to 90 cm
Widespread throughout most of
Britain and Ireland.

IDENTIFICATION

Tall relative of the hollyhocks, found on wasteland and verges. Flowers are 2.5–4 cm in diameter, with five dark-lined purplish-pink petals that are narrow at the base and slightly indented at the tip. Central stamen stalks are united into a short tube, branching at the tip into a tuft of pollen-bearing anthers. Basal leaves are rounded, up to 10 cm in diameter, hairy, and crinkly or wrinkled. Stem leaves are smaller and more deeply lobed.

CHARACTERISTICS

Perennial, with thick, tough stems and strong, deep roots. Flowers June–September. Attractive flower, sometimes left for ornamental value. Seeds are large and wrinkled.

IN THE GARDEN

Flowers are visited by many insects, especially bees for pollen. The large seeds are eaten by mice and voles. Food plant for caterpillars of the Mallow moth and Painted Lady butterfly.

NOTE

Musk Mallow, *M. moschata*, is often grown in gardens. Flowers are similar to Common Mallow, but are paler pink or white, and leaves are deeply dissected. Dwarf Mallow, *M. neglecta*, is smaller and creeping: an annual weed of disturbed ground.

Soft Cranesbill *Geranium molle*

Height 10–40 cm
Common in Britain and Ireland.

Occurs in cultivated parts of the garden, and in lawns, where its low growth withstands mowing.

IN THE GARDEN

Flowers are visited by smaller insects. The small seeds are eaten by sparrows, finches and Dunnocks. It is also a food plant of general plant-feeding moth caterpillars.

IDENTIFICATION

Often grows close to the ground. Flowers are small and pinkish-purple, with five petals that are 3–6 mm long and with a deep notch at the tip. Leaves are rounded, and cut into several lobes by some deep and some shallow divisions and covered with soft pale hairs.

CHARACTERISTICS

Annual, producing flowers April–September. Fruit is a capsule with a narrow, pointed beak, 5–8 mm long. Its base is enclosed by hairy sepals so that it appears wider, and it is held at an angle on the stalk. The whole fruit suggests the neck, head and bill of a crane.

NOTE

Herb Robert, *G. robertianum*, has larger flowers and its stems are often reddish.

BLACK MEDICK *Medicago lupulina*

Prostrate, spreading up to 50 cm
Widespread in Britain and Ireland.

IDENTIFICATION

Creeping plant resembling a small, yellow clover. Leaves have three leaflets, like clover. Each leaflet is roundish, although pointed at the tip, and its outer edge has small, finely pointed teeth. Flowers are small (2–3 mm long) and bright yellow, like narrow, miniature pea flowers, and are arranged in a small globular head like clover flowers. Fruits are different from those of clover: each is small (2 mm long), turns black, is coiled into a tiny disc and clustered at the tip of the stem.

CHARACTERISTICS

A very small member of the pea family, which grows in short grassland and on lawns, where its low, creeping habit is resistant to mowing. Usually annual. Flowers May–September.

IN THE GARDEN

The seeds are eaten by sparrows and finches, while flowers are visited by very small insects. Sometimes a food plant of caterpillars that feed on larger members of the pea family, including the Common Blue.

WHITE CLOVER *Trifolium repens*

(DUTCH CLOVER)

Low-growing with creeping stems
up to 50 cm long
Found in grasslands throughout
Britain and Ireland.

IDENTIFICATION

Flowers are white or slightly pink. The globular flower heads, up to 2 cm across, are made up of numerous florets. Each individual floret is like a small, rather narrow pea flower, 8–10 mm long. Leaves are borne on thin stalks, each in the form of the familiar trefoil with three roundish leaflets that often have a pale V-shaped mark.

CHARACTERISTICS

Low-growing perennial with long, creeping stems. Petals form a narrow tube, making the nectar accessible only to insects with long tongues. Flowers June–September. Common on lawns and resistant to mowing.

IN THE GARDEN

An important source of nectar for several insects, especially bees. Leaving White Clover to flower and not mowing it too short or too frequently will benefit these insects. Food for a number of caterpillars, including Common Blue butterfly and Garden Dart, Hebrew Character and Silver Y moths.

> **NOTE**
>
> Red Clover, *T. pratense*, is common in grassland but less common on lawns. The flower heads are larger than White Clover and are purplish pink. The leaves also have larger leaflets (10–30 mm long).

BRAMBLE *Rubus fruticosus*

(BLACKBERRY)
Height up to 4 m
Widespread in Britain and Ireland.

IDENTIFICATION
Long, arching stems become tough and woody. Has numerous sharp flat thorns on the stems, and smaller prickles on the leaf stalks and leaf undersides. Flowers are white, sometimes pinkish, usually with five petals and shorter green sepals showing between these. There is a central mass of yellow stamens. Fruit is the blackberry, which changes from green to red to black. Leaves have three or five leaflets with toothed edges.

CHARACTERISTICS
A dense, perennial bush. Individual shoots are biennial, growing in one year and flowering the next, before dying back. Stems scramble up with the aid of the thorns. Shoots root where they touch the ground.

IN THE GARDEN
A useful shrub if there is space in the garden. Flowers provide nectar and pollen for bees and butterflies; fruit is eaten by Wood Mice, Bank Voles, Foxes and many birds, and several butterflies drink the juice from damaged berries. Seeds are eaten by tits and Bullfinches; leaves are eaten by many moth caterpillars; and the bush provides cover for hibernating Commas and nest sites for birds and Hedgehogs.

DOG ROSE *Rosa canina*

(BRIAR)
Height up to 3 m
Widespread in Britain
and Ireland.

IDENTIFICATION
This wild, native rose has long stems with sharp curved thorns that allow it to scramble through other shrubs. The five to seven oval, slightly toothed leaflets are arranged in pairs on a thin stalk. Flowers are 45–50 mm across, vary from white to pink and have five notched petals. The orange-red fruits, called hips, often last through the winter and are flask-shaped.

CHARACTERISTICS
Flowers June–August. A woody plant that climbs to reach the light, sometimes getting to the crowns of smaller trees. It spreads through root suckers. Unlikely to arrive in a garden naturally unless near countryside or wasteland, or is specially introduced. Some cultivated roses are grafted onto Dog Rose stock, and suckers may be this species.

IN THE GARDEN
A good plant to have in the garden, especially in a boundary hedge to provide nest sites for birds. It is also home for many small insects, including gall wasps: the striking Robin's Pincushion Gall (*see* p127), and pea galls on the underside of leaves. It also attracts aphids, which in turn provide food for many creatures, including ladybirds, lacewings and small birds. The leaves are food for several moths, the flowers provide nectar for butterflies such as the Gatekeeper, and the hips are winter food for thrushes, Greenfinches and other birds, and also for mice and voles.

BITING STONECROP *Sedum acre*

(WALL PEPPER)

Height 2–10 cm
Found throughout most of Britain and Ireland.

IDENTIFICATION

Low-growing plant. Flowers are bright yellow, 12 mm across and star-shaped, with five petals. Leaves are tiny (3–6 mm long), fat and fleshy, in the form of a short cylinder, and held closely against the stem.

CHARACTERISTICS

Grows in dry, open places. A perennial and evergreen, with both erect and creeping stems. Stonecrops are succulent plants, with fleshy leaves that are adapted for storing

water, and can survive in dry places with poor or thin soil. In gardens, Biting Stonecrop grows on paths, rockeries, walls and roofs. It spreads easily from small detached fragments of plant.

IN THE GARDEN

The pretty clusters of flowers are visited by small flies and bees, which pollinate them. It is also the food plant of a few moth caterpillars, including (in coastal areas) the Northern Rustic.

NOTE

Two stonecrop species with white flowers may also be found in gardens: English Stonecrop, *S. anglicum*, is low-growing with reddish leaves; and White Stonecrop, *S. album*, has flowers borne on stalks in a branched head.

BROAD-LEAVED WILLOW-HERB *Epilobium montanum*

Height 20–69 cm
Common in Britain and Ireland.

IDENTIFICATION

Slender and erect, often with a pinkish stem. Small flowers with four pale pink petals are

4–7 mm long with a deep notch at the tip. Each flower is at the tip of a long, thin capsule 4–8 cm long and covered with soft hairs, which becomes a seed pod. Leaves are narrow, oval and pointed, with toothed edges.

CHARACTERISTICS

A small relative of the Rosebay Willow-herb, or Fireweed, of wasteland. The most common of the small-flowered willow-herbs occurring in gardens. Perennial, dying down in autumn to a dense rosette of leaves close to the ground. Flower is often self-pollinated. Seed capsule, when ripe, splits lengthwise into four segments, exposing the seeds. These are small (1 mm long) and have a plume of fine hairs. When dry, seeds disperse on the wind. Flowers June–August.

IN THE GARDEN

The flowers are occasionally visited by small insects and the seeds are eaten by Goldfinch. Leaves are sometimes eaten by moth caterpillars such as those of Elephant Hawkmoth.

IVY *Hedera helix*

Climbs to a height of 30 m
Common and widespread throughout
Britain and Ireland.

IDENTIFICATION

Glossy dark green leaves have three to five triangular lobes, although those on flowering shoots are diamond-shaped or oval. Climbing stems become woody. Flowers are borne on the end of stalks, in round clusters and are small (petals 3–4 mm long), greenish, with yellow anthers. Fruits are berries, green turning dull black when ripe in early spring.

Ivy berries are eaten by Blackbirds.

CHARACTERISTICS

A familiar climber on trees, in woods and hedges, on rocks and walls, and also along the ground. The underside of the climbing stem has a thick mat of short roots, used for attachment. Autumn flowering, with berries ripening in early spring.

IN THE GARDEN

Has a high conservation value if allowed to mature and flower, e.g. along a wall. Provides nest sites for small birds and hibernation sites for Brimstone butterflies. Flowers provide nectar for late-season flying insects and are often covered with flies, hoverflies, Hornets, wasps and butterflies. Ivy berries ripen only in early spring, when they are useful food for Blackbird and Blackcap. Woodpigeons eat them at any stage for the sake of the seeds. The flowers and developing berries are food for Holly Blue caterpillars.

COW PARSLEY *Anthriscus sylvestris*

Height up to 1 m
Abundant throughout Britain
and Ireland.

IDENTIFICATION

Tall, with somewhat branched, erect stems. Typical umbellifer flowers, arranged in wide, fairly flat heads (the umbels of the group's name). Individual flowers are white, small (3–4 mm across) and arranged in groups about 1 cm across. These groups are further arranged in flattish clusters of 8–10, about 10 cm across, which in turn are borne on stalks to form a large, loose head. Leaves are much divided, looking rather like fern leaves, and are up to 30 cm long and slightly hairy.

CHARACTERISTICS

Frequent on verges, this typical member of the carrot family is usually the commonest of the group that includes Hogweed, Hemlock and Parsnip. Stems often have a purplish tinge and are hollow and grooved. Has a strong taproot. Perennial, but seeds easily in garden soil. Flowers April–June.

IN THE GARDEN

Flowers are visited by many insects for nectar and pollen, conspicuously hoverflies and Soldier Beetles. Seeds are large (5 mm long), and are taken by sparrows and finches as well as mice and voles. It is a food plant of the Single-dotted Wave moth and other non-specilised plant-feeding caterpillars.

GROUND ELDER   *Aegopodium podagraria*

Height 40 cm
Found throughout Britain and
Ireland.

IDENTIFICATION

Has an erect, hollow, flowering stem with narrow grooves. Flowers are white, borne in flattish heads or umbels 2–6 cm across and made up of small round groups. Individual flowers are tiny, 1 mm across. Leaves resemble those of Elder. They are oval with a finely toothed edge, grow on a stalk from the ground, and are divided into oval leaflets that are each 4–8 cm long.

CHARACTERISTICS

A member of the carrot family, believed to have been introduced originally by the Romans as a herb, but now naturalised. It is still sometimes known as Goutweed, after the condition it was supposed to cure. Usually found around buildings and especially in gardens. Long, creeping underground stems (rhizomes) send up new shoots to form clumps of plants. Flowers May–July.

IN THE GARDEN

Well known, even infamous, as a persistent garden weed of flower-beds. The strong underground growth of the rhizomes makes it difficult to control. The flowers are visited by small insects such as hoverflies.

PETTY SPURGE   *Euphorbia peplus*

Height 10–30 cm
Very common throughout Britain
and Ireland.

IDENTIFICATION

Short, erect plant, with a wide, flat head of pale green flowers. The flowers are unusual, lacking petals, and have four or five green glands within the cup, each with a pair of slender horns. The male and female parts are surrounded by small leaves called bracts. The upper leaves are roughly triangular, while the lower ones (0.5–3 cm long) are oval and narrow at the base. The fruit is a capsule (2 mm long) containing three compartments.

CHARACTERISTICS

Annual on arable land and in gardens, where it is the commonest of several wild spurges (there are also several cultivated forms of *Euphorbia*). Like other euphorbias, the stem produces a milky white sap when broken.

IN THE GARDEN

The flowers are visited and pollinated by various flies, the seeds are eaten by sparrows and Dunnocks, and it is also a food plant of the Drab Looper moth.

> ### NOTE
> Sun Spurge, *E. helioscopia*, is similar to Petty Spurge, but the flowers are yellowish. The leaves below the flower head form a whorl or ring, and have small teeth towards the tip.

COMMON KNOTGRASS   *Polygonum aviculare*

Creeping stems up to 100 cm long
Common and widespread throughout
Britain and Ireland.

IDENTIFICATION

Low-growing plant that creeps close to the ground. Flowers are tiny, pink or white, and usually have five petals. They are borne on short stalks or grow directly from the stem in small groups, from silvery sheaths that enclose the base of the leaf stalks. Leaves are narrow, oval and pointed, 5 cm long, growing singly along the stem.

CHARACTERISTICS

Annual, growing on arable land, roadsides and wasteground. Stems are tough and sometimes slightly angled at the joints. Fruits are small and remain enclosed within the dead petals. In gardens, it is usually on neglected bare ground, or on or alongside paths, where it withstands some trampling but not competition. Flowers June–November.

IN THE GARDEN

The flowers are visited by very small insects and the seeds eaten by House Sparrows and Dunnocks. Listed as a food plant of many moth species, including Blood Vein, Tawny Wave, Vestal, Gem, Flame, Green Arches, Dark Brocade and Bird's Wing.

PERSICARIA   *Polygonum persicaria*

(REDSHANK)

Height 25–75 cm
Common throughout Britain
and Ireland.

IDENTIFICATION

Has erect reddish or purplish branched stems, with flower heads at the tips. Flowers are pink, borne in a short cylindrical cluster; individual flowers are very small. Leaves are narrow and pointed (lance-shaped), 5–10 cm long and usually have a large dark mark in their centre. A short frilly sheath grows around the stem at leaf junctions, from which the side branches emerge.

CHARACTERISTICS

A close relative of the garden bistorts. Found on arable and disused land and beside rivers. In gardens, grows in cultivated and neglected ground. Annual. Flowers June–October.

IN THE GARDEN

The flowers are visited by small insects and the seeds are eaten by sparrows, finches and Dunnocks. A main food plant of Gem and Light Brocade moth caterpillars and also eaten by other small plant-feeders.

BROAD-LEAVED DOCK *Rumex obtusifolius*

Height 50–100 cm
Widespread in Britain and Ireland.

IDENTIFICATION
Long, broad leaves (up to 25 cm), with rounded tip and oval or heart-shaped at the base. They grow from a sheath at the base of the stalk. Flowers are on tall, branched spikes, arranged in whorls. Individual flowers are small, pink and green, dangling on short stalks. Each has tiny petals (5–6 mm), pressed against the fruit with teeth on their edges. Produces substantial seeds (3 mm long).

CHARACTERISTICS
Perennial in hedges, field edges and waste-ground. Has a strong taproot, from which it regenerates if cut. Flowers are wind-pollinated. Crushed leaves soothe nettle stings.

IN THE GARDEN
Flowers have no nectar, but some insects feed on the pollen. Seeds eaten on the stem by Goldfinch and Bullfinch, and on the ground by sparrows, finches and Dunnocks. Leaves are food for caterpillars of the Small Copper and various moths, including Garden Tiger, Garden Dart, Angle Shades and non-specialist feeders.

STINGING NETTLE *Urtica dioica*

Height 30–180 cm
Abundant in Britain and Ireland.

IDENTIFICATION
Medium to tall plant. Famous for the stinging hairs on the stem and leaves, used as a defence against browsing mammals. Leaves (4–8 cm long) are oval with a broad base, pointed and strongly toothed, and arranged in opposite pairs. Tiny flowers are green with yellow stamens, and borne on thin tassels.

CHARACTERISTICS
Well-known perennial of hedges, woods and places where the ground has been disturbed or enriched. Spreads by creeping stems. Flowers June–September. Male and female flowers are on separate plants.

IN THE GARDEN
Used by bugs, leafhoppers, weevils and many other insects. Food of Red Admiral, Small Tortoiseshell and Peacock caterpillars. Important to moths, including Snout, Burnished Brass and Angle Shades.

These need rich, new growth in a fertile, sunny spot; if possible, leave a patch in your garden, cutting a small area to allow for fresh shoots. Restrict growth by surrounding it with a sunken barrier of plastic.

HEDGE BINDWEED
Calystegia sepium

(CONVOLVULUS)
Trailing, or climbing to 3 m
Abundant and widespread in most of
Britain and Ireland.

IDENTIFICATION
Flowers are white, large (4 cm across), funnel-shaped and close at night. The five sepals are each 1 cm long and partly overlapped by two pale bracts at the base of the flower. Leaves are heart- or arrow-shaped, up to 15 cm.

CHARACTERISTICS
Perennial of hedges, the edges of woods and wasteland, and also in gardens, around the edges or in neglected areas. The stems are long and weak, and may trail or twine anticlockwise up larger plants and shrubs. The shoot-tips push into the ground and take root. The underground rhizomes grow down to 30 cm. These are yellowish-white and brittle, and are easily broken, making it difficult to control.

NOTE
Great Bindweed, *C. sylvatica*, has even larger white flowers (6–7.5 cm across), and the bracts overlap and cover the sepals. Introduced from southern Europe and now common in city gardens and railway embankments.

IN THE GARDEN
Flowers are visited by bees and other insects for pollen and nectar. It is a food plant for caterpillars of the Convolvulus Hawkmoth. The large wrinkled seeds are eaten by mice and Bank Voles.

LESSER BINDWEED
Convolvulus arvensis

(FIELD BINDWEED)
Climbing to a height of 75 cm
Common throughout Britain, except in
northern Scotland. Local in Ireland.

IDENTIFICATION
Slender stems, either trailing or climbing. Single flowers are funnel- or trumpet-shaped, up to 3 cm across, slightly scented, and white, pale pink or variegated with both colours. They have five pointed sepals. Leaves are usually arrow-shaped and 2–5 cm long.

CHARACTERISTICS
Flowers June–September. Perennial of arable land, roadsides and wasteground. Climbs by twining anticlockwise up other plants. Has long, strong, twisted underground stems (rhizomes) as well as roots, penetrating far into the soil, sometimes to more than 2 m. Seeds are contained in a small capsule.

IN THE GARDEN
The flowers are visited by a variety of insects for nectar and pollen, and its seeds are probably eaten by sparrows, Dunnocks, mice and voles. The leaves are eaten by the caterpillars of the Four-spotted Moth and Convolvulus Hawkmoth, and by other non-specialised plant-feeding caterpillars.

Ivy-Leaved Toadflax *Cymbalaria muralis*

Trailing to 60 cm
Common in most of Britain and Ireland.

IDENTIFICATION
Small to medium plant, trailing or hanging and usually growing on a vertical surface. Has tiny Snapdragon-like flowers, 8–10 mm long, growing singly on thin stalks. The lilac flowers have upper and lower lips, and a curved

backwards-pointing spur. They are darker on the upper lip, and the central part is white with a yellow spot. Small purple-tinged leaves (2.5 cm long) are rather thick and have blunt lobes (giving a passing likeness to Ivy). Stems are often purplish.

CHARACTERISTICS
Perennial. Flowers May–September. Has slender trailing stems and takes root in small crevices with little soil, often growing on old walls. Flowers are held towards the light, but when flowering is over the stalks bend back into the shade. This helps to shed the seeds into cracks where they can grow. Originally introduced from southern Europe in the 17th century as an ornamental wall plant.

IN THE GARDEN
In gardens it is found in crevices in walls where few other flowering plants can grow. The flowers are visited mostly by small bees, which act as pollinators.

Ground Ivy *Glechoma hederacea*

Height 10–30 cm
Common in Britain and Ireland, but rare in northern Scotland.

IDENTIFICATION
Low-growing plant. Flowers are blue and small (15–20 mm long), and are very similar to those of a dead-nettle, with upper and lower lips. They are arranged in whorls of two to four along the stem in the leaf axils. Leaves are rounded or kidney-shaped, 1–3 cm across, with roundly toothed edges. In sunny sites, the whole plant shows a purplish tinge.

CHARACTERISTICS
A perennial that flowers March–June. Grows in woodland, hedges and along verges. Despite its name, it hardly resembles true Ivy and is not related to it, but is so called for the way it grows across the ground. Stems are thin and creeping, sending out roots at frequent intervals so that the plant spreads. Flowers are borne on vertical, short shoots. Plants are slightly hairy and aromatic when crushed. Seeds are formed in groups of four at the base of the sepals when the petals have fallen.

IN THE GARDEN
The flowers are visited by bees and are an important resource for these insects in early spring. The seeds are eaten by House Sparrows and Dunnocks. The species is also a food plant of a number of leaf-feeding insects.

Speedwells

Low-growing plants with small, usually blue flowers that have four petals of slightly unequal size (the bottom petal is the smallest). Found in a variety of habitats including aquatic environments. Several species are common in gardens.

Flowers are visited by small insects, and seeds are taken by seed-eating birds. Leaves are eaten by general plant-feeders. A gall midge causes swelling of the terminal buds.

Common Field Speedwell

Veronica persica

Trailing stems 10–40 cm long
Widesprerad in Britain and Ireland.

Small and trailing with several branches. Small flowers (8–10 mm), bright blue with paler bottom petal, and borne singly along the stem. Leaves are 1–3 cm, triangular to oval, lack stalks and have hairy undersides.

Flowers January–December. Most common speedwell, found on bare soil. Introduced in 19th century from Asia. Annual. Germinates quickly and may have two generations a year. Flowers do not need to cross-pollinate.

> **Note**
> The Germander Speedwell, *V. chamaedrys*, is similar to the Common Field Speedwell. Brighter blue, white at the centre, and borne on loose spikes. Stems have two rows of hairs running along their length.

Ivy-Leaved Speedwell

Veronica hederifolia

Trailing stems 10–60 cm long
Common in Britain and Ireland.

Long, very weak trailing stems. Flowers are very small, pale lilac in colour, with sepals that are longer than the petals. Small leaves have bluntly pointed lobes, reminiscent of those of Ivy, borne singly along the stem. Found on cultivated soil. Small, round fruit capsule ripens and sets seed very quickly. Flowers March–August. Can self-pollinate.

Slender Speedwell

Veronica filiformis

Trailing stems 5–20 cm long
Locally common in Britain and Ireland.

Thin, creeping stems forming thick patches on the ground. Flowers more mauve than those of Common Field Speedwell, and on long, thin stalks. Leaves are small, round or kidney-shaped on short stalks. Introduced from the Near East as a garden plant and still spreading. Is found on lawns, where it can dominate large areas. Reaches new areas when broken fragments are carried on people's or animals' feet. Flowers April–May.

SELF-HEAL *Prunella vulgaris*

Height 5–30 cm
Common in Britain and Ireland.

IDENTIFICATION
Has short (5 cm) vertical flowering shoots. Flowers are violet, 10–15 mm long and resemble dead-nettles, with upper and lower lips. Borne in a group at the top of the stem as a stumpy, short head, with the individual flowers arranged all around and the leaves below them. Because of the colour of the sepals, the whole head often looks purplish. Stem is square in cross-section. Leaves are oval and pointed, 2–5 cm long.

CHARACTERISTICS
Perennial of grassland and woodland clearings. Flowers June–November. Short shoots grow along the ground, while vertical flowering shoots may be very compact on a mown lawn, almost like rosettes (even when mown they usually retain a few flowers). Small seeds develop in groups of four in the base of the sepals. In gardens, it is found on lawns or adjacent footpaths. Traditionally it was used in herbal remedies.

IN THE GARDEN
Flowers mainly visited by bees, for which it can be an important food. It needs a little height to flower well. Seeds are eaten by House Sparrows and Dunnocks, while leaves are food for a few plant-feeding insects.

HEDGE WOUNDWORT *Stachys sylvatica*

Height 30–100 cm
Found throughout Britain
and Ireland.

IDENTIFICATION
Member of the dead-nettle family. Flowers are a very dark reddish-purple, 13–15 mm long, and divided into upper and lower lips. They are arranged in whorls of about six around the stem, forming a flowering spike above the leaves. Stem is solid and is square in cross-section. Leaves are an elongated heart shape and are covered with rough hairs, making the plant almost prickly to the touch. Has a strong smell when crushed.

CHARACTERISTICS
Perennial of woodlands and hedgerows (there are also garden varieties). Flowers July–August. Spreads by creeping stems (rhizomes), which send up erect shoots. Seeds are in groups of four, hidden inside the tube formed by the sepals. Common name alludes to its use in traditional herbal remedies.

IN THE GARDEN
Grows in neglected, undisturbed areas, usually shady places around the edges. Visited by bees for nectar, and its seeds are eaten by sparrows and Dunnocks. A food plant of the caterpillars of a few moths, including the Sub-angled Wave, Rosy Rustic and Plain Golden Y, as well as other plant-feeders.

RED DEAD-NETTLE *Lamium purpureum*

Height 10–40 cm
*Abundant and widespread throughout
Britain and Ireland.*

IDENTIFICATION

Short with pinkish-purple flowers, 10–15 mm long, and arranged in whorls around the upper stem. Each has a tubular base, with

the upper part divided into two lips: the upper lip forms a curved hood, sheltering the stamens and stigmas; while the lower lip is flatter, divided into two lobes. The stem is square in cross-section. Leaves are heart-shaped or triangular, 1–5 cm long, and have toothed edges. The whole plant may appear purplish.

CHARACTERISTICS

Found in cultivated and disturbed ground, especially gardens. A member of the mint family, and not related to the Stinging Nettle. Annual, with short, erect stems, several arising together from the base. Slightly hairy, but the hairs do not sting. The sepals are joined to form a narrow funnel with five long teeth, and the group of four seeds that develop are neatly arranged inside the base of this. Flowers March–October, but especially spring.

IN THE GARDEN

Important as an early source of nectar and pollen, especially for bumblebees. The seeds eaten by sparrows, Dunnocks and other small birds. The leaves are food for a number of moth caterpillars, including Burnished Brass.

WHITE DEAD-NETTLE *Lamium album*

Height 20–60 cm
*Common in Britain except northern
Scotland, and in Ireland.*

IDENTIFICATION

Medium-height plant. White flowers are 20–25 mm long, arranged in whorls down the stem, each whorl above a pair of leaves. Each flower has a tubular base, with the upper part divided into two lips: the upper lip forms a curved hood covering the stamens and stigmas; while the lower lip is flatter, with small teeth. Stem is square in cross-section. Leaves resemble those of Stinging Nettle.

CHARACTERISTICS

Found in hedges and verges, and in gardens in areas that are only occasionally dug. Related to the mint family, and not a nettle. Perennial, with creeping shoots on or under the ground that send up vertical stalks. Flowers May–December. Flowers bear the weight of heavy insects, whose backs receive pollen and transfer it to the next flower.

IN THE GARDEN

Pollinated by long-tongued bumblebees, for which it is an extremely important food source, especially in spring and early summer. Seeds are eaten by sparrows and Dunnocks, and the leaves are the food of a number of moth caterpillars, including Burnished Brass and Setaceous Hebrew Character.

GREATER PLANTAIN *Plantago major*

Height 10–15 cm
Widespread in Britain and Ireland.

IDENTIFICATION

Leaves are a broad oval, 10–15 cm long. They narrow to a distinct leaf stalk and form an obvious flat rosette. Flower head is long, tall and narrow, growing longer as the flowers and

fruits develop. Tiny yellowish-green flowers are insignificant. Anthers are conspicuous as the flowers develop, initially purple and turning yellowish-brown.

CHARACTERISTICS

A perennial, usually found in open areas. Flowers are wind-pollinated, so the stamens protrude from the flower spike but produce no nectar. In gardens, sometimes found on short-mown lawns, where the leaf rosette withstands mowing. Can withstand considerable trampling, and often occurs on or bedside garden paths. Elsewhere, not able to avoid competition with taller plants, even in grassland.

IN THE GARDEN

The flowers are visited by insects, mainly small bees, for their pollen. The seeds are eaten by sparrows, finches and Dunnocks. Not the specific food plant of any species, but eaten by a number of moth caterpillars that rely on various plantains or are generalist feeders, including Garden Dart, Heart and Dart, Barred Chestnut, Setaceous Hebrew Character, Dot, Rustic and Common Swift.

RIBWORT PLANTAIN *Plantago lanceolata*

Height up to 50 cm
Abundant in Britain and Ireland.

IDENTIFICATION

Leaves are narrow, pointed and lance-shaped, usually 10–15 cm long and tapering gradually to base. Each has three or five strong ribs on the underside. In short turf, they form a flat rosette, while in longer vegetation they are more upright and longer. Flowers are borne on tall single stalks above the leaves, and form an oval head (1–3 cm high) that is blackish-green, turning brown after flowering. Individual flowers are tiny and insignificant, but during flowering the stamens and their anthers stick out of the head in a ring, and new ones emerge as the flowers develop.

CHARACTERISTICS

Perennial of grassland, verges and wasteground. Flowers are wind-pollinated, and stamens protrude conspicuously, but there is no nectar. In gardens, usually on lawns, where the leaf rosette withstands mowing.

IN THE GARDEN

Flowers are visited by insects (mainly small bees) for pollen, and the seeds are eaten by sparrows and Dunnocks. Food plant of the Six-striped Rustic and also eaten by the same moth caterpillars as Greater Plantain.

GOOSEGRASS *Galium aparine*

(CLEAVERS OR STICKY WEED)
Stem height up to 120 cm
Widespread and abundant throughout
Britain and Ireland.

IDENTIFICATION
Goosegrass is known for the plant itself rather than its tiny flowers. It has long, thin, straggling stems, which are sharply squared in cross-section. Leaves are 1–5 cm long, narrow but slightly wider towards the tip, and end in a fine spine. They are arranged in rings or whorls of 6–8 around the stem. Flowers are tiny (2 mm), creamy white and are carried in small clusters on short side shoots.

CHARACTERISTICS
Annual, with new green shoots appearing early in spring. Found in hedgerows and wasteland, with many local names. Tiny, backwards-pointing bristles on the stems and leaves help the weak stems climb up or through other plants, and also cause the whole plant to stick to animals or human clothing. The small, round fruits, up to 6 mm across, are formed in pairs and are also equipped with hooks to aid dispersal.

IN THE GARDEN
Mammals disperse the seeds on their fur. Seeds are also eaten by Wood Mouse and Bank Vole, and by seed-eating birds such as sparrows. Leaves eaten by moth caterpillars.

COMMON GROUNDSEL *Senecio vulgaris*

Height 8–25 cm
Common and widespread throughout
Britain and Ireland.

IDENTIFICATION
Small plant. Flower heads are small (4 mm in diameter) and cylindrical, like tiny shaving brushes with yellow tips, and are borne in small clusters. The heads are made up of minute disc florets and lack the ray florets found in most other composites. When ripe, the seed heads are like very small and fluffy Dandelion heads. Leaves are narrow and finely lobed.

CHARACTERISTICS
Annual plant of bare and cultivated ground and is an abundant and widespread garden weed. Grows rapidly to the flowering and seed-production stage. Develops a large number of small seeds that carry a simple parachute and so can be spread by wind. The seeds germinate when exposed to light in disturbed soil. Flowers throughout the year.

IN THE GARDEN
The seeds are gathered from the seed heads by House Sparrows, Goldfinches and Linnets. A few caterpillars eat the leaves, including those of the Cinnabar and Setaceous Hebrew Character moths. The plant is sometimes host to a conspicuous rust fungus, which causes orange patches on the undersides of the leaves.

SCENTLESS MAYWEED *Tripleurospermum inodorum*

Height 15–60 cm
Widespread in Britain and Ireland.

IDENTIFICATION

Composite daisy-like flower with both ray and disc florets. Has medium-sized, upright branched stems. Flower head resembles a Daisy but larger (2–3.5 cm across). Ray florets are white and number 12–30, while disc of yellow florets is slightly domed. Leaves are dissected and feathery. Little scent is produced when the plant is crushed.

CHARACTERISTICS

Usually annual, growing as a weed in cultivated parts of the garden. Seeds form in the disc of the flower head, are elongated (2–3 mm long) and lack the fluffy parachutes of some composites. Flowers July–September.

IN THE GARDEN

The flowers are visited by bees and flies for nectar and pollen, and the seeds are eaten by sparrows, finches and Dunnocks.

NOTE

Stinking Mayweed, *Anthemis cotula*, is similar but only locally common in southern Britain and Ireland. Its white, ray florets are strongly downturned, and the plant is very strong-smelling when it is crushed. Lawn Chamomile, *Chamaemelum nobile*, is also similar and sometimes grown as a lawn for its fragrance.

PINEAPPLEWEED *Matricaria discoidea*

(RAYLESS MAYWEED)

Height 5–30 cm
Abundant in most of Britain and Ireland.

IN THE GARDEN

The flowers are not much visited by insects, but the small seeds are eaten by sparrows, finches and Dunnocks. It is a food plant of the Chamomile Shark moth.

IDENTIFICATION

Small to medium-sized plant with erect, branched stems. The greenish-yellow flower heads (5–8 mm) are not very conspicuous. Although it is a composite like the Daisy, it has only the central disc florets and lacks the rays of most members of the family. Flower therefore looks like the centre of a Daisy, although more domed. Leaves are feathery, sometimes quite dense. A strong Pineapple-like scent is released when crushed.

CHARACTERISTICS

An annual. In gardens, occurs in cultivated ground such as a vegetable patch. Also found on roadsides and wasteland, especially in trampled areas beside footpaths and gateways. Originally an introduced species, probably from Asia. Flowers May–November.

DAISY *Bellis perennis*

Height 12 cm
Widespread and abundant throughout Britain and Ireland.

IDENTIFICATION

Single flower heads, 16–25 mm across, on thin upright stalks. Outer part of head (ray florets)

is white, sometimes tinged pink, while central part (disc florets) is yellow and slightly raised. Leaves form a rosette close to the ground. They are spoon-shaped, broad and rounded near the tip, and narrowing to the base, with blunt-toothed edges.

CHARACTERISTICS

Well-known member of the Asteraceae family, with composite flowers made up of numerous small florets. It does not compete well with taller plants, so the species is helped by grazing or mowing and is usually found in short grassland. Flower heads open in the daytime and close in the evening, which gave the plant its original name of 'Day's Eye'. After flowering, the head bears small seeds (1.5–2 mm long).

IN THE GARDEN

Grows on lawns, although mowing that is too frequent or too close will reduce the number of flowers. A source of nectar and pollen for small insects. Has been eliminated in many gardens by selective weedkillers.

MUGWORT *Artemisia vulgaris*

Height 60–120 cm
Common throughout Britain and Ireland, in hedgerows and on wasteland.

IDENTIFICATION

Tall, conspicuous plant with contrasting dark green and silvery grey on the leaves. Flowers grow in dense leafy spikes, at or near the tip of the stem. Although they are small (2–3 mm long) and oval, they are not individual flowers but are small composite heads. They are grey, with tips ranging from yellow to pale brown. Leaves are 5–8 cm long, deeply divided and toothed, dark green above, and grey or white and hairy below.

CHARACTERISTICS

Stems are tough (almost woody) and erect, flowers are wind-pollinated and seeds are very small (c. 1 mm long). Flowers July–September, although the flowers are not obvious. Its common name comes from its traditional use as a flavouring in ale. It is a close relative of the notorious Wormwood and of some garden species of *Artemisia*.

IN THE GARDEN

Flowers contain no nectar, and are visited by insects for pollen. The seeds are taken by Goldfinches on the stem, and by sparrows and Dunnocks from the ground. It is the food plant of a few moth caterpillars, including Common Emerald (before hibernation), Wormwood Pug and Wormwood, and is also eaten by generalist caterpillars, although the bitterness may deter some species.

CREEPING THISTLE *Cirsium arvense*

Height 30–90 cm
Abundant in Britain and Ireland.

IDENTIFICATION

Flower head comprises lilac-coloured florets that are divided, so that it appears to be made up of many filaments. Base of head is expanded, round or oval, and covered in purplish scales (bracts). It is wider at the tip when in flower (to 15–25 mm). Leaves are basically lance-shaped, narrower at the base, but have divided or wavy edges with numerous stiff, sharp spines. They form an erect rosette in non-flowering plants, and at the base of flowering shoots. Stems lack spines.

CHARACTERISTICS

Perennial, flowering July–September. Our most common thistle, found in fields, on verges and on waste ground, and the one most likely to grow in gardens. Has erect flowering shoots and a deep taproot. It sends out creeping side roots that form new plants and give it its common name. Seeds (4 mm long) are packed together and each carries a tuft of long feathery hairs (thistledown) at one end, allowing them to be dispersed by wind.

IN THE GARDEN

Flowers are visited by bees for pollen and nectar, and by many other nectar-feeding insects, notably butterflies (especially skippers and browns). Birds (especially Goldfinches) take its seeds. It is also an important food of caterpillars of the Painted Lady and of moths, including the Knot Grass, Frosted Orange and other generalist feeders. It is a host to rust fungi of the genus *Puccinia* and produces several galls, notably a swelling in the stem caused by the fly *Euribia cardui*.

NIPPLEWORT *Lapsana communis*

Height 20–90 cm
Common in Britain and Ireland.

IN THE GARDEN

The flowers are visited by small bees and flies, for pollen and nectar, and the seeds are eaten by sparrows, finches and Dunnocks. Not a specific food plant of any moth species, but used by generalist plant-feeders.

IDENTIFICATION

Member of the daisy family, with small dandelion-like flowers. Has tall, thin, upright stems, branched to form loose clusters of flower heads. These are yellow, 10–20 mm across, and have rather few (8–15) ray florets, with no central disc florets. Buds are neat and oval. Leaves are oval and pointed, with toothed edges. Lower leaves may have divisions at their base. Seeds are elongated, 3–4 mm long, and lack a parachute.

CHARACTERISTICS

Annual. Commonly found in hedges, along roadsides and on waste ground. In gardens, often occurs along hedges and beside walls. Lacks the milky sap of many yellow composites. Flowers close in the afternoon, and often stay closed during dull weather.

DANDELION *Taraxacum officinale*

Height up to 20 cm
Widespread in Britain and Ireland.

IDENTIFICATION

Found in grassland, along roadsides and on wasteground. Has flat, bright yellow single flower heads on bare erect stalks. Flowers 35–50 mm across comprise straight-edged ray florets surrounded by rings of green bracts, the outer ones turned down. Hollow stalk and leaves are with filled with milky sap. Leaves form a flat rosette and are lance-shaped, narrowing at the base, but with large, deep, backwards-pointing teeth (*dents de lion* of the common name). Seeds are narrow and crowded, each bearing a parachute of hairs. When ripe, these form the familiar round Dandelion 'clock'.

CHARACTERISTICS

Grows in lawns as well as on cultivated ground. Perennial, flowering April–June, although can be found in any month. Has a strong, deep taproot that re-grows even when

broken. Parachutes are an effective method of seed dispersal by the wind. Seeds are set without fertilisation.

IN THE GARDEN

Flowers are visited for pollen by many insects, including small pollen beetles. Seeds are taken by Goldfinches and sparrows. It is a food of many moth caterpillars, including Large Yellow Underwing, Red Chestnut, Hebrew Character and White Ermine.

COMMON SOWTHISTLE *Sonchus oleraceus*

Height 20–150 cm
Common in Britain and Ireland.

IDENTIFICATION

Medium-height plant. Pale yellow flower heads like a Dandelion, but these are smaller (20–25 cm), bulbous below with green bracts (like a thistle head). Leaves are pointed, toothed and indented, with soft spines. They clasp the stem at the base with pointed wings. Lower leaves are more divided. Seed heads resemble miniature Dandelion clocks.

CHARACTERISTICS

Flowers May–August, but sometimes found later. Annual plant of wasteland and cultivated ground, although sometimes survives the winter. The hollow stems contain milky sap, and seeds are dispersed by wind.

IN THE GARDEN

Flowers are visited by insects, especially for pollen. Seeds are taken by Goldfinches from the heads, and by sparrows, finches and Dunnocks from the ground. It is a food of several moth caterpillars, including Gothic.

NOTE

Prickly Sowthistle, *S. asper*, is also commonly found in gardens. It differs from Common Sowthistle in having much sharper spines and less divided leaves, which clasp the stem at the base in a long, rounded lobe.

YELLOW COMPOSITES

A number of similar-looking composite species with yellow flowers and confusing names occur in gardens.

IDENTIFICATION

Many resemble the Dandelion, although most have a solid rather than a hollow stem.

CHARACTERISTICS

Like Dandelion, the seeds are dispersed by means of parachutes and colonise bare ground. Low-growing leaves allow them to grow on lawns, where they survive mowing.

COMMON CATSEAR

Hypochaeris radicata

Height 20–60 cm
Common in Britain and Ireland.

Flowers June–September in drier grassland and verges. Large, bright yellow flower head (2.5–4 cm), sometimes on branched stalks; outer florets have green underside. Leaves (7–25 cm) form a rosette; they are narrow, lance-shaped, with indented edges (not as deep as Dandelion) and blunt ends. They are narrow at the base, rough and hairy.

AUTUMN HAWKBIT

Leontodon autumnalis

Height 50–60 cm
Abundant in Britain and Ireland.

Flowers later in the season than Common Catsear (July–October), and is found in meadows and along verges. Flower heads are smaller than Catsear (1–3.5 cm across) and a bright golden yellow. Outer florets streaked red beneath. Flowering stems are tall and usually branched. Leaves are hairless and shiny, with deeply lobed edges, resembling Dandelion leaves but with pointed tips. Plant is divided to form several rosettes.

IN THE GARDEN

Flowers are visited by insects, especially for pollen. Seeds are eaten by sparrows and Goldfinches. They are the food for several moths, including Clouded Buff, Small Ranunculus and Marbled Clover, as well as other generalist plant-feeders.

SMOOTH HAWKSBEARD

Crepis capillaris

Height 20–90 cm
Common throughout Britain and Ireland.

Flowers June–September in grassland, walls and on wasteland. Flower heads are 1–1.3 cm across and yellow, with the outer florets reddish beneath. Stem branches to carry several flower heads in a loose cluster.

Leaves are long, shiny, narrow at the base and deeply toothed, growing as a rosette and also carried further up the stem. Upper leaves are smaller, not toothed, and clasping the stem with pointed bases.

MOUSE-EAR HAWKWEED

Hieracium pilosella

Height 20–30 cm
Locally common in Britain and Ireland.

Found May–October in short turf and bare places. Flower heads are 2–3 cm across, pale lemon-yellow, and outer florets may be reddish beneath. Bracts beneath flower head are densely hairy. Stems are shorter than other plants covered here, and support single flower heads. Oval leaves narrow at the base, are hairy, and white and downy beneath; all grow in a basal rosette, with none on the stem. Other stems creep along the ground and form new rosettes.

GRASSES

Grasses are so familiar as the main constituent of lawns that it is hard to appreciate that they are individual flowering plants of several species.

IDENTIFICATION

Individual flowers, or spikelets, are small and narrow, with a number of green parts. They are either close to the stem, or form a loose, open panicle. Long, thin leaves are known as blades. Grasses produce large amounts of pollen, which is carried by the wind.

CHARACTERISTICS

Growing points are not at the tips of the shoots, but at the bases of the stems and leaf blades. This is an adaptation to grazing – if part is bitten off, the plant continues to grow. This makes grasses ideal for mown lawns.

IN THE GARDEN

Long grass provides a home to a community of animals, with Field Voles and many invertebrates living among the stems and roots. Sparrows, finches, mice and voles feed on seeds, and leaves are eaten by Field Voles, and by insects such as grasshoppers and plant bugs. They are also eaten by the caterpillars of various butterflies and moths, especially grass moths from the family Pyralidae.

PERENNIAL RYE-GRASS

Lolium perenne

Height 3–20 cm
Found in most of Britain and Ireland.

Frequently sown as part of the grass mixture of new pastures, and extensively as a lawn grass. Forms loose tufts of narrow, dark green blades, glossy on the upper surface. Spikelets lack stalks, are flat and oval, and are arranged alternately along the stem to form a flat spike. In lawns, it is valued for its toughness and resistance to trampling.

ANNUAL MEADOW-GRASS

Poa annua

Height 1–14 cm
Abundant in Britain and Ireland.

Forms small, compact tufts, with pale or bright green blades. Spikelets are borne on stalks and arranged in a loose, roughly triangular panicle. Unusually for a grass, it is an annual. Continuous seeding means dead plants are constantly replaced.

In gardens, it grows on cultivated soil. Not good for lawns, but grows where there are bare patches.

COUCH GRASS

Elytrigia repens

Height 30–120 cm
Widespread in arable farming areas.

Invasive grass, taller and with slightly broader leaf blades than the other species described. Spikelets are stalk-less and flattened, as in Perennial Rye-grass, but are arranged in the spike at right angles to the stem. Its extensive creeping stems (called rhizomes) can re-grow into new plants if broken.

GARDEN PLANTS

SUNFLOWER *Helianthus annuus*

Height up to 2.4 m
Any soil, but prefers clay loam
Flowers late summer – early autumn

IDENTIFICATION
The most common variety of Sunflower grows as a single-stem plant with a single flower that may be up to 30 cm in diameter. The flowers are usually brilliant yellow with dark brown or purple centre. Leaves are heart-shaped.

CHARACTERISTICS
Annual or perennial. Easily grown from seed and a hardy plant. Some may set naturally around a bird feeder or in parts of the garden were seeds have been 'hidden' by Coal Tits.

Grows well in direct sunlight or partial shade and may need support as the large and heavy flower develops, especially in windy positions. The flower heads will turn to face the sun.

IN THE GARDEN
Most wild species of sunflowers are native to North America. Cultivated Sunflower seeds are

a familiar ingredient of commercial bird food and frequently grown in the British countryside. If left to flower and form seeds naturally they are likely to become food for garden birds, especially Greenfinch. The flowers are also attractive to bees. Smaller varieties can be grown in tubs or window boxes.

HIMALAYAN HONEYSUCKLE *Leycesteria formosa*

(FLOWERING NUTMEG)
Height up to 2 m
Will grow on most soils.

IDENTIFICATION
A medium- to large-sized shrub. Flowering shoots hang over at the tips. Flowers are white, funnel-shaped (15–20 mm), with five petals that hang downwards, surrounded by a long cluster of reddish or purple bracts. Fruits are dark purple berries. Stems are smooth and hollow, swollen at the joints. Leaves are dark green, oval, pointed and arranged in pairs.

September. Flowers are formed on the year's new growth, so they can be encouraged by pruning in the early spring.

CHARACTERISTICS
Introduced as a garden plant from China and the Himalayas. Deciduous, usually dying back in winter. Likes a fertile, well-drained soil in full sun. Propagated from cuttings. Flowers July–

IN THE GARDEN
Flowers are a good source of nectar for long-tongued insects, particularly bumblebees, butterflies and moths. The fruits are eaten by berry-feeding birds, especially Blackbirds.

COMFREY   *Symphytum* species

Height up to 150 cm
Will grow on most soils.

IDENTIFICATION

Tall perennial. Garden varieties usually shorter than wild plants. Flowers grow in a short spiral at the end of the stem, opening in succession, with the youngest at the tip. Flowers (10–18 mm long) are tubular at the base and bell-shaped at the tip. Depending on the species, they are pink (Common Comfrey), pink turning to blue (Russian Comfrey) or white (White Comfrey). There are also cultivated varieties. Leaves are large, oval, pointed and, like the stem, covered in rough hairs.

CHARACTERISTICS

Several species, some occurring wild, have become naturalised in Britain and Ireland. Perennials, flowering April–August depending on the species. White is early, Russian is later. Grows in a range of soils, from damp (Common and White) to drier (Russian). Traditionally a medicinal herb, once widely used as a treatment for breaks and sprains (hence its common name of Knitbone).

IN THE GARDEN

A valuable source of nectar, especially for long-tongued bees. A food plant for the Garden Tiger moth and other plant-feeding insects. It is also a beneficial addition to garden compost.

TEASEL   *Dipsacus fullonum*

Height up to 2 m
Prefers dry soils and a sunny aspect.

IDENTIFICATION

Tall with upright stems. Flowers are borne in large oval heads, up to 8 cm long, densely spiky and with long, curved spines (bracts) cupping the base. They are purplish-pink, flowering around the head in bands. Leaves at the base are oval and stalked, forming a flat rosette on the ground, while the upper leaves are more pointed. Each pair is joined at the base, where they surround the stem in a cup that often contains water. Stems and underside of the leaf's midrib are spiny.

CHARACTERISTICS

A biennial, flowering July–August in its second year, when the leaves at the base wither. The seed heads then stand through the autumn and winter. The water held in the leaf bases often contains the bodies of drowned insects. As these decay, the plant may absorb some of the resulting nutrients. A long-headed variety was once used for combing wool and napping the finished cloth.

IN THE GARDEN

A plant that can be useful in the garden. Flowers are visited by butterflies, bees, hoverflies and other insects. Seeds are famously taken by Goldfinches, whose long pointed bills can reach between the protective spines.

HONEYSUCKLE *Lonicera periclymenum*

May climb to 6 m
Prefers slightly acid (lime-free) soil.

IDENTIFICATION

Climbs with thin, twisted, woody stems. Oval leaves are arranged in pairs along the stem, dark green above and paler beneath. Flowers are long tubes, 35–55 mm in length, with petals that curl open at the tip to expose the stigma and stamens. They are creamy white or pale yellow, often tinged pink, and are arranged in a circle at the tip of the shoot. Fruits are small clusters of red berries.

CHARACTERISTICS

Tolerates shade, but flowers better in sun. Perennial. Climbs trellis, other shrubs, etc. Flowers are heavily scented, mainly in the evening and at night. Flowers June–October. Leaves often show pale galleries of the Honeysuckle Leaf Miner.

IN THE GARDEN

Native species, useful for covering vertical surfaces. Important for night-flying moths, which are its main pollinators. Hummingbird Hawkmoth and long-tongued bumblebees visit by day. Berries are taken by Robins, Blackbirds, Song Thrushes and Blackcaps.

BROOM *Cytisus scoparius*

Height up to 2 m
Prefers acid soils and a sunny aspect.

other insects. Seeds have small sweet-tasting outgrowths, attractive to ants, which carry them off, helping seed dispersal.

IDENTIFICATION

Erect shrub with stems that are thin, straight, green in colour and five-sided in cross-section. Bright yellow flowers, 16–18 mm long, like those of a pea. They are in loose spikes with small trefoil leaves between them. Leaves begin small and simple, and become larger and three-lobed. Fruits are like small, hairy pea-pods, first green and then black.

CHARACTERISTICS

Native Broom is useful in gardens, where coloured cultivated varieties are also grown. Does best in a sunny position. Perennial, but short-lived. Flowers are pollinated by bumblebees. Seeds and foliage are poisonous. Ripe pods burst with a 'snap'.

IN THE GARDEN

Flowers are visited mainly by bees and foliage is eaten by several moth caterpillars and

GOLDENROD *Solidago canadensis*

(CANADIAN GOLDENROD)
Height up to 1.5 m
Prefers well-drained soils.

IDENTIFICATION
A medium to tall plant that grows as a dense clump of single stems. The composite flowers are small (5 mm across) and bright yellow with 10–15 short ray florets. They are arranged in rows along the upper sides of sideways-spreading shoots at the top of the stem. Leaves are narrow and pointed, with two prominent veins. Old stems become woody.

CHARACTERISTICS
The usual species found in gardens was originally introduced from North America. Flowers August–October. Perennial, dying down in winter. Underground stems (rhizomes) spread and expand the clump.

IN THE GARDEN
Useful as a source of pollen and nectar late in the season. Flowers are visited especially by Honey Bees, bumblebees and hoverflies, and also by butterflies such as the Small Copper. It is a food plant of a number of general plant-feeding insects. The dead woody stalks may be used by hibernating insects, so it is worth leaving them standing until spring.

MICHAELMAS DAISY *Aster novi-belgii*

Height up to 1.2 m
Needs a rich soil, well drained but moist in summer.

IDENTIFICATION
Medium height with erect stems that branch towards the tips. A member of the daisy family. Flower heads are 25–40 mm across, with yellow centres (disc florets) and blue ray florets, although garden cultivars may also have white, purple or reddish rays. The heads are borne in rather flat clusters at the stem tips. Leaves are dark green, long and pointed, clasping the stem at their base.

CHARACTERISTICS
Perennial, spreading by underground roots and rhizomes. Introduced to gardens from North America, but also found growing wild. Flowers September–October. Many garden cultivars are available, with different heights, colours and flower sizes. After a few years, plants grow into a thick, extensive clump, which can be split. Woody stems remain standing in winter.

IN THE GARDEN
A useful source of nectar late in the season, for bees, hoverflies and butterflies, especially Small Tortoiseshell and Small Copper. (Not all garden cultivars are of equal value in this respect.) Seeds are eaten by Goldfinches and other seed-eating birds. Leaves are food for general plant-feeding insects. Dead standing stems and seed heads may be used by hibernating insects such as ladybirds if left uncut.

GREAT MULLEIN   *Verbascum thapsus*

(AARON'S ROD)
Height up to 2 m
Prefers well-drained soil and full sun.
Wild in England and Wales but rare in
Scotland and Ireland.

IDENTIFICATION
Tall, striking single spike. Flowers are bright yellow, 15–30 mm across, with five spreading petals and orange stamens. Flowers and buds are densely packed up a considerable length of the upper stem. Leaves and buds have a woolly coating of whitish hairs. The leaves are oval and pointed, forming a large rosette at the base and smaller higher up.

CHARACTERISTICS
Biennial, with only a rosette of leaves on the ground in the first

year. Flowers June–August. Our largest native mullein. Other mulleins, native and introduced, are also cultivated.

IN THE GARDEN
The flowers are visited for pollen and nectar, mainly by bees and hoverflies. The species is also the food of the specialist caterpillar of the Mullein Moth. This is a large, striking caterpillar (up to 50 mm long), whitish tinged with pale green or blue, and with a pattern of yellow bands with black spots.

FOXGLOVE   *Digitalis purpurea*

Height up to 1.5 m
Prefers acidic soils.

IDENTIFICATION
Tall single spike, with dense flowers on the upper part, opening from the bottom upwards.

Each flower is a downwards-pointing tube, 40–55 mm long, expanded at the mouth and narrow at the base. Flowers are light purple or pink (occasionally white), with white and dark spots inside the lip. Leaves are greyish-green, oval and pointed.

CHARACTERISTICS
Familiar native species found throughout Britain and Ireland, and popular in gardens. A rosette of leaves shows in the first year, with the flowering spike appearing a year later. The plant lives for only a few years.

They are pollinated by bumblebees, which crawl up the flower tube, emerge with pollen on their backs, and then transfer it to an older flower where the stigma is receptive. Cone-shaped seed capsules produce large numbers of tiny seeds (estimated at 750,000 a plant). Foxgloves are poisonous, containing toxins that act on the muscles of the heart.

IN THE GARDEN
A source of pollen and nectar for bumblebees. It is the food plant of the caterpillar of the Foxglove Pug moth, and is eaten by a few other insects, including caterpillars of the Lesser Yellow Underwing moth.

HEMP AGRIMONY *Eupatorium cannabinum*

Height up to 120 cm
Prefers damp conditions. In the wild,
widespread in England, Wales and
Ireland, but scarce in Scotland.

IDENTIFICATION

A medium to tall plant. Has stout, erect reddish stems. Flowers form a dense flattish head comprising many clusters of tiny florets. Individual florets are tubular, purple at the base and pink at the tip. The projecting styles are white, creating a pale pink effect overall. Leaves are toothed and completely divided into several narrow, pointed lobes.

CHARACTERISTICS

Perennial, dying down in winter. Grows in damp or wet places, so does well in marshy ground beside garden ponds. Will tolerate some shade, but flowers better in direct sun. Flowers July–September. Leaves resemble those of cannabis, thus its scientific name.

IN THE GARDEN

Flowers are a popular source of nectar for butterflies, including Red Admiral, Peacock, Small Tortoiseshell, Gatekeeper and Holly Blue, and for many bees, hoverflies and other insects. It is the food plant of the caterpillar of the Scarce Burnished Brass, and for a few more generalist moth caterpillars.

FIELD SCABIOUS *Knautia arvensis*

Height 25–100 cm
Prefers well-drained soil and a
sunny position.

IDENTIFICATION

Erect stems and round, slightly domed flower heads, 30–40 mm in diameter. Flowers are pale blue or lilac (cultivated scabious may be pink, crimson, purple, cream or yellow). Individual flowers, or florets, have four petals, these unequal in size: the outer florets are larger (sometimes much larger) than those towards the centre. Leaves are slightly hairy, those at the base elongated with short stalks and forming a rosette. Stem leaves are more elongated, with a few long lobes along the sides. Stem is covered with fine bristles.

CHARACTERISTICS

Native to Britain and Ireland, often grown in gardens (most other cultivated species and varieties of scabious belong to the genus *Scabiosa*). Perennial. Prefers an open, sunny situation and well-drained lime-based soil. The stamens protrude above the florets, where they deposit pollen on the heads of feeding insects. The seeds, hidden within the sepals, are quite large (5 mm long) and hairy. Flowers July–September.

IN THE GARDEN

A good source of food for butterflies and bees (many of the garden varieties are also useful in this respect). The leaves are eaten by general plant-feeding insects, and the seeds are eaten by sparrows and finches.

RED VALERIAN *Centranthus ruber*

Height up to 80 cm
Grows well in poor, limy soil.

IDENTIFICATION

Erect plant with a branched stem. Has red flowers, although these are occasionally white or pink. Each flower is a small, thin tube, about 5 mm across and 8–12 mm long, opening up as five small petals. Below is a thin spur, 4–7 mm long. Individual flowers make up a loose, oval flower head. Leaves are oval and pointed, narrowing into a stalk. The upper leaves have toothed edges and

no stalks, clasping stems at their bases. Leaves and stem are a pale blue-green colour.

CHARACTERISTICS

Introduced as a garden plant from the Mediterranean, but also found naturalised on cliffs, old walls, banks and wasteground. Perennial, mainly dying back in winter. Scented flowers attract long-tongued insects, which reach the nectar. Stamens protrude above the flower so that pollen is removed on the heads of insects, and transferred to an older flower where the stigma is receptive. Flowers June–August. The fruit produces a single seed, which has a cluster of hairs so that it is easily dispersed by the wind.

IN THE GARDEN

Attracts butterflies and Hummingbird Hawkmoths by day, and other moths at night.

LUNGWORT *Pulmonaria officinalis*

Height 10–30 cm
Prefers moist but well-drained soil.

IDENTIFICATION

Resembles a low-growing comfrey, but with short flower spikes. Flowers are tubular at the base, 15 mm long, with five petals expanding into a bell shape. These start as pink buds and turn through purple to blue, and are arranged as a loose cluster at the top of the stem. Leaves at the base are oval and pointed, almost heart-shaped, with winged stalks. Stem leaves lack stalks. All are dark green and covered with pale round blotches. Both leaves and the stems are rough and hairy.

CHARACTERISTICS

A continental species introduced to gardens, but occasionally found naturalised. Other species and varieties are cultivated. A perennial, spreading by creeping underground shoots. Flowers March–May. Stamens are hidden inside the tubular part of the flower, where they are reached by nectar-seeking bumblebees. Fruit comprises four nutlets, hidden at the base of the sepal tube. Prefers 'woodland' conditions and grows best in humus-rich soil and tolerates shade.

IN THE GARDEN

The value of this plant for wildlife is its very early flowers, which provide an important source of nectar for emerging queen bumblebees and early Honey Bees. Early-flowering cultivated varieties can also be useful.

MINTS *Mentha* **species**

Height 15–100 cm
Prefer well-drained soil.

IDENTIFICATION

Small- to medium-sized plants, with erect, branched stems. Flowers are pink or purplish, in dense heads and interspersed with small leaves at the tip of the stem. Individual flowers are small and tubular, with small spreading petals at the mouth. Leaves are oval and pointed, triangular or elongated, with small teeth, and are arranged in opposite pairs. Stems are square in cross-section.

CHARACTERISTICS

Known for a strong mint scent when crushed but smell differs in some species. Native Water Mint, *M. aquatica*, can usefully be grown around a pond. Garden mints are usually introduced species or cultivated varieties grown as culinary herbs. Perennials that spread by vigorous underground rhizomes, and may be invasive. Flower July–September.

IN THE GARDEN

A useful source of nectar for bees, but also occasionally for butterflies. Most varieties are useful if the plants are allowed to flower.

NOTE

Catmints (genus *Nepeta*) grow close to the ground. Their flowers are usually pale blue and borne in small clusters. They flower earlier than *Mentha* species and have a longer season. Catmints are also a useful nectar source for bees and are the food plant of the Mint Moth.

LAVENDER *Lavandula angustifolia*

Height up to 50 cm
Prefer well-drained soil.

IDENTIFICATION

Small, dense shrub. Flower spikes are borne on thin straight stems that grow above the foliage. Flowers are blue or purple, arranged tightly in a vertical group close to the stem. Each is about 14 mm long, the base comprising a thin tube that opens at the mouth as five petals. Of these, two join to form a hood at the top, and the three remaining smaller petals form a lower lip. After flowering, elongated oval fruits persist on the stem for several months. Leaves are long, narrow and greyish green, with edges folded underneath.

CHARACTERISTICS

A well-loved garden plant, popular for its scent. Most garden varieties are this species, or French Lavender, *L. dentata*. Features such as the coating of scaly grey hairs and the rolled narrow leaf prevent water loss in dry conditions. It also contains fragrant oil. Flowers July–September.

IN THE GARDEN

Needs trimming after flowering to maintain the shape and quality of the flowers for the following year. A source of nectar for bees and butterflies; its midsummer flowers are well timed for the new generation of Small Tortoiseshells. The seeds are taken by sparrows and finches, particularly Bullfinches.

BARBERRY *Berberis vulgaris*

Height up to 2.5 m
Will grow in most soils.

IDENTIFICATION

A dense shrub. Flowers are bright yellow, small (6–8 mm) and globular, hanging from the twigs in bunches. They develop bright orange-red, sausage-shaped berries. Leaves are small and oval, dark green and glossy, with small sharp teeth along the edge. (Other forms are cultivated for their different foliage.) Twigs are yellowish, with grooves or ridges. They bear very sharp, strong spines.

CHARACTERISTICS

Continental species, probably introduced as a hedge or garden plant. Other species and cultivars are grown. Deciduous, but some are evergreen. Flowers in May–June. The stamens flick inwards if touched at the base, ensuring contact with visiting insects.

IN THE GARDEN

Flowers provide nectar for bees and small insects. Berries are eaten by Blackbirds, thrushes and Robins. The dense, spiny bush is a good nesting site for Blackbirds, Song Thrushes, Dunnocks and even Long-tailed Tits.

FIRETHORN *Pyracantha atalantioides*

Typical mature bush is 1.8 m high
x 1.5 m wide
Grows in most well-drained soils.

IDENTIFICATION

A commonly grown evergreen garden shrub; with small, oval, dark green leaves and strong fierce spines. Groups of small white flowers appear in early summer and clusters of red berries form in late summer. There are various other species and varieties of *Pyracantha*, with berries varying from scarlet to orange and also yellow.

CHARACTERISTICS

This shrub may grow as a dense, free-standing bush or be planted as a hedge. Most commonly it is grown against a wall where it can reach a height of 4.5 m.

IN THE GARDEN

The dense cover is good for nesting birds such as Blackbirds and Song Thrush. The flowers are attractive to a variety of insects including flies, beetles and bees. The colourful berries can be an important winter food for thrushes, even migrant species such as Redwing and Fieldfare.

TREES AND SHRUBS

HAZEL *Corylus avellana*

(COBNUT)
Height to 6 m
Common across England, Wales, Ireland and the lowlands and west coast of Scotland and the Hebrides.

IDENTIFICATION

Bushy shrub that only rarely develops into a tree. Best known for the yellowish 'lamb's tail' catkins of late winter, which are groups of male flowers that appear before the leaves, and mostly shed their pollen in February. The female flowers are tiny, red bud-shaped growths. Leaves are quite coarse, almost round with a blunt point, and appear in April and turn yellow in autumn. Fruit is the well-known hazel or cob nut, which starts green and becomes brown as it ripens in late summer. It is contained in a ragged green case.

CHARACTERISTICS

Grows in woodland edges and hedges, and sometimes also planted in gardens for its popular nuts. Hazel was once important in the rural economy, and extensive copses of the species once grew in many parts of Britain to provide poles or rods for fencing and other local crafts. The shrubs were cut almost to the ground in a seven-year rotational process known as coppicing, in which a seventh of the copse was cut each year to ensure an annual supply of wood. Even today, Hazels in woodland and along old hedge-lines may be ancient coppiced shrubs.

IN THE GARDEN

Hazel is an interesting plant to introduce to a garden. Cultivated varieties produce larger nuts, although the simple native variety is probably of greatest benefit to wildlife overall. Hazel can be introduced to a mixed garden hedge or can even be used for a whole hedge. Alternatively, it may be planted as a single specimen shrub. It can be cut regularly to produce pea- or bean-sticks, or for small timber to add to a log pile.

The foliage is eaten by a number of moth caterpillars, including the Pale Eggar, Large Emerald and Winter Moth. The nuts may be taken by crows such as Jays, and Nuthatches, Great Spotted Woodpeckers and Grey Squirrels, and by smaller mammals such as mice and voles.

NOTE

Blackthorn, *Prunus spinosa*, is a thorny shrub that is widespread in the English, Welsh and Irish landscapes, but is more local in Scotland. It produces the frosty purple berry known as the sloe. It is frequently found alongside roads and is most obvious in early spring, when its white blossom smothers the hedgerows. Blackthorn can be introduced to a larger garden, where it will attract insects and may become a home for nesting birds. However, it does produce suckers and in some locations may be difficult to control.

SILVER BIRCH *Betula pendula*

Height to 25–30 m
Common in Britain, although more
thinly distributed in upland Scotland
and in Ireland.

Older trees may attract gall wasps, which lay their eggs in the growing buds. The tree then reacts to this invasion by growing distorted bushy twigs and branches, commonly known as 'witches' brooms'.

IN THE GARDEN

Windblown seeds may arrive in gardens naturally. The species is relatively easy to grow on light soils and is suitable for all but the smallest gardens. More than 500 species of invertebrates, including many moths, have been known to feed on this tree, and over 100 of these are exclusive to the species. When mature, Silver Birches may provide nest sites for woodpeckers and other small birds may sometimes nest in their branches, especially in a fork. The seeds are an important food supply for many birds such as tits, Goldfinches, Redpolls and Siskins, which will feed acrobatically on the hanging branches, and sparrows and finches, which will pick them up from the ground. The decaying wood from Silver Birch often supports fungi, so it is good to leave fallen branches *in situ*.

IDENTIFICATION

Graceful deciduous tree with white paper-like bark, sometimes peeling on older trees, blackish protrusions (especially around the base of old trees), and shiny reddish-brown twigs that droop gently at the tips. Young trees have reddish bark. In late winter, branches may appear purplish before the leaf buds break open. Leaves have been likened to an 'ace of spades' shape with small serrations along the edges, and they turn yellow before falling in autumn. Yellowish 'lamb's tail' catkins form in early spring, with the male flowers hanging down and the females initially more upright.

CHARACTERISTICS

A tree of light, sandy and acidic soils. In the countryside it sometimes forms pure woodland, or it may occur singly within a wood of other species. Relatively fast-growing and popular with wildlife. Does not produce dense shade and therefore other plants will grow in its shadow. Its tiny seeds have small papery wings and form within the ripening catkins during the summer. They are released in large numbers in late summer and autumn, and may be carried long distances on the wind.

CULTIVATED APPLE   *Malus domestica*

Height to 10 m
Common in gardens throughout
Britain and Ireland.

IDENTIFICATION

Familiar yet highly variable tree, with rather small, broad, rounded leaves that have a blunt point and downy underside. Flowers (blossom) in spring are pale pink, becoming white, and grow in small clusters. Small green fruits develop in summer and ripen from late summer through autumn depending on the variety. Some varieties remain green while others turn red.

CHARACTERISTICS

A relative of the wild Crab Apple, *M. sylvestris*, which is relatively common in England, Wales, parts of Ireland and southern Scotland. The fruits of the cultivated form are much larger than those of the wild form and vary in size, colour and taste. The cultivated form needs to cross-pollinate with another variety to produce fruit, and the seeds may revert to a different type altogether. There are thought to have once been more than 6,000 varieties of apple, and although many of the old varieties have died out there may still be around 2,000 surviving today.

The shape of the tree may vary depending on the way it is trained and pruned. Aside from varieties that grow as bushes or low trees, and larger specimens that are more traditional tree shapes, the Cultivated Apple may be grown as a fan or espalier.

IN THE GARDEN

This is a win-win species for the wildlife gardener: it is a tree that produces an edible crop for humans, and there is usually enough fruit left over to supply birds such as thrushes with food in autumn. Even butterflies like the Red Admiral will be attracted to the rotting fruit if it is left where it falls.

Mature trees may provide nesting sites for birds, and if trained to grow along a wall, will not only look particularly attractive but are more likely to be used by species such as Spotted Flycatchers. Cultivated Apple trees are also host to a number of moths, especially the Winter Moth and Codling Moth. The female Codling Moth flies in May and lays her eggs on the outside of the newly formed fruit. The caterpillars then eat their way into the soft flesh, and there they eat and grow until they are ready to emerge before the apple falls.

DOGWOOD *Cornus sanguinea*

Height to 4 m
Widespread in England, Wales and
southern Scotland; local in Ireland.

IDENTIFICATION

It is usually the red stems in winter and early spring that draw attention to this plant. The four-petalled flowers are borne in rounded clusters and are creamy white. Berries appear in bunches in late summer and are small and black. Leaves are oval with obvious veins and a point at the tip. They grow on stalks on opposite sides of the stem and are often colourful in autumn, turning red before falling.

CHARACTERISTICS

In the wild, Dogwood is a shrub of woods, thickets and hedges. Leaves form early in the year and the clusters of flowers follow later in June, but are not as obvious as other wild blossom and have a rather unpleasant scent. The berries start green and later become glossy black. The white wood was traditionally used for making meat skewers.

IN THE GARDEN

Ornamental species of Dogwood are available, but these are less beneficial for wildlife than the native plant. The flowers are attractive to small beetles and flies, and the berries, although bitter to humans, are popular with birds such as Blackcaps and Blackbirds. The bush can become large, but is relatively easy to control by cutting it back in late winter. Try to stagger pruning by cutting back some branches one year and the remainder the next. The new shoots grow quickly from the old wood and are a deep red, especially when young.

GUELDER ROSE *Viburnum opulus*

Height to 4 m
Widespread in England and Wales; local
in Scotland and Ireland.

IN THE GARDEN

An attractive-looking shrub that is also useful to wildlife: its flowers are visited by insects and its berries eaten by birds. The berries ripen slowly, providing food in the coldest months of the year for thrushes (especially Mistle and Song Thrushes) and Bullfinches, the latter taking them for both the ripe flesh and seed. Privet Hawkmoth caterpillars have been observed feeding on this plant.

IDENTIFICATION

Shrubby deciduous bush or small tree. Leaves become red before falling in autumn, and have three or five lobes and a ragged edge, not unlike those of a maple. In May–July it produces white flowers that grow in flat-topped clusters and are sweet-smelling. The brilliant white outer flowers are large but sterile, while the inner flowers are smaller, duller and pollen-producing. Bunches of waxy red berries ripen in autumn and may remain on the bush into the winter.

CHARACTERISTICS

Found in fens, hedgerows and woodlands, and also in gardens. It is the wild ancestor of the cultivated 'Snowball Tree' of parks and gardens.

GOAT WILLOW *Salix caprea*

(PUSSY WILLOW, GREAT SALLOW)
Height to 10 m or more
Common and widespread in Britain;
more scattered in Ireland.

IDENTIFICATION
May grow into a tree but more often occurs as a bushy shrub. Best known for its male flowers, which start life as the silky grey 'pussy willows' of early spring, breaking open before the leaves and later becoming yellow-green catkins. Yellow female flowers release white tufted seeds that float on the wind in May. Leaves are oval with well-marked veins, are often wrinkled and grow on reddish stems. They are downy at first and soft to the touch, and remain downy on their undersides.

CHARACTERISTICS
A plant of wetlands and riverbanks, although it also occurs widely in drier localities, including woodland margins and even field hedges. The species is fast-growing and its shoots can increase in length by as much as 4 cm a day. Like other willows it was often traditionally coppiced or pollarded to remove its branches, although these had relatively little commercial value as they are more brittle than those of

many other willow species. The plant is used in the religious festival of Palm Sunday in some countries, where pussy willow is traditionally used instead of palm fronds at church services a week before Easter.

IN THE GARDEN
This is a good plant for insects. Bees and other insects are attracted to its flowers in early spring, and many caterpillars feed on its leaves, especially the Feathered Thorn, Puss Moth and Red Underwing.

The Goat Willow may be planted as a bush in a hedge-line to screen an untidy feature such as a compost pile. Alternatively, it can be allowed to grow naturally into a large bush or tree, but may be cut back regularly, which will encourage new shoots. Traditionally, the species was cut back to 50 cm above ground level to form a stool (coppice), but if the plant resembles a tree, the branches should be pruned back to the trunk (pollard).

NOTE

The Weeping Willow, *S. babylonica*, was originally introduced from China, but the familiar ornamental tree of parks and larger gardens is usually a hybrid. It provides few natural benefits and grows rapidly to a very large size, so its introduction to the garden needs careful consideration.

ASH *Fraxinus excelsior*

*Height to 37 m
Common in Britain and Ireland
except on the highest land.*

IDENTIFICATION

Deciduous tree that is usually the last to come into leaf. Trunk is quite smooth and greyish when young, but ridged and furrowed as it gets older. Mature trees are tall and slender, and form dominant landmarks in the countryside. The large leaves are dark green, with 5–13 leaflets that

have slightly serrated edges and grow in pairs along a single stalk, giving the tree a feathery appearance. In autumn they become pure yellow before falling. The following year's leaves at this time are obvious as small, hard, pointed black buds that become larger and blacker as winter progresses, finally opening in April or even May. The flowers, which appear before the leaves, are tufts of small catkins that become green in March or April. The fruits, known as keys, have paper-like wings and hang in bunches through the autumn and winter, until about March.

CHARACTERISTICS

Since the decline of the English Elm the Ash has become a much more significant tree in the landscape in many parts of southern Britain. Ashes have bisexual flowers, some of them hermaphrodite, while others, even on the same tree, are either male or female. Pollination is by the wind and not by insects. The Ash keys float freely on the wind, and young trees germinate easily, even in gardens.

IN THE GARDEN

29 species of invertebrates are dependent on the Ash, which is considerably less than most other native trees. However, it is relatively fast-growing and the keys are an important food for Bullfinches. A healthy standard also provides useful structure to a garden, a site for nest boxes, and a place for garden birds to forage and even occasionally nest.

Traditionally, Ash trees were managed by either pollarding (removing the upper branches) or coppicing (sawing off to leave a 'stool' just above ground level). In both operations, new vigorous growth springs up, producing straight poles that were traditionally used in the countryside. This management could also be used in a garden setting.

ASH DIEBACK

Hymenoscyphus fraxineus

This fungal disease was first recorded in Britain in 2012. It is spread by spores from the fruiting bodies of the fungus produced on fallen Ash leaves. On affected trees, the shooting tips of twigs become black and shriveled. Young trees die quickly, while older trees appear initially resistant, but then become weaker and die. It is not known what the long-term effect will be across Britain. New cases should be reported to the Forestry Commission.

ROWAN *Sorbus aucuparia*

(MOUNTAIN ASH)
Height to 18 m
Found throughout Britain and Ireland, although less common in central England.

IDENTIFICATION

Graceful medium-sized deciduous tree that tends to grow singly rather than forming woods or copses. In the wild it often occurs in rocky places, where it benefits from peaty soil. The bark is shiny grey-brown. Leaves are composed of several leaflets with serrated edges, each leaflet oval and slightly toothed. It is not particularly colourful in autumn. In spring it produces clusters of small creamy-white flowers that give off a rather acrid scent. Berries set during the summer and are at first green, turning orange and finally red as they ripen.

CHARACTERISTICS

Rowan is a popular amenity tree, with several cultivated varieties, some of which have orange (not red) berries. In the countryside it is often associated with wild places, such as the edges of moorland and upland crags. Here it will sometimes grow amongst rocks where there appears to be little soil and no other plants, and it can even survive the ravages of grazing sheep. In Scotland and Northern England it is reputed to have been planted close to cottages to deter witches.

IN THE GARDEN

This is a good tree for the garden as it grows relatively quickly and is not too large. Seeds may arrive naturally in bird droppings. More than 150 insect species have been recorded feeding on Rowan, 14 of which are exclusive to the species. The flowers are pollinated by insects, especially flies, which are attracted to the heavily scented blossom. The red berries are popular with many birds, and the trees are usually stripped of their fruits very quickly. Starlings are especially attracted to them, but Blackbirds, Song Thrushes and Mistle Thrushes will also search out these trees.

The berries are rich in vitamin C and are used in jam-making, although in the wildlife garden the fruits are best left on the tree to help birds, especially juveniles, survive. Any berries remaining into the winter become increasing valuable as other natural food sources are used up. If you are especially fortunate, winter migrants such as Redwings, Fieldfares and even Waxwings from northern Europe may descend and devour a late crop.

ELDER *Sambucus nigra*

Height to 10 m
Common in Britain and Ireland
except in upland areas.

IDENTIFICATION

Deciduous shrub that usually grows as a bush, although some plants have the proportions of a small tree. Bark of older plants is rugged and fissured. Dark green leaves have five or seven leaflets: one large leaflet, plus two or three smaller ones on either side of the stalk, opposite each other. They have a rather unpleasant smell, and they turn yellow and fall earlier than those of many other native shrubs. In May and June the bushes may be covered with tiny white flowers, which grow in large, flat-topped clusters. The green fruits gradually turn red and then black as they ripen in early autumn.

CHARACTERISTICS

Elder often grows on disturbed ground and may be the first shrub to colonise a site that is newly cleared. Although it grows in hedgerows, it is not a traditional hedging plant, being too brittle to be properly stock-proof.

The seeds contained in the berries are carried by birds, and it is not unusual to find self-set Elders growing as garden 'weeds'. Mammals also carry the seeds; in the countryside Elder bushes are often associated with Badger setts, the seeds having germinated in the latrines close to the sett entrances. Elder also survives grazing by Rabbits, as they do not eat the young plants. Both the flowers and fruits are frequently used in wine-making, and the plant has a long tradition in folklore and magic.

IN THE GARDEN

The Elder has considerable wildlife value, but it is not suitable for very small gardens. However, where there is space it makes a useful addition. It provides nectar for insects in spring, and in summer small birds search for tiny invertebrates among its leaves and branches. In autumn its berries are an important food for many birds, including Starlings and thrushes. Warblers such as Blackcaps also eat the berries before their autumn migration. Even butterflies like the Red Admiral are attracted to overripe berries.

HAWTHORN *Crataegus monogyna*

(MAY)

Height to 15 m
Common throughout Britain and
Ireland except on the very highest hills.

IDENTIFICATION

Familiar and variable thorny species that will grow into a small, rounded tree if left alone. More often it is a dense shrub or is clipped into a traditional farmland or roadside hedge. It flowers mainly in May (hence its alternative common name). The fragrant white blossom is made up of many individual flowers that grow in a cluster and turn pink as they fade. Leaves form before the flowers and are relatively small, with three or five distinct lobes. The red berries contain a single seed and form in late summer. The smooth trunk of young trees becomes more rugged and fluted with age.

CHARACTERISTICS

Hawthorns naturally grow thickly with intertwining branches, which not only explains why they are popular for hedging, but also why they are good for wildlife, especially nesting birds. The species has a long tradition in our countryside and is the tree most often mentioned as marking Anglo-Saxon boundaries. There is also evidence that it was grown in gardens during the Roman occupation of Britain.

IN THE GARDEN

While Hawthorn may not be a natural choice for the garden, it is well worth considering this species for hedging. As well as attracting insects to its blossom, and birds for nesting and to eat its berries, it has the additional benefit of being thick and thorny, hence providing security. It may be left to grow as a bush or tree, or cut regularly. If you do prune it, cut alternate sides annually so that you will continue to have blossom and berries each year, and avoid cutting it when birds may be nesting.

If you decide to establish a Hawthorn hedge, it is worth taking professional advice and having it laid properly – the process requires partly cutting through the main stem, pulling it back at an angle and fixing it in place. The final result will be an attractive and very dense hedge. Ornamental varieties are less useful.

> **NOTE**
> The very similar Midland Hawthorn, *C. laevigata*, is found mainly in southern and central England and will hybridise with the common Hawthorn. It is less thorny and its leaves are shinier, with generally only three lobes. The flowers do not fade to pink, and they have two styles in their centre from which two seeds (rather than the single seed of Hawthorn) develop.

PEDUNCULATE OAK *Quercus robur*

(ENGLISH OAK)

Height to 40 m
Common in most of Britain and Ireland,
except on the highest hills.

IDENTIFICATION

Tall, broad, rounded tree. Familiar, lobed oblong leaf has almost no stalk and turns yellow-brown in autumn. Male and female flowers grow on the same tree, after the first leaves have started to open in April and May. Male flowers hang down as yellowish-green catkins while the female flowers are upright and borne on shorter stalks. Acorns develop from the female flowers and several grow on a long stem. Trunk becomes furrowed and gnarled with age, and attains a huge girth.

CHARACTERISTICS

No other British tree has as many invertebrates dependent on it as the Pedunculate Oak. Gall wasps lay their eggs in the developing tissue of new shoots and the tree reacts by forming a gall. The slightly spongy oak apple is a gall that looks more like a fruit; marble galls are hard and round; spangle galls form on the leaves, currant galls on the catkins (see p127), and knopper galls deform the symmetry of acorns, sometimes taking them over completely. Inside the galls, the wasp larvae develop until they are ready to tunnel out.

Tortrix moth larvae are looper caterpillars that may decimate the leaves of the Pedunculate Oak in some years. Luckily, the tree is resilient enough to withstand these occasional insect attacks. The caterpillars are food for tits and other birds, and even those that escape by dangling on their silken threads may be snatched by a passing Swallow.

IN THE GARDEN

It is an ambitious gardener who introduces this tree, given that its maximum value is likely to be 100 years after planting. It is also totally unsuitable for most gardens, given the proportions it will eventually reach. Nevertheless, in larger gardens it has a place both now and in the future, and some gardeners may be fortunate enough to inherit a Pedunculate Oak from previous occupants.

Little management is needed aside from prudent pruning. The tree scores highly for insects, these feeding on its foliage and using the fissured bark for hiding and hibernating. The acorns attract iterant Jays in autumn, and mature trees provide nesting and feeding sites for many birds, from woodpeckers to warblers.

NOTE

The Sessile Oak, *Q. petraea*, is very similar to the Pedunculate Oak, but is more often found in the north and west, especially in Wales and Ireland. Its leaves grow on longer stalks but the acorns it produces are almost stalkless.

HOLLY *Ilex aquifolium*

Height to 23 m
Widespread, though most plentiful in the west; only locally distributed in Scotland under 300 m.

IDENTIFICATION

An evergreen species that is usually seen as a dense bush but may form a tall tree. The familiar glossy, prickly leaves are slightly curled or twisted. Those that grow higher on the tree have fewer prickles and some are completely oval with no prickles at all. The tiny white flowers have four petals and grow in bunches. They appear May–August, and male and female flowers usually occur on different trees. Berries form only on the female bushes and ripen in late autumn.

CHARACTERISTICS

A valuable wildlife plant, providing food and shelter for many creatures, including the Holly Blue butterfly, which lays its first brood of eggs on this species. Holly leaves have a very high calorific value, and the tops of trees were once lopped in winter to provide cattle feed. Being broadleaved but evergreen is an unusual characteristic among British trees, and it presents the problem of moisture potentially being lost through the leaves during cold spells in winter, when the ground is frozen. The plant has overcome this by evolving leaves that have a tough, waxy coat, which helps prevents water loss.

IN THE GARDEN

The Holly is a good addition to any medium-sized or large garden. It can, of course, be used for Christmas decorations, but its chief benefit in terms of wildlife is that the flowers attract pollinating bees and flies, and the berries attract thrushes and other birds. A wide variety of Hollies are available to the gardener, so care is required to select berry-producing (female) plants. Choosing the native type is probably the best way to ensure maximum wildlife value. The plants may be left to grow into standards or can be incorporated into a hedgerow and lightly trimmed annually. As with other shrubs used for hedging, cutting the sides of the hedge in rotation will help the development of berries the following year.

FUNGI AND NON-FLOWERING PLANTS

STINKING PARASOL   *Lepiota cristata*

(STINKING DAPPERLING)
Diameter 3–8 cm, height 2–8 cm
Widespread on lawns, pasture and
woodland paths in Britain and Ireland.

IDENTIFICATION
Rather delicate-looking fungus. Has a slender, pale brown stem, a ring of membrane near the top of the stem and a large cap. Cap is often tilted and has concentric rings of small brown scales and an obviously darker reddish-brown centre. Gills under the cap are whitish but become brown with age. Fungus starts bell-shaped, with the cap flattening out as it matures.

CHARACTERISTICS
A close relative of the Shaggy Parasol that grows in the leaf litter of woods. Found in summer and autumn. It has an unpleasant scent, and while some say that it is quite good to eat, others say it should be avoided.

IN THE GARDEN
Although essentially a woodland species, this toadstool may sometimes appear in gardens and on disturbed ground, where it will help in the decay of leaves and other organic material.

YELLOW STAINER   *Agaricus xanthodermus*

Diameter 8–20 cm, height 5–15 cm
Widespread in Britain and Ireland in
woods and grassy areas.

IDENTIFICATION
Pale mushroom that is almost spherical as it emerges from the ground, but becomes a traditional mushroom shape as it matures, finally having an almost flat cap. Resembles the

Horse Mushroom in appearance: the cap is off-white and very slightly scaly, and the gills under the cap turn from white to pink and finally brown. However, if bruised, the damaged area becomes bright chrome-yellow, especially towards the edges and base. Stem is thicker at the base, which is also often yellow, and is circled by the remains of an obvious membrane that breaks away from the cap as it opens out.

CHARACTERISTICS
A close relative of the mushrooms we commonly purchase for consumption. This species is seen in summer and autumn in grassy places and along hedgerows. It is known to be poisonous to many people and so should be avoided.

IN THE GARDEN
This is not a very common mushroom, but it will sometimes be found in gardens, often on bare soil or short grass. If it is not a hazard to children it can be left, in which case it will probably attract flies and beetles and even be nibbled by small mammals.

SULPHUR TUFT *Hypholoma fasciculare*

*Diameter 4–8 cm, height 4–10 cm
Widespread and common in Britain
and Ireland.*

IDENTIFICATION

Striking fungus that grows in profusion on rotten wood such as tree stumps, in large clumps of 100 or more. Has a bright sulphur-yellow cap, merging into orange or brown at the centre. Stems are variable in length and may be curved; they are also mainly yellow but have a brownish base. Gills on the underside of cap are also yellowish but later turn green or brown. Most of the caps retain their rounded umbrella shape.

CHARACTERISTICS

A succession of different fungi may colonise rotting timber, of which Sulphur Tuft is one of the larger and later species. It grows on all kinds of tree stumps, both coniferous and deciduous. It is variously described as bitter or inedible, so is probably best left alone. May be found year-round.

IN THE GARDEN

A fungus like this is a reminder of the value and interest that lies in rotting wood. Naturally a woodland species, the Sulphur Tuft will grow on a rotten tree stump left in a garden. Such stumps can also provide homes for a variety of small invertebrates and thus increase the garden's biodiversity.

PLUMS AND CUSTARD *Tricholomopsis rutilans*

*Diameter 4–12 cm, height 3–5 cm
Common in Britain and Ireland.*

IDENTIFICATION

Striking and colourful fungus. Yellow with an extensive covering of reddish or purplish scales over most of the cap, especially at the centre. Gills beneath the cap are also yellow, and the yellow stem is mainly covered in fine purplish scales. The cap, as it opens, may be convex or bell-shaped.

CHARACTERISTICS

This fungus clusters on or around the stumps of old conifers and smells of rotten wood. It is usually seen in late summer and autumn.

IN THE GARDEN

Not uncommon in gardens that contain, or have contained, conifer trees. Like other fungi, it plays an important role in the decomposition of old timber and is also likely to attract invertebrates that will help return the rotting wood back to the soil.

FAIRY RING CHAMPIGNON *Marasmius oreades*

Diameter 2–5 cm, height 2–10 cm
Widespread in Britain and Ireland.

IDENTIFICATION

Small, with a flattened cap. Buff coloured with a darker centre to the cap and a longish pale stem. Grows in groups, these forming a circle that gets larger year by year. Often the circle

is disturbed and the result is an asymmetrical pattern, semicircle or even wavy lines. Gills are white or cream. Said to smell of sawdust.

CHARACTERISTICS

This is the common 'fairy ring' of toadstools found on lawns, even those that are quite new, and other areas of short grass. It is generally seen after rain in summer or autumn. Even when the toadstools are not obvious, the area has noticeable rings of poor-quality grass surrounded by lush grass; these are caused by the release of nitrogen from the mycelium (vegetative stage) of the fungus. The species is edible, but care is needed as it is very similar to poisonous species of the genus *Clitocybe*, which often grow in similar areas.

IN THE GARDEN

Unpopular with gardeners as it is difficult to eradicate, but it does little harm and grass grows stronger and greener on the outside of the ring.

HONEY FUNGUS *Armillaria mellea*

(HONEY TUFT, BOOTLACE FUNGUS)
Diameter 4–12 cm, height 5–15 cm
Very common and widespread in woodland in Britain and Ireland.

IDENTIFICATION

Grows in clumps on the trunks and stumps of trees. Yellowish-brown and variable in shape, some with bulbous stems and others tapering off near the base as they grow taller. Cap has some darker scales and opens out to become slightly rounded, sometimes with a dip in the centre or rather wavy in profile. Stem starts pale and becomes reddish-brown with age. Gills start white, later becoming yellow and spotted. Has a strong smell.

CHARACTERISTICS

The Honey Fungus is an aggressive root parasite that attacks many plants, including trees. It spreads through the soil or under bark by means of black bootlace-like rhizomorphs (the fungal equivalent of roots), which may be 3 m or more in length and are able to penetrate plant roots, causing considerable damage.

Wood containing Honey Fungus mycelium may glow faintly in the dark. Can be eaten, but it is known to cause stomach upsets in some people.

IN THE GARDEN

This fungus is a curse of gardeners as it attacks a wide range of trees and other plants. For these reasons it is probably best not to introduce it artificially into a garden.

BONNET MYCENA *Mycena epipterygia*

Diameter 2–5 cm, height 2–10 cm
Common in Britain and Ireland.

IDENTIFICATION

Found in clumps on deciduous wood. Cap may be cone- or bell-shaped as it first emerges, and then expands and flattens out. Colour is variable, from pale grey to pale brown, and it has a paler margin that is distinctly lined. The relatively long, often yellow stems tend to be paler near the cap, and the gills under the cap are whitish at first and gradually become pinkish.

CHARACTERISTICS

Bonnet Mycena is just one representative of the 100-plus delicate *Mycena* fungi found in Britain and Ireland, but is the species that is sometimes found in gardens. It may be seen year-round on tree stumps or fallen branches. Its stem is hollow but quite strong, and if crushed is said to smell quite mealy.

IN THE GARDEN

A wildlife garden will not generally be over-tidy and will probably contain some dead wood,

either in the form of a log pile, fallen branches, or the stumps of dead trees or shrubs. In these conditions fungi have a chance to bring different colour and shapes to the garden, as well as attracting small invertebrates.

SHAGGY PARASOL *Chlorophyllum rhacodes*

Diameter 8–15 cm, height 6–7 cm
Widespread in Britain and Ireland.

IDENTIFICATION

Starts as a smooth reddish-brown ball or oval as it emerges from the ground, and ends up as a long stalk with a nearly flat cap. The latter has dark brown or grey curling, symmetrically arranged scales on a whitish background, except at the centre, where it remains smooth and brown. Stem is long and pale grey. Gills on the underside of the cap are white or cream, but darken with age.

CHARACTERISTICS

Found in shady areas of gardens, often on bare and humus-rich soil, or in open grassy places on moist rich soil and especially around compost heaps. Edible, but perhaps best avoided as it can apparently cause

stomach upsets in some people. Appears in late summer and autumn, and may be associated with conifer trees.

IN THE GARDEN

One of a number of toadstools that appear near compost heaps and that help in the decay of plant material in the soil.

Dryad's Saddle   *Polyporus squamosus*

Diameter 15–35 cm
Widespread where there are trees in Britain and Ireland.

Identification

Hard annual growth on the sides of trees and stumps. Starts as a small semicircular growth and expands until it is almost a complete circle or ellipse. It is supported by a short, hard, pale stem, and is yellow-brown with darker brown marks. Gills on the underside are very pale. General profile is wavy with some of the edges turned down. Has a faint sweetish scent.

Characteristics

One of a group known as bracket fungi. It is found from spring onwards and is apparently edible when young. It grows either high on a trunk or close to the ground on a variety of trees, including Sycamore and English Elm. It has been estimated that this species may release 50–100 billion spores, which are sometimes visible as clouds around the fungus. It is a destructive parasite on living trees, as its white mycelium causes a wet rot under the bark. It was once used to make razor strops, although was less popular for this purpose than some other larger bracket fungi.

In the garden

Dryad's Saddle will only occur in gardens where there are mature trees or where trees have been cut down and the trunks and roots left behind. It is sometimes host to one of our 26 species of fungus beetle.

Varicoloured Bracket   *Trametes versicolor*

(Many-zoned Polypore)
Diameter 4–10 cm
Common in Britain and Ireland.

Identification

One of the most common bracket fungi. Forms a series of overlapping, roughly semicircular caps, which, although thin, are remarkably hard and leathery. They appear initially to have a velvety texture and show a well-defined, multi-coloured pattern of concentric zones of brown, yellow, grey, purple, green and black, generally with a pale cream outer margin.

Characteristics

Found year-round on a variety of species of decaying deciduous wood and timber, and may form large clusters on a tree stump or on dead wood on a log pile.

In the garden

The presence of this fungus indicates that decay is under way and that the wood, whether

natural or sawn, is on its way to being returned to the soil. The wood will also be a target for invertebrates that are agents of decay and natural recycling.

CANDLE-SNUFF FUNGUS *Xylaria hypoxylon*

(STAG'S HORN)
Height 1–7 cm
Common in Britain and Ireland.

IDENTIFICATION

This distinctive fungus has been likened to a snuffed-out candle wick, hence its common name. It is tall, thin and often flattened, and usually branches like a deer's antlers near the top. It grows in clusters. At first it is black at the base, grey in the middle and white at the top, but it becomes blackish all over with age. The stem has a hairy texture, while the tip is powdery with spores. Later on, some black spores are also produced.

CHARACTERISTICS

It may be found in any season of the year on tree stumps and rotting wood, although it is most frequently seen in autumn and winter. It is a flask fungus belonging to the class Pyrenomycetes, meaning 'fire fungi', members of which appear blackened as if burnt. It is not edible.

IN THE GARDEN

Effective conservation management requires a measure of untidiness, such as leaving dead wood where it falls. Dead tree stumps and logs will attract fungi, as these organisms start the essential process of decay. The Candle-snuff is one of the most common fungi of both woodland and gardens.

CORAL SPOT FUNGUS *Nectria cinnabarina*

Diameter up to 2 mm
Widespread in areas with trees in Britain and Ireland.

IDENTIFICATION

Obvious and very distinctive fungus. Comprises tiny cushions that may be bright orange, red or pink. Pushes through the bark of branches and twigs, and is sometimes found on other wooden objects. Usually grows together in large groups.

CHARACTERISTICS

The Coral Spot likes moist conditions and is commonly found on the branches of Sycamore, other maples and other trees, on fallen branches and on other wood such as fences. It is found year-round and grows communally, usually in very large numbers. It is a flask fungus, the hard, colourful cushions each containing a large number of tiny flask-shaped cavities that themselves contain spores that are released when ripe. It is not edible.

IN THE GARDEN

This tiny fungus is common in gardens where there are fallen branches or log piles. It plays a part in the decay and decomposition of dead and dying wood.

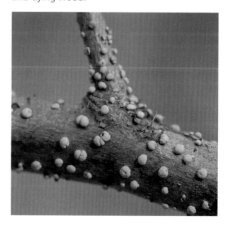

LICHENS

Lichens are simple growths comprising a symbiotic partnership between a fungus and an alga. They form on rocks and building stone, slates, tiles and concrete, and on the bark and twigs of trees.

IDENTIFICATION

May appear flat and crusty, flat and leafy, or branched and mossy. Often grey, but may be greenish, yellow, orange or black. Some grow only 1 mm per year, but they are tolerant of harsh conditions, including drought or extremes of heat or cold.

CHARACTERISTICS

The main body of the lichen is a fungus, within which are the individual cells of an alga (or sometimes a cyanobacterium, or blue-green alga). The fungus takes up nutrients in rainwater, while the alga uses sunlight to synthesise organic materials. This partnership allows the two organisms to live as if they were one.

IN THE GARDEN

Lichens are the first living colonists of many bare surfaces. Because they absorb nutrients from rainwater, some species are particularly sensitive to atmospheric pollution and are thus good indicators of cleaner air.

Lichens are food for a number of moth caterpillars, especially the Common Footman. Some are also gathered by birds as nesting material.

CALOPLACA FLAVESCENS

Spreading
Common in England (especially the south-east) and Wales. Also found in Ireland and southern Scotland.

Flat, crusty growth, usually forming a circle or part of a circle. The centre may be missing. Bright orange, usually with a whitish zone inside the rim. Small, flat, round, orange fruiting bodies occur on the surface. Grows in exposed situations on stone and cement, and especially on roof tiles.

HYPOGYMNIA PHYSODES

Spreading
Common throughout Britain and Ireland.

Grey 'leafy' lichen that is quite resistant to atmospheric sulphur dioxide pollution. Forms either a round or irregular-shaped patch, made up of branched lobes radiating from the centre. These are not flat, but rather crinkly, and may resemble dead seaweed. The lobes are attached by their undersides at the centre to the bark below. They may be curled up at the tips, where the spores develop as a floury powder. Grows on the bark, branches and twigs of trees.

EVERNIA PRUNASTRI

Spreading
Common throughout Britain and Ireland.

'Mossy' form of lichen. Erect or drooping tufts are formed from long, flattened, branched filaments. These are greenish-grey or yellowish-grey with white undersides. The similar-looking *Ramalina farinacea* lacks the white underside.

Moderately tolerant of pollution. Found growing on the bark, branches and twigs of deciduous trees, and on old fenceposts. In the past, this lichen had many uses, including making powder for wigs and as a dye. It is often used by Long-tailed Tits to camouflage their nests.

LIVERWORTS

Liverworts are simple green plants that do not flower. They also lack the conducting tissues, or veins, found in flowering plants. Because they are not resistant to drying out, liverworts are confined to damp, usually shady conditions.

IDENTIFICATION

The most obvious liverworts consist of flattened lobes that are rounded, irregular or strap-shaped, and often divided. Others have a row of thin leaf-like structures along each side. They are attached to the substrate by fine root-like structures called rhizoids.

CHARACTERISTICS

Reproduction takes place in two stages. Male and female cells are produced within small organs that are usually hidden in the plant. Fertilisation requires water so that the male cells can swim to the female cells. The fertilised egg produces a thin stalk bearing a small capsule like a pinhead, which releases spores that are dispersed and can grow into new liverworts.

Some liverworts reproduce by vegetative means. They produce small green structures called gemmae, which resemble seeds but are more akin to tiny buds. These are dispersed mainly by water and grow into new plants.

IN THE GARDEN

These ancient plants deserve a place in our gardens, where they are part of the complete ecosystem we should be trying to create. Tiny invertebrates live on some species or are sheltered by them.

CRESCENT CUP LIVERWORT
Lunularia cruciata

Lobes up to 2.5 cm long and 1 cm wide
Common in Britain and Ireland, although rarer in the north.

Bright green, with overlapping, shiny, rounded or irregular lobes, slightly divided at the tips. The surface is covered with pale, slightly raised spots. The best means of identification are the gemmae cups, if present. These are crescent-moon-shaped flaps, within which are a cluster of green gemmae.

Usually found in gardens. Possibly originally introduced to our region from the Mediterranean with garden plants. Found on stone or brick paths or walls, sometimes on soil or in flowerpots, always in damp, shady parts of the garden. Rarely produces spores, so reproduction is mainly by means of the gemmae.

COMMON LIVERWORT
Marchantia polymorpha

Low and spreading, up to 10 cm long and 1.3 cm wide
Common throughout Britain and Ireland.

Large, branched liverwort. Dark green, but brownish towards the middle of the plant. Surface has conspicuous pale spots, which with magnification are seen to be set in a pattern of hexagons. The small gemmae cups are distinctive, round and cup-shaped. The gemmae within them are disc-shaped.

The species' male and female reproductive organs are distinctive. Both have a long stalk with a flat, parasol-like structure at the top, but the male's has a lobed edge while female's is star-shaped with about nine pointed rays. Male and female grow on separate plants.

In gardens, this species is usually found in flowerpots and greenhouses. It is often introduced with potted plants bought at garden centres.

Mosses

There are many species of moss, which are simple flowerless plants. All are small and will need to be magnified to reveal any detail.

IDENTIFICATION

Mosses have stems, along which are small leaves that have a midrib. The leaves have none of the veins found in higher plants.

CHARACTERISTICS

The male and female parts of the plant are small, hidden at the tip of the stem in a rosette. Once the female has been fertilised, it grows a tall, thin stalk carrying the spore capsule.

IN THE GARDEN

Mosses often colonise bare surfaces and provide an important microhabitat for very small invertebrates. Some are used in nest-building by birds such as tits, by small mammals such as mice and voles, and by bumblebees. In spring, small dry clumps can usefully be left if the lawn is raked. Any control should not involve chemicals.

WALL SCREW MOSS

Tortula muralis

Height 10 mm, diameter up to 50 mm
Common in Britain and Ireland.

Forms small, dense clumps or tufts, rather grey in appearance. Individual plants are single stems with narrow leaves. Each leaf carries a long projection at its tip, which gives the grey appearance. The spore capsule is cylindrical, and is carried upright on a 2 cm-long stalk.

Common in exposed places, including the tops of walls, roofs and paths. Withstands desiccation, when the leaves become narrow and twisted. The capsules are seen in spring and summer.

SILKY WALL FEATHER MOSS

Homalothecium (Camptothecium) sericeum

Forms thick mats on the ground
Common in Britain and Ireland.

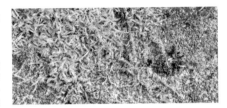

Grows in a thick mat, which is tinged yellow or gold and has a silky texture. Stems are long and creeping, and have many short branches. The leaves are small, with a long point. Spore capsules are oval and are held upright.

Common in gardens on the lower part of tree trunks, stumps and walls, and on footpaths.

DROOPING-LEAVED FEATHER MOSS

Rhytidiadelphus squarrosus

Forms thick mats on the ground
Locally abundant in grasslands in Britain and Ireland.

Pale green or yellowish. Has long branched stems, trailing or erect, but these are weak and need to be supported by other plants. With slight magnification, the species' identity is easily confirmed as the narrow, pointed leaves can be seen to curve backwards along the stem.

Often forms large patches on lawns. Rarely produces spore capsules.

DIY IN THE GARDEN

NEST BOXES FOR BIRDS

Many gardens are short of natural nest sites, especially for birds that nest in holes, so erecting nest boxes can be an important step towards maintaining a viable population. The garden species most likely to use such boxes are shown in the table below. Some species – especially Wrens, tits and House Sparrows – will also use nest boxes as winter roost sites.

MATERIALS

Nest boxes can be made from hardwood, softwood, marine plywood or external plywood, but not chipboard. The wood used should be at least 15 mm thick.

DESIGN

There are no definitive rules for nest box design. Two basic styles are shown here, one with a hole and the other open-fronted, and these can be scaled up to suit larger birds. The sizes given are approximate, although the hole size for smaller species may be critical (see table below). Species such as Blackbirds and Spotted Flycatchers can sometimes be helped by the erection of a simple shelf or platform in a suitable position within a climbing plant.

POSITION

Boxes placed in the open should face north or east, out of full sun and driving rain. Aspect is less important for boxes that are sheltered by trees and bushes. Birds such as Robins, Wrens

A nest box with a hole offers a substitute for the natural tree holes used by tits.

Common bird species that use artificial nest boxes.

Species	Height of box from ground	Box with hole	Open-fronted box	Platform	Internal dimensions (D × W × H)	Hole size
Blackbird	1–4 m		✓	✓	130 × 130 × 300 mm	—
Blue Tit	2–4 m	✓			100 × 100 × 150 mm	28 mm
Great Tit	2–4 m	✓			100 × 100 × 150 mm	30 mm
House Sparrow	2–8 m	✓			100 × 100 × 150 mm	35 mm
Jackdaw	5–10 m	✓			200 × 200 × 450 mm	150 mm
Starling	3–10 m	✓			130 × 130 × 300 mm	52 mm
Spotted Flycatcher	1–3 m		✓	✓	100 × 100 × 150 mm	—
Robin	0–0.5 m		✓		100 × 100 × 150 mm	—
Wren	0.5–8 m		✓		80 × 80 × 80 mm	—

and Blackbirds like to be hidden or have some cover, while tits and sparrows are happy to nest in boxes in the open. Boxes for tree-nesting species such as Jackdaws or Starlings should be among lower tree branches, although these birds are also likely to use buildings, so a box on an outbuilding may be successful if it is positioned high enough. Of the regular garden breeders that will use boxes, only the House Sparrow is colonial and likes to have several similar boxes close together.

CARE OF NEST BOXES

External surfaces should be treated with a water-based non-toxic wood preservative and allowed to dry thoroughly before use. All boxes should be cleared out at the end of the breeding season and cleaned with a five per cent disinfectant solution.

COMMERCIAL PRODUCTS

A wide variety of ready-made boxes are available for purchase. Many of these are sold by specialist providers such as the RSPB, but beware unusual designs that are sold at some garden centres, pet shops and the like. In particular, avoid the combined bird table and 'bird house'.

Open-fronted boxes are used by birds such as Robins and Spotted Flycatchers.

(above) These varieties should be avoided since food on the table may attract predators to a nest.

BIRD TABLES

It is not essential to have a bird table in order to feed garden birds, and not all species will use one anyway. However, a bird table does provide a focus for watching wild birds in the garden, especially if it is positioned where it can be seen from a window. At times it can become the centre of a frenzy of activity, especially if bird feeders are hung from it.

To make a bird table, you will need to attach a flat tray to the top of a pole that stands at a height of 1.5 m. Depending on your carpentry skills, you may or may not choose to add a roof. Ensure the post is firmly bedded into the ground before using the table, and if it has a lip around the edge remember to make gaps or drill reasonably large holes in it to allow for drainage.

Keeping food off the ground helps to deter mice and rats, which might otherwise be attracted to a regular food source, and positioning a table in the open will encourage birds to feed away from cover where cats may lurk. If Sparrowhawks raid your garden, position the table near thick bushes where the birds can take shelter. An open table probably attracts more birds, but a roof helps to protect food and the birds will get used to being under cover.

Tables can become soiled with stale food and droppings, so regular hygiene is essential. Clean and wash the bird table using five per cent disinfectant solution, and move portable feeding stations to a new area every

Taller tables protect both birds and bird food from mammals like foxes.

month to prevent droppings accumulating below. Finally, remember that species such as Dunnocks and Song and Mistle Thrushes are more likely to feed on the ground, so put out some food for them where they can find it (watching out for rodents).

Many garden birds can be watched and enjoyed while they are feeding on a well-stocked bird table.

Hedgehog Boxes

One of the most popular but more elusive garden visitors is the Hedgehog, often seen searching lawns and flower beds after dark on a summer's evening. It is a good idea to try to encourage them to stay around the garden, and the best way to do this is by constructing a Hedgehog house. This may be used by the animals during the daytime in summer, or for hibernating in winter.

There is no single design, but a box measuring approximately 300 × 300 × 200 mm and positioned off the ground on bricks, with a tunnel that slopes down from the entrance, is all that is really needed. The box needs to be made from good-quality timber or exterior plywood, and must have some ventilation/drainage holes drilled in the base. If you prefer to buy a ready-made box, these are available from conservation organisations and commercial suppliers.

To provide insulation, dry leaves should be placed inside, together with dry grass or straw. The box should then be

positioned in a part of the garden where it is unlikely to be disturbed, perhaps under cover in a corner close to where Hedgehogs are known to have a run. An alternative is to build the box into the base of a compost heap, close to one of their feeding areas.

If you are successful in attracting Hedgehogs to your garden, always check that they have not moved into the base of a bonfire, especially in autumn. And if you want to encourage them further you can try feeding them. However, do not put out bread or milk as these are actually harmful; instead, supply these carnivores with a small amount of wet cat or dog food (puppy food is particularly suitable). *See p26.*

A secure Hedgehog box can encourage Hedgehogs to stay in the garden, and perhaps to hibernate or even to breed.

Dense cover surrounding the box is the finishing touch to an ideal nest.

GARDEN PONDS

Prepare the hole by removing sharp stones and placing sand, newspaper or old carpet to protect the lining. Anchor the pond lining with stones or turf around the edge after filling it with water.

Ideal plants for a garden pond	
Submerged	Water Starwort *Callitriche stagnalis* (has some floating leaves)
	Water Milfoil *Myriophyllum spicatum* (has emergent flower spikes)
Floating	Frogbit *Hydrocharis morsus-ranae*
	Fringed Waterlily *Nymphoides peltata*
Waterside	Marsh Marigold *Caltha palustris*
	Water Forget-me-not *Myosotis scorpioides* (some leaves in water)
	Amphibious Bistort *Polygonum amphibium* (some leaves floating, emergent flower spikes)
	Flowering Rush *Butomus umbellatus* (emergent)
	Water Plantain *Alisma plantago-aquatica* (emergent)
Good in marshy edges	Hemp Agrimony *Eupatorium cannabinum*
	Meadowsweet *Filipendula ulmaria*
	Purple Loosestrife *Lythrum salicaria*
Avoid	Large aggressive species such as Reedmace (*Typha*)
	Duckweed *Lemna* spp. (will probably colonise anyway).

A variety of water plants – submerged, floating and emergent – will greatly improve your pond. An adjacent marshy area will provide good insect food plants and cover for amphibians.

Top tips for garden ponds

- Shallow edges allow birds to drink and bathe, and amphibians to get in and out of the water

- A deeper area (minimum 0.5 m) helps aquatic animals survive if the surface of the pond freezes

- A rockery nearby provides daytime hiding places for toads and newts. Spoil from digging the pond can be a basis for this

- Marshy edges allow marshland plants to grow

- Paving along part of the edge allows access without trampling wildlife

- Native species should be acquired from a reputable source

- Long grass near the pond provides hiding places for small creatures

- Emergent plants allow dragonfly nymphs to climb out of the water. A variety of submerged plants provide shelter and breeding places for pond animals

- Branches should not overhang the pond, as their leaves would otherwise fall into the water and break down, causing de-oxygenation

- Partial shade from nearby trees is desirable

- Goldfish should not be introduced to a garden pond, as they will eat native wildlife

- Muddy edges can be used by Song Thrush and House Martin for nest construction

INSECT HOMES

Insects are at the heart of the wildlife garden, being both prey and predator, but despite this, we don't usually do enough to help their survival. Many of them need crevices or holes as shelters, hibernating sites or for breeding. Before the days of double glazing, it was not unusual to find clusters of ladybirds and lacewings around window frames. Today, the same effect can be achieved by leaving herbaceous plants standing in autumn, allowing their hollow stems to become winter homes for these insects.

Commercial insect shelters are available on the market, but it is also possible to make your own. Simply gather 20 or 30 hollow stems of plants that would otherwise be cut down and tie them together securely (if hollow stems are not available, paper drinking straws will probably work just as well). Hang the resulting cluster in a sheltered part of the garden. Hopefully, insects and spiders will crawl inside to shelter in summer or hibernate in winter.

Consider designing your own 'Insect Hotel'. You can choose a size to suit your garden and use recycled material. Use timber off-cuts and old bricks for a framework and in-fill with a variety of materials such as old wool carpet, straw, flower-pots, logs of various sizes, pine cones and perhaps even a few roofing tiles.

Many insects will use tubes or slots for nesting or hibernation sites. Hollow tubes are ideal for nesting solitary bees, but will not attract the hive species.

BAT BOXES

Just as birds lack nest sites in urban areas, so bats often lack suitable cavities to hide away in. Some enter our roof spaces, but others will use bat boxes erected in gardens as summer roosts or for winter hibernation. Certain species of bat, such as the pipistrelles, are colonial when breeding but solitary at other times of year, and six bat species have been recorded using boxes for breeding. This is more likely to occur in a box that has been used as a roost for a few years.

Ready-made bat boxes are available from conservation organisations and commercial suppliers, although it is relatively easy to make your own. The one shown below is a simple box and uses sawn timber that is more than 15 mm thick. Note that the timber should not be treated with wood preservatives. The entrance to the box should be on the bottom, at the back, and should comprise a narrow slit measuring 1.5–2 cm. The rear interior should be rough or have grooves cut into it to allow the bats to hang easily.

The boxes should be positioned well off the ground, as high as 5 m. They should not be in dense cover, so that the bats have a clear flight path in and out. They often also work best when placed in groups, so that the bats can move from one box to another as the temperature changes. One recommended method is to put three boxes up around a single tree trunk, all facing in different directions. Alternatively, they can be placed on the walls of buildings, under the eaves.

Bat boxes have a slot on the underside as the entrance. Grooves on the inside walls allow the bats to cling easily. The box should be about 15 cm across the front.

GLOSSARY

Abdomen The hindmost, and usually the largest, of the three body sections of an insect.

Amphibians A group of cold-blooded animals that are active on both land and in the water. They generally breathe through gills when young and with lungs as adults. Frogs, toads and newts are in this group.

Annual A plant that lives for one growing season.

Antenna (plural **antennae**) Sensory structures on an insect's head.

Anther The part of the male reproductive body of a flower (stamen) that contains pollen.

Arachnids A group of invertebrates that includes the spiders.

Arthropods A subdivision of animals with segmented bodies and jointed appendages (legs). The group includes crustaceans, spiders, insects and millipedes.

Biennial A plant that lives for two growing seasons.

Biodiversity The variety of life on Earth.

Carnivore A meat-eating animal.

Composite A plant of the Asteraceae family (e.g. daisies and thistles) whose flower heads comprise dense clusters of small florets surrounded by a ring of bracts.

Coppicing The traditional method of pruning of trees by removing the trunk down to ground level, or just above it, to encourage new growth to develop.

Cornicle A tube or horn at the rear end of an insect.

Deciduous A tree or shrub that loses its leaves in winter.

Evergreen A plant that keeps its leaves year-round.

Gall A plant growth caused by the presence of a parasite.

Honeydew A sticky, sugary secretion, such as that made by aphids.

Insectivores A group of small mammals that eat mainly invertebrates. In Britain, this group comprises the Hedgehog, Mole and shrews.

Invertebrates Animals that do not have a backbone.

Larva (plural **larvae**) The young stage of an insect, generally appearing very different from the adult form, e.g. a caterpillar is the larva of a butterfly or moth.

Metamorphosis Physical transformation from one stage in a life cycle to another, e.g. from a tadpole to a frog.

Migrant A bird or other animal that moves between different summer and winter grounds.

Mycelium The vegetative part of a fungus.

Nocturnal Active at night.

Nymph The immature form of some insects, especially dragonflies and damselflies.

Omnivorous Feeds on a wide variety of food, both vegetable and animal.

Ovipositor Egg-laying organ at the rear end of some female insects.

Parasite A plant or animal that is dependent on another species for part of, or all of, its life.

Perennial A plant that lives for more than two growing seasons.

Pollarding The traditional method of pruning trees by removing limbs above the trunk and forcing a mass of dense new growth.

Pollen Tiny structures that contain a plant's male sex cells.

Proboscis A feeding appendage, often a tube used for sucking up fluids.

Pupa (plural **pupae**) The life stage that some insects pass through as they develop from a larva into an adult. Known as a chrysalis in butterflies and moths. Generally, the pupa case is hard and is sometimes contained within a cocoon or other protective structure.

Rhizome Underground stem.

Rhizomorph Root-like structure of a fungus.

Roost A place where a bird or bat sleeps, or the act of sleeping.

Sepal One of the usually green, leaf-like outer parts of a flower.

Spore Reproductive body of a fungus, fern, moss or alga.

Stamen The male reproductive part of a flower.

Stigma Part of the female reproductive part of a flower (style) that receives the pollen.

Style The female reproductive part of a flower.

Thorax The middle of the three body sections of an insect, carrying the wings and legs.

Umbellifer Plant whose flowers form in clusters on stalks, resembling an umbrella (also known as the parsley family).

INDEX

PICTURE CREDITS

Key: G = Getty; SS = Shutterstock; NPL = Nature Picture Library; AL = Alamy; i = iStock; UIG = Universal Images Group; BZG = Bildagentur Zoonar GmbH

Front cover & spine M.Lane45/i; **back cover** t I.Redding/i, b Abi Warner/SS; **half title** uleiber/SS, R.P.Long/SS, A.Hakola/SS, Adrian_am13/SS; **4** V.Vasily/SS; **5** kievith/i; **6** coastalrunner/i; **7** troyka/SS; **8** R.P.Long/SS; **9** J.Smalley/AL; **10** t T.Gowanlock/SS, b P.Miguel/FLPA; **11** t A.Fletcher/SS, inset A.Bailey/FLPA; **12** t N&S.Aldridge/FLPA, b G.Ferrari/FLPA; **13** C.Mckie/SS; **14** T.Graham/G; **15** Reinhard/NPL; **16** D.Harris/AL; **17** b S.Dalton/NPL, inset H.Clark/FLPA; **18** b Jausa/SS, inset R.Zwerver/SS; **19** t R.Becker/FLPA , b M.Fowler/SS; **20** t Reinhard/NPL, b I.Arndt/NPL; **22** t HOMONSTOCK/SS, b S.Day/SS; **23** C.Ning/SS; **24** D.Norton/NPL; **25** Arterra/G ; **26** t uleiber/SS, b W.Weenink/FLPA; **27** Grandpa/SS, b KOO/SS; **28** t G.Farkas/SS, b H.Clark/FLPA; **29** t L.Campbell/NPL, b I.Kuzmin/FLPA; **30-31** R.Zwerver/SS (3), MYN/NPL (4); **32** t Erni/SS, b D.Middleton; **33** t N.Hardwick/SS, b R.Zwerver/SS; **34** t P.v Hoof/FLPA, b D.Middleton/FLPA; **35** t S.Dalton/NPL, b E.James/NPL; **36** t W.Howe/SS, b Giedriius/SS ; **37** t P.Maguire/SS, b G.Farkas/SS; **38** t M.Caunt/SS, b F.Cahez/NPL; **39** t Erni/SS, b K.J.Keatley/NPL; **40** t Erni/SS, b C.Rouso/FLPA; **41** M.Gaellman; **42** t FotoRequest/AL, bl M.Olszewski/SS, br Erni/SS; **43** tl BZG/SS, tr MAC1/SS, b A.Astbury/SS; **44** t P.Krzeslak/SS, b T.Graham/G; **45** tl B.Coster/FLPA, tr kojihirano/i; bl&r P.Sawer/FLPA; **46** t&br M.Bridger/SS, bl M.Caunt/SS; **47** t D.Duckett/FLPA, b F.Desmette/FLPA; **48** Diamond Shutter/SS; **49** t garmoncheg/SS, b FotoRequest/SS; **50** t A.Williams/NPL, b R.Wilmshurst/FLPA; **51** t V.Shinde/SS, b S.Jamsa/SS; **52** t Imagebroker/FLPA, b M.Flowler/SS; **53** t W.Osborn/NPL, b C.O'Reilly/NPL; **54** t Gallinago/SS, b N.Hardwick/SS; **55** t B.Coster/FLPA, b garmoncheg/SS; **56** t D.Bevan/NPL , b N.Hardwick/SS; **57** t D.Tipling/NPL, b P.Sawer/FLPA; **58** t D.Usher/FLPA, b A.Rouse/NPL; **59** t G.Hooijer/SS, b Erni/SS; **60** t R.Zinica/SS, b KOO/SS; **61** t F.Christoffers/FLPA, b R.Schols/FLPA; **62** t-b: cmnaumann/SS, P.Miguel/FLPA, YK/SS, A.Sand/NPL; **63** l photomaster/SS, r Varesvuo/NPL, b M.Wilkes/NPL; **64** t W.Osborn/NPL, b P.Clement/SS; **65** t U.Bild/G, b J.Hallett/NPL; **66** t K.Wothe/FLPA, b photomaster/SS; **67** t Varesvuo/NPL, b A.Parkinson/NPL; **68** t V.Tyakht/SS, b I.Duffield/SS; **69** t De Meester/NPL, b H.Brehm/NPL; **70** t Em-Jott/SS, b S.Widstrand/NPL; **71** t M.Gaellman/SS, b S.Dalton/NPL; **72** t T.Brindley/SS, b M.Lane/FLPA; **73** t J.Hawkins/FLPA, b R.P.Long/SS; **74** t-b E.Isselee/SS, muratart/SS, xpixel/SS; **75** t R.Steel/FLPA, b A.Karpenko/SS; **76** t Varesvuo/NPL, b B.Vijeikiene/SS; **77** t S.Knell/NPL, b J.Wenger/FLPA; **78** t B.Natalia/SS, b S.Dalton/NPL; **79** t N.Dowsett/SS, t S.Dalton/NPL; **80** t A.Karpenko/SS, b J.Hallett/NPL; **81** t Tobyphotos/SS, b M.Shuurman/FLPA; **82** Varesvuo/NPL; **83** t A.Hakola/SS, b S C.Brown/FLPA; **84** t M.Mekel/SS, b D.Kjaer/NPL; **85** S.Uryadnikov/SS; **86** t T.Hunt/NPL, b D.Heuclin/NPL; **87** t V.Hulai/SS, b L.Campbell/NPL; **88** t vnlit/SS, l DJTaylor/SS, r N.Upton/NPL; **89** t Pan Stock/SS, l I.Protsiuk/SS, r D.Hosking/FLPA; **90** t&b G.Farkas/SS; **91** t D.Ercken/SS, b T.Marent/FLPA, **92** t rpage11/SS, m E.Giesbers/NPL, b JDCarballo/SS; **93** Photo Fun; **94** t B.Oxana/SS, b J.Herder/FLPA; **95** t H.Lansdown/SS, l Ezume/SS, r G.Braid/SS; **96** t C.Moody/SS, l K.Taylor/NPL, r McPHOTO/AL; **97** t V.Hulai/SS, b E.Isselee/SS, **98** t-b C. Moody/SS, M.Rodrigues/SS, paulrommer/SS; **99** tl M.Cole/FLPA, tr P.R.Sterry/AL, bl pzAxe/SS, br I.Redding/SS; **100** t H.Larsson/SS, l C.Moody/SS, r E.Isselee/SS; **101** t Natural History Museum/AL, b irin-k/SS; **102** t T.Dietrich/SS, b M.Velechovsky/SS; **103** R.Stothard/G; **104** t kezza/SS, m S.Dalton/NPL, b N.Upton/NPL; **105** A. van Dulmen/SS, b P.Clement/NPL; **106** t A. de Wilde/FLPA, b LFRabanedo/SS; **107** M.Fowler/SS; **108** t N.Cattlin/FLPA, m K.Taylor/NPL, b S.Dalton/NPL, **109** t P.Krasensky/SS, b E.Isselee/SS; **110** t Yon Marsh Natural History/AL, UIG/G; **111** t U.Bild/G, b UIG/G; **112** tl B.Barthelemy/NPL, tr P.Pittorino/NPL, m R.Cooper/NPL, bl S.Knell/NPL, br R.Williams; **113** tl R. Williams, tr K.Elsby, m&br R.Hoddinott/NPL, bl M.Graul/SS; **114** t H.Lansdown/SS, b U.Bild/G; **115** t U.Bild/G, b J.Abbott/NPL; **116** t J.Miko/SS, l D.Pressland/FLPA, r J.Hamrsky/NPL; **117** t B.Yeniceri/SS, b K.Taylor/NPL; **118** t N.Upton/NPL, l A.Hakola/SS, r PHOTO FUN/SS; **119** t N.Cattlin/FLPA, b A.Hakola/SS; **120** t E.Ayupov/SS, b A.Sandy/NPL; **121** t D.Pressland/FLPA, b E.Butter/SS; **122** t D.Bindemanis/SS, m M.Velechovsky/SS, b K.Taylor/NPL; **123** t J.Chua/SS, b J.Aalbers/SS; **124** t SunTime/SS, m E.R.Harold/SS, b Visuals Unlimited/NPL; **125** l I.Redding/SS, r D.Vesely/SS, b J.Visser/SS; **126** t skynetphoto/SS, l thatmacroguy/SS, r Sarah2/SS; **127** t L.Campbell/NPL, b E.Bantin/SS; **128** l M.Cole/FLPA, r Tomatito/SS; **129** t E.Kartis/SS, b E.Philipps/SS; **130** t Arco Images/AL, m H.Paves/SS, b R.

Becker/AL; **131** t E.Isselee/SS, m G.Farkas/SS, b H.Francic/SS; **132** t A.G.A/SS, l S.Robinson/SS, b thatmacroguy/SS; **133** l alsutsky/SS, r Meul/NPL; **134** t Gecko1968/SS, m A.Hakola/SS, b R.Becker/FLPA; **135** t M.Ruckszio/SS, m BZG/SS, b C. Gomershall/NPL; **136** t Naturepix/AL, l C.Manci/SS, r H. Lansdown/SS; **137** t InsectWorld/SS, gstalker/SS, b iPics/SS; **138** t A.Mangoni/SS, m M.Graul/SS, b mahey/SS; **139** t K.Taylor/NPL, b H.Larsson/SS; **140** t schankz/SS, l J.Aalbers/SS, r Jojoo64/SS; **141** tl D.Tabler/SS, tr P.Alexander/SS, ml kurt_G/SS, mr R.Becker/FLPA, bl D.Kitwood/G, br M.Pettigrew/SS; **142** t C.Morrow/AL, b C.Varndell/NPL; **143** t E.Isselee/SS, b N.Cattlin/FLPA; **144** t&m M.Pelanek/SS, b N.Philipps/AL; **145** t N.Cattlin/FLPA, b P.Hobson/NPL; **146** t&b Lebendkulturen/SS; **147** R.Williams; **148** t H.Clark/FLPA, l T.Graham/G, P.McLean/FLPA; **149** t G.Dore/NPL, b K.Taylor/NPL; **150** t krisgillam/SS, b chris2766/SS; **151** t A.Hyde/NPL, b K.Taylor/NPL; **152** t NNehring/i, b U.Bild/G; **153** t S.Colmer/NPL, t T.Graham/G; **154** t S.Colmer/NPL, b Digital Camera Magazine/G; **155** t MARKBZ/SS, l G.Dore/NPL, r M.Vydrak/SS; **156** t thatmacroguy/SS, b R.Cooper/NPL; **157** t alslutsky/SS, b M.Payne-Gill/NPL; **158** t Russell Cooper/NPL, b David Kjaer/NPL; **159** thatmacroguy/SS; **160** all N.Cattlin/FLPA; **161** t N.Upton/NPL, m I.Kimber, b A. Darrington/AL; **162** t D.Pressland/FLPA, l A.Hyde/NPL, r R. Thompson/NPL; **163** t I.Redding/AL, b B.Castelein/NPL; **164** tl A.Hyde/NPL, tr D.McEwan/NPL, m E.Isselee/SS, b G.Edwardes/NPL; **165** t A.Sands/NPL, m A.Darrington/AL, b D.Chapman/AL; **166** t N.Cattlin/FLPA, b R.Thompson/NPL; **167** t A.Hyde/NPL, b R.Thompson/NPL; **168** t I.Redding/SS, b A.Hyde/NPL; **169** t BZG/SS, b A.Darrington/AL; **170** l I.Redding/SS, r J.Stuurman/FLPA, b S&AParker/AL; **171** tl, ml, bl&r A.Hyde/NPL, tr S.Bidouze/SS, N.Hardwick/SS; **172** t K.David/SS, b Colette3/SS; **173** tl A. van Dulmen/SS, tr N.Hardwick/SS, bl R.Becker/FLPA, br D.Baker/SS; **174** tl N.Benvie/NPL, tr F.Paul/FLPA, m R. Thompson/NPL, b D.Pressland/FLPA; **175** t N.Upton/NPL, b R.Becker/FLPA; **176** t N.Cattlin/FLPA, b ARCO/NPL; **177** t C. Manci/SS, b blickwinkel/AL; **178** t-b N.Cattlin/FLPA, Sarah2/SS, S.Dalton/NPL, U.Bild/G; **179** t alslutsky/SS, m R.Thompson/NPL, b V.Hulai/SS; **180** t R.Thompson/NPL, b HHelene/SS; **181** BZG/SS; **182** t V.Lavra/SS, b T.Graham/G; **183** t dadalia/SS, b N.Upton/NPL; **184** t BZG/SS, b N.Hardwick/SS; **185** t C.Varndell/NPL, b M.Ruckszio/SS; **186** t K.Burdett/AL, b B.Gibbons/FLPA; **187** l P.Clement/NPL, r N.Cattlin/FLPA, b Alexander62/SS; **188** t H.Rau/SS, l S.Colmer/NPL, r Meister Photos/SS; **189** t M.Fowler/SS, b S.Chimphoolsuk; **190** tl&r D.P.Ronneberg/SS, bl U.Bild/G, br De Agostini/G; **191** t M.Ruckszio/SS, b Florapix/AL; **192** t-b S.Alfio/SS, BZG/SS, WILDLIFE GmbH/AL, V.Abrahamyan/SS; **193** l M.Ruckszio/SS, r BZG/SS, b mimohe/SS; **194** t B.Gibbons/FLPA, b blickwinkel/AL; **195** t BZG/SS, b Brzostowska/SS; **196** t LFRabanedo/SS, b dadalia/SS; **197** t A le Moigne/SS, b M. Hlavko/SS; **198** tl S.Pvan/SS, tr P.R. Sterry/AL, b R.Biedermann/SS; **199** t H.Rau/SS, b J.Roy/SS; **200** t UIG/G, b B.Gibbons/FLPA; **201** t R.Maximiliane/SS, b M.Kuchenbecker/SS; **202** t BZG/AL, b mr_coffee/SS; **203** t ChWeiss/SS, b Imageman/SS; **204** t U.Bild/G, b G.Pisotckii/SS; **205** t Brzostowska/SS, b N.Cattlin/FLPA; **206** t AS Food Studio/SS, b BZG/SS; **207** tl S.Colmer/NPL, tr M.Fowler/SS, bl T.Volgutova/SS, bl I.Vagnerova/SS; **208** t U.Bild/G, l M.Heighes/SS, r De Agostini/G; **209** P.Entwhistle/FLPA; **210** t Aflo/NPL, b islavicek/SS; **211** t M.Ruckszio/SS, b BZG/SS; **212** t D.Pike/NPL, b BZG/SS; **213** t UIG/G, b S.Pavan/SS; **214** t lavtushenko/SS, b W.Cushman/SS; **215** t BZG/SS, b UIG/G; **216** t E.Sekowska/SS, b L.Anton/SS; **217** t I.Redding/SS, b Visual China Group/G; **218** tl A.Tkacenko/SS, tr BZG/SS, b SergeyIT/SS; **219** Klein&Hubert/FLPA; **220** t Maleo/SS, l osoznanie.jizni/SS, r K.Maksim/SS; **221** l TV/SS, r Robyn Mackenzie/SS, b bjonesphotography/SS; **222** tl&br UIG/G, tr Fotofermer/SS, bl Hulton Archive/G; **223** t Adam J/SS, bl Madlen/SS, br De Agostini/G; **224** t grahamspics/SS, m vvoe/SS, b Mariusz Jurgielewicz/SS; **225** t M.Fowler/SS, b garmoncheg/SS; **226** t A.Alekseev/SS, b K.Weiss/SS; **227** t Adam J/SS, b unpict/SS; **228** t Ilya Images/SS, b unpict/SS; **229** t 1000 words/SS, b unpict/SS; **230** t M.Fowler/SS, b M. Barbone/SS; **231** M.Alexander/SS; **232** t ImageBroker/FLPA, b A.Darrington/AL; **233** t U.Bild/G, b Adrian_am13/SS; **234** t LFRabanedo/SS, b A.Koturanov/SS; **235** t D.Pressland/FLPA, b J.Navajo/SS; **236** t vladis.studio/SS, b KanphotoSS/SS; **237** t&b A.Davies/NPL; **238** t HHelene/SS, m A.Wynn/NPL, b R.Thompson/NPL; **239** t S.Colmer/NPL, b A.Davies/NPL; **240** t egschiller/SS, m R.Thompson/NPL, b D.Hosking/FLPA; **241** V.Lawless/SS; **242** ian600f/i; **243** t P.Dunn/AL, b D.Watts/NPL; **244** t W.Sloss/NPL, b UIG/G; **245** t P.Hobson/NPL, b G.Smith/FLPA; **246** eZeePics/SS; **247** T.Graham/G; **248** t Anjes/i, b lcrms/SS; **249** jeromewhittingham/i